Old Ways to New Days

Shane Lehane is a lecturer and course director in Cultural and Heritage Studies at Cork College of FET and teaches Folklore at University College Cork. With over 35 years' experience, he is known for his engaging lectures on Irish folk custom, tradition and belief – exploring festivals, the life cycle and vernacular life. Passionate about folklife, he highlights the significance of everyday objects, architecture and food in Irish heritage.

Shane has published widely, including influential works on beekeeping and the Skelligs, and frequently contributes to local journals and history societies. A familiar face on Irish media, he is the resident folklorist on RTÉ's *The Today Show*, sharing insights on Irish folk traditions.

Away from academia, Shane enjoys life in the countryside with his partner, tending to his bees, growing rare tomato varieties and crafting traditional furniture and currachs – pursuits that reflect his deep connection to Ireland's material and cultural heritage.

Sara Baker has been illustrating for over 30 years. A native of Northern Ireland, she studied art in Brighton and Chelsea College of Art in London. She has illustrated everything from Bibles and maths books to children's picture books, greeting cards, posters and packaging. She has two grown up daughters and lives in West Cork with her husband and two dogs.

Old Ways to New Days

The **FOLKLORE, TRADITIONS**
and **EVERYDAY OBJECTS** *that*
SHAPED IRELAND

Shane Lehane

HACHETTE
BOOKS
IRELAND

Copyright © 2025 Shane Lehane

The right of Shane Lehane to be identified as the Author of
the Work has been asserted by him in accordance with the
Copyright, Designs and Patents Act 1988.

First published in Ireland in 2025 by
HACHETTE BOOKS IRELAND

All rights reserved. No part of this publication may be reproduced, stored in
a retrieval system, or transmitted, in any form or by any means without the
prior written permission of the publisher, nor be otherwise circulated in any
form of binding or cover other than that in which it is published and without
a similar condition being imposed on the subsequent purchaser.

Cataloguing in Publication Data is available from the British Library

ISBN 9781399736473

Typeset in Baskerville by Slick Fish Design

Printed and bound in Great Britain by
Clays Ltd, Elcograf S.p.A

Hachette Books Ireland policy is to use papers that are natural, renewable and recyclable
products and made from wood grown in sustainable forests. The logging and manufacturing
processes are expected to conform to the environmental regulations of the country of origin.

Hachette Books Ireland
8 Castlecourt Centre
Castleknock
Dublin 15, Ireland
(email: info@hbgi.ie)

Authorised representative in the EEA

A division of Hachette UK Ltd
Carmelite House, 50 Victoria Embankment, London EC4Y 0DZ

www.hachettebooksireland.ie

For Máire

mad for road, yet a rock of sense,
a woman of never-ending patience, encouragement and love

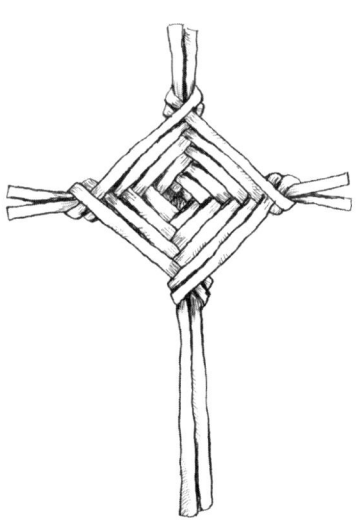

Artist note: The illustrations for this book were hand drawn with a dip pen and Indian ink, with the natural imperfections and unpredictability that this method produces. I wanted them to be accessible, humorous and in the vernacular style to reflect the themes and language of Shane's delightful writing.

Contents

Foreword/Réamhfhocal by Dáithí Ó Sé   11
Introduction   17

PART ONE
The Rituals of the Cycles of Life   21

New Beginnings   27
In the sop   28
The *Brat Bríde* • Birthing in the Straw • Fairy Changelings

Love and Marriage   45
'Would you like to be buried with my people?'   46
Matchmaking • Fortunes and Dowries • Skellicking
• Salting, Punching and Chalking • The Skellig Lists
• Shellicking Day

Future Loves   63
Love Divination and Charms • Coax-ee-orums

Runaway Weddings and Wedding Rituals   71
The Newest of Food and the Oldest of Drink • Strawing
• The Hauling Home

Death   83
Stopping the Clock   84
The Time of Passing • Women and the Rituals of Death
• The Merry Wake and Games • Burial

PART TWO
Folk Life: The Extraordinary in the Everyday   99

At Home   105
Dead From Tea and Dead Without It   106
   The Early Days of Tea • The Tay-Man • A Cup Out of Your Hand

A Place to Sleep   117
   Straw and Rushes • Toss the Feathers • Hot Jars and Bri-Nylon

The Fear of God   128
   A Rebounding Faith • Sacred Hearts and Chalky Gods • Down on our Knees

In the Community   141
The Forge: Men's Shed   142
   The Heart of the Village • Cures and Curses

'Have Ye No Homes to Go to?'   153
   Shebeens and Ale Poles • The Pub Comes of Age

The Fat of the Land   166
   Churn and Market • Piseogs and Charms • The Butter-Stealing Hare

Natural Expression   179
'When Spiders From their Cobwebs Creep'   180
   Vernacular Meteorology • 'It's Only a Shower' • The Ash Before the Oak • The Weather Year

'English That for Me'   198
   Beyond the Aboriginal • The Gaeltacht • English Woven on a Gaelic Loom

PART THREE
Instruments of Change   213

Lighting the Dark   217
Illuminations   218
  Rushlights • The Christmas Candle
  • Paraffin Oil and Tilley Lamps

Pole Men and Sacred Heart Lamps   228
  The Coming of the Electric • Light and Water • On the Farm

Freedom   247
'The Horse that Eats No Hay'   248
  'The Devil on Wires' • The Freedom Machine
  • Messenger Boys and Punctures

Communication   259
Drop Me a Line   260
  Pen • Paper • Post • The Picture Postcard

Black and White and Read All Over   272
  The First Mass Media • Keeping an Eye on Russia
  • A Way with Words • Lighting the Fire and Killing Flies

New Age of Entertainment   285
The Wireless   286
  2RN: Ireland Calling • Sport and Talk • Jazz and the Pirates

Going to the Pictures   299
  The Flicks • Jam Jars and Usherettes
  • Jumbos, and Cowboys and Indians

Turning on the Telly   313
  Telefís Éireann • 'What's on the Box?'
  • *The Late Late Show* and Beyond

Epilogue   327
Glossary of Irish Words and Phrases   329
Acknowledgements   335

Foreword
Réamhfhocal

———— ✥✥✥ ————

Bhí an t-ádh liom, I was very lucky to have been born in the west Kerry Gaeltacht where folklore and *seanachas* seeps out of every rock and mountain, where the echoes of days gone by can be not only heard, but also felt in your bones.

I was always blown away with the stories I heard when I was growing up, and then, years later in Galway, hearing the same story with a different twist. These stories, legends and customs don't belong exclusively to any one townland or county, even though we thought they did, so we all claim them. The beauty of the oral tradition is that the storyteller had the right to add, subtract and embellish the story each time it is told to meet the demands of his audience.

You can only imagine, then, my excitement when I see Shane Lehane coming into *The Today Show* in RTÉ with his bag of *giuirléidí*, his box of tricks. He is a natural storyteller full of pure passion for old customs and traditions of times gone by. I remember the first time he came in, he did so with the bounding enthusiasm of a seventeen-year-old Cork fan leaving Killarney after beating Kerry in a Munster final.

Shane's folklore is a celebration of and a rejoining with all the people he has met along the way. In folklore and in life today, if you take the people and the community out of the equation, what are you left with? The pace of today's world is faster than it's ever been, which sometimes means that the lessons of the past seem further away, and even forgotten. With that, we can lose sight of who we are, where we have come from and what we have learned.

Up until recently we were not, in the traditional sense of the word, an educated people. It is not that long ago that we were not allowed to go to school and very young children had to work as part of a household. We did not have the freedom to do as we pleased. Nevertheless, our minds and imaginations were never conquered or controlled. We always had the ability to let our minds soar and dream, and these flights of imagination were played out in our songs and especially in our stories. Today, people hold up the stories of Disney or Narnia as great examples of how to catch people's imaginations and keep them entertained. However, if you look back to what we have always had in Irish folklore, between fairy changelings being swapped for children or fishermen falling in love with mermaids by the sea, the modern stuff would not get a look in with us. Take Halloween as another example, it all started here in Ireland, landed in America, came back to us and now people here have bought into it not realising where it all began.

Foreword/Réamhfhocal

I know Naomh Bríd or St Brigid had, and still has, a very strong imprint in Kildare, Louth and Cork. Growing up in west Kerry, I remember my mother, who is from Cordal just outside Castleisland in the county, telling us about her going on the Biddy with a baby doll around to all the neighbours when she was a child in the 1940s. They didn't have much to get from them – only an apple or whatever they could give. This story inspired us to do the same and, once or twice, I went on the Biddy, taking with me my sister's Cabbage Patch doll, which was more like a Halloween doll, an unholy sight. Every year, as long as I can remember, I have put the *brat Bríde* out and I still believe in its power. St Brigid has made a huge resurgence in recent years; she has been reborn. I hear people say 'this is amazing' and it is, but some of us knew that a long time ago. St Brigid was always very important to me. I find great solace in her.

I had dinner with Kerry great, Mick O'Dwyer, one evening, most of the night was spent talking about football and the other part about *piseoga*. The Mayo football curse was mentioned, as you might imagine. He was a great storyteller. All the way home, I was wondering why we went out the back door when we had finished when the big front door was straight in front of us. I got my answer the following day when I went into Dingle to meet a friend for a pint. It was before opening time, so we went in the back door as the front one was closed. When it was time to go, I was heading for the front door and the man who was with me let out a roar, 'Out the door we came in, a *bhuachaill*.'

Not only does this book explore and explain the world of *piseoga* and the many beliefs and customs we had, but it also gives us a moment in time of what life was like in Ireland down through the years. It is that connection between our generation and that of my parents and theirs before them, that shows how rooted we are in this country. People are amazed when Americans, for example, want to go see a ruin of an old cottage, in the middle of a field, in the middle of the Irish countryside. Sometimes, we forget how lucky we are because we can just walk down the road, point at a field and say my great-great-great-great grandmother was born there. Others cannot do this, they do not have that legacy or heritage at hand. I see it all the time on the Rose of Tralee. It is like a broken link, and I do think it is a big part of their lives that they are missing.

In his gentle style and fascinating accounts, Shane brings us from darkness to light and literally from the spoken to the written word. His great understanding of the Irish language is always a great help when trying to get to grips with the old ways in these new days in particular. When speaking about the language to people today they almost automatically mention the *modh coinníolach*, they are worrying about something that might never happen in one sense. Even when we speak English today, we do so through an Irish prism and we have a great skill of being able to put meat on the bone while not losing anything in translation. Folklore is often where the Irish and English language worlds meet in harmony. It is a safe place for both with no stopped the clock on the wall for either.

This book is also a great escape from the worries of today, just like the stories of yesteryear took minds off some of the harsh realities that surrounded those who listened. The only thing better than reading this book is hearing the stories from the man himself. I did feel like he was reading it to me, which is a skill in itself when writing.

'*Tá sé in am sip*' as my father would say, Now I'm off to play the fiddle in front of the young fella and see if he was swapped years ago. I must also look for the *bean an tí*, she was off looking for some leather cloak down by the shore, I hope she went out the door she came in!

Dáithí Ó Sé
September 2025

INTRODUCTION
Finding Folklore

Two lovely sisters, Madge and May Kennedy, lived without electricity in a mud-walled thatched house on the shore of Lough Beg, in a forgotten corner of Cork harbour. I remember with fondness my first meeting with these two gentle ladies back in 1986, when they, with big smiles, welcomed me into their extraordinary home. They swung open their red half-door and, when I entered, I felt as if I had stepped back in time.

I was a young undergraduate student of archaeology and, for my final-year dissertation, I had taken it upon myself to survey and record the extant vernacular houses in the Ringaskiddy hinterland. This area was soon to become one of Ireland's most intensely developed industrial zones, with gargantuan pharmaceutical plants and a new deep-water berth.

Madge and May cooked over the open fire, their cooking pots black on the outside but scoured clean and gleaming on the inside. They had a beautiful dresser packed with shining delph, old photographs, and a lifetime of ornaments and mementos. They shared their house with a cat and a few kittens, and it was into the small shallow hollows of their earthen floor that they poured the milk for the cats to enjoy. At night, their only source of light came from a double-burning oil lamp set on their kitchen table and, as their cotton wick was nearly spent, I remember their relief when I sourced a new one for them in the hardware shop in Macroom Square.

When people ask me how I first got interested in Irish folklore and folk life, I think back to my encounters with Madge and May, and the countless other marvellous people that I have had the pleasure of meeting over the past forty years or so. Somehow, I have always been drawn to, and feel most at home, in that other Ireland; that slightly esoteric anachronistic place and its inhabitants, whose way of life is a step or two behind the ever-increasing waves of perpetual change.

I have fond memories of when, as a young folklorist, I visited a small house near the top of the mountain at Bauracaurin in County Cork's Boggeragh Mountains. I was delighted to sit with my little tape-recorder in the kitchen, recording Johnny Katie Looney and his sister Hannie talking about their memories of cutting turf. There was yellow lino on the floor, the enchanting smell of turf burning in the range, and I was made welcome with endless cups of tea and slices of jam Swiss roll. Their stories of the lightning that killed two men coming from the bog and detailed accounts of finding and tasting bog butter, and the strange activities of the hares from Inchamay bog had me enraptured.

Introduction

The same kind of lore and intricate detail of a different way of living and seeing the world was present when I visited my aunt and uncle every summer on their small farm between Cahersiveen and Portmagee in County Kerry. There, with my brothers, sister and cousins, we drew water from the well in white enamel buckets, rode on donkeys, and bound and stacked sheaves of oats in golden sun-drenched meadows. We sat under cows, milking them by hand, and marvelled at my uncle turning horseshoes on the anvil before searing them into a horse's hoof. At night, we were regaled with story after story until we went off to bed, wide-eyed and half-paralysed with wonder, our heads full of stories of the fairies and the púca.

It was the intimate moments of such experiences that lit the fire of intrigue and wonder in me, and that led me to what is now close on forty years of study and lecturing in the field of folklore and ethnology.

I have had the pleasure of learning from the inspiring insights of accomplished academics at university, while simultaneously building up a substantial library and archive of my own folkloric research. I am deeply indebted to the innumerable local historians and enthusiasts whom I have met while giving lectures around the country. They, along with my many adult students, have shared a wealth of personal memories and fascinating stories with me. I am privileged to have enveloped myself in this wonderfully stimulating and intriguing discipline and to have been granted opportunities to share and illuminate this aspect of our heritage.

This collection of musings and memory is a concentrated mixum-gatherum of intriguing detail that seeks to illuminate the distinct elements and traditions that have shaped Irish life and character. It concerns itself with the changes and technologies that brought Ireland rapidly – almost too rapidly – from an almost medieval way of life to one of extraordinary modernity. Tradition and change are neither static nor linear; they are dynamic and often cyclical.

The transition from a peasant subsistence economy of 1750 to the commodity-fandangled, more convenient life of the present day was not without its problems, nor was it universal. Many held on to old traditions and customs. Life in the Irish countryside was an open social contest between the haves and have-nots, and conveniences and things new were met with anything from eagerness to suspicion to outright disdain. Change is inexorable, but the nature of tradition is to maintain the old order and to be conservative; an approach that is sometimes dictated by economic, religious or social circumstances.

This book will chart these great changes in Irish life by exploring how different technical innovations have changed people's inherited survival skills and broadened their lives and their worlds. It is a window on our past that demonstrates how many of our traditions and ways of being have had a lasting impact, while some, for good or for bad, have been lost over the passage of time.

PART ONE

The Rituals of the Cycles of Life

Some thirty years ago, I sat in the pub in Rossaveal, County Galway, trying to dry out following a soaking that I'd got on a rough ferry-crossing back from Inis Meáin – the 'middle island' of the Aran Islands. There were a few Connemara trawlermen in the pub, waiting for the bad weather to pass and, as I warmed up by the fire, I got chatting to one of them. I asked him about fishing lore, and he had a number of interesting stories about red-haired women and hares, and how they were not things any fisherman wanted to see or mention before he set sail. He was a fine storyteller, and I asked him if he had any stories about mermaids or seals. There are many folktales about seals taking human form and he told me one, the memory of which has stayed with me. I had no tape recorder or notebook, but such was the clarity of his storytelling, that the detail has remained crystal clear. I wrote it down as soon as I got home. It went as follows.

There was a man one time; he was unmarried and lived with his elderly parents. He had built himself a fine currach and spent most of his time working from the seashore, fishing,

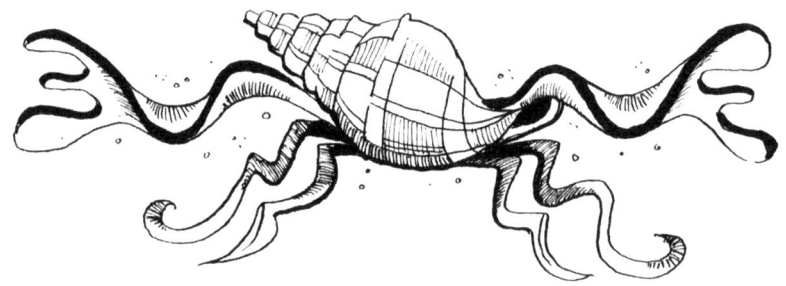

gathering seaweed and collecting periwinkles. He would often stop in his work, look out to the bright light reflected on the sea and wonder what would come of his life, for he was lonely. He never didn't see the head of the young seal breaking the water, whose two eyes used to watch his hard toil every day.

One day following a fierce storm, he went walking the shore collecting the wrack thrown up by the sea. There was always something of value in the flotsam and jetsam that came after a storm. Then, what did he come across but a beautiful sealskin folded on the beach. It was the finest piece of supple leather he had ever seen. He knew it would be very handy and he took it into his small storage shed at the corner of the beach. He hid it carefully away in the back and covered it over so no one could find it.

When he emerged from his shed, he was absolutely astonished to see a beautiful woman sitting on the rock close to where he had found the skin. He was very shy and did not know what to do. She was naked to the world except for her long hair, which she was combing with a seashell comb. She looked at him with her big dark eyes and put out her hand to take his. He put his jacket around her shoulders. He knew by the smile on her face and the look in her eyes that it was love at first sight for both of them. She did not speak a word, but there was an immediate deep understanding between them.

She gladly went with him back to his house and, in no time, and with his parents' permission, the man married the woman, and she took over the running of the house.

From that day on, his pots and nets and fishing lines were never empty and, over the next number of years, they were as happy as any couple could be. She bore him a large family of nine hardy children. Every now and again, however, the man would find his wife missing and would always come across her sitting on the rock with tears in her eyes, looking out to sea. He knew that, despite her sincere love for him and their smiling contented children, there was a great and unbearable sadness deep within her. As time went on, she began to look pale and sick, and he became greatly worried.

One day, he was returning from a day's fishing, his currach full of mackerel, when a wave gashed the boat against the rocks and ripped a big hole in its skin. On landing his currach, he immediately set about boiling the tar to patch the hole. He remembered the fine skin he had found on the beach all those years ago and, without thinking, he asked his wife to go down to the shed by the shore to fetch it. When she took down the skin, her true nature and instinct came rushing back to her, for this was the skin that she had taken off when she had left the sea. She opened out the skin on the shore and rolling it tight around her, she returned to her seal shape and slipped back into the water.

Her husband came to the shore to look for her, but all he could see was the head of the seal breaking the water and the two dark eyes staring back at him. He could not but recognise the beautiful eyes that had been so loving. He knew the seal was his wife and while he was heartbroken, he nodded and smiled at her to put her at her ease. He knew he had been lucky to have had her for so many years, but that she had no choice but to return to her own world.

This folktale carries some amazing folk imagery, not least the notion that a seal, by casting off its skin, can shapeshift into the form of a woman. There is also the idea of the horizontal threshold of the sea as a liminal barrier under which the fisherman cannot follow, for humans cannot survive in that otherworld. The tale is full of mythological conceits and symbolisms, but I have always looked at it as a simple love story, the detail of which would have resonated with many in the time when this tale was told. The loneliness and lack of opportunity of the poor fisherman living with his elderly parents was commonplace. The wonder of finding true love and fulfilment, even in such a fantastical and magical way, would have been truly appealing. The need for the parents' agreement to bring an unknown woman into the home, who consequently took over the running of the house, corresponds to seminal moments in the lives of many.

Instructively, the stark contrast between the pre-marriage hardship and the subsequent good fortune and ample provisioning that followed the marriage was seen as a direct consequence of the quality of the union. A full family of no less than nine healthy children born from the love match, is an idyll in itself. Finally, the sudden and somewhat unexpected departure of the seal woman is a cause of sadness, yet there is the clear sense that her exit from the life of the man and the family was not unusual and was borne with the solace of good memories.

This intriguing narrative is punctuated by the life transitions that centre on love, marriage, birth, prosperity, and, finally, death and loss. In the cycle of life between birth and death, the prospect of finding love and securing a good marriage, having children, and enjoying health and prosperity were far from guaranteed. In addition to the usual uncertainties of life, a person's luck might be altered by supernatural intervention.

Amongst the pre-industrial, rural peasantry of the eighteenth, nineteenth and early twentieth centuries, there was a deep investment in established folk beliefs and rituals, specifically at these liminal points of transition of birth, love, marriage and death. Despite a dedicated and public adherence to the doctrine of their Catholic faith, there remained the vestiges of a private belief system of a powerful otherworld. People were tied to superstitious observances and bound by rituals to court good fortune and ward off any potential bad luck. In Ireland, it is still considered a portent of bad luck to put shoes on a table or to hand someone a knife or to go out a different door than the one you came in. No matter how sophisticated we might think we are, remnants of our folkloric inheritance are still deeply rooted in our personal and communal psyches.

NEW BEGINNINGS

In the Sop

Many years ago, I interviewed Charlie Twomey, the sacristan in Macroom. He was responsible for modernising the access to St Berrihert's Holy Well, which is situated just outside the town on the road to Inchigeelagh. Charlie told me that he organised the building of the new entrance because, many years earlier, as he was passing the well, he saw two women trying to hoist a pregnant woman over the ditch so that she could gain access to the holy water.

In Ireland, many holy wells were the folk *loci* for popular medicine and cures, with some being considered essential for pregnant women facing the ordeal of labour. The miracle of new life is timeless, but its success was often a very complicated and dangerous affair, particularly before the advent of modern gynaecological and obstetric medicine. In rural Ireland, from 1700 until the early twentieth century, the ability – or not – to become pregnant and to give birth to children was strewn with widely held and deeply superstitious beliefs and rituals.

Brigid is the great mother figure in Ireland and the most revered of all the Irish female saints. In the folk tradition, on the eve of her feast day of 1 February, complex sets of rituals were performed in people's homes that promoted fertility and the safe delivery of new life.

The Brat Bríde

For as long as anyone can remember, on the eve of St Brigid's Day, it was customary to take a piece of cloth or a ribbon and hang it on a bush outside the house overnight. It was believed that the 'Blessed Bridie', as she was known, blessed the items and the following day the cloth or ribbon – the *brat bríde* and *ribín bríd* respectively – now bestowed magical properties, imparting health and well-being to the family.

This little piece of cloth had a wide variety of applications: everything from easing the creaking of old bones and rheumatic pains to helping reluctant ewes to accept their newborn lambs. The *brat* was placed on the backs of cows both during and after parturition to ensure that all would be well and there would not be any complications.

In the human realm, little pieces of the cloth were sown into petticoats and were thought to protect the virginity of young girls, while the *brat* was also the go-to item for couples who were having difficulty conceiving a child – as one man said to me some years back, 'It was used to polish up the apparatus!' The *brat* was much sought after when women were in labour as its presence was considered crucial for a safe delivery.

The *ribín* had similar attributes and functions, often tied as a girdle around the waists of women to protect virginity – and also those who were pregnant. The *ribín* is still a core traditional feature extant in Baile Bhuirne, County Cork, where Gobnait, the patron saint of beekeepers, who has the same fertility attributes as Brigid, is celebrated on her feast day of 11 February. It is on this day that people in the community will measure their ribbon against a medieval wooden statue of Gobnait and anyone who carries Gobnait's measured ribbon with them will be safe on all journeys and when travelling on water. This attribute also applies to the *brat Bríde*, which takes on the magical properties associated with the 'caul'. On rare occasions, a baby is born with a 'caul' (a part of the amniotic sac) covering their heads and this membrane was collected as a charm to protect against drowning. Such was the popularity of these cauls amongst the merchant and navy seamen in England, that midwives would advertise them in the local newspapers, selling them for a high price. In Ireland, other than the caul, the *brat Bríde* was considered the most effective protection against drowning and was very popular amongst fishermen. Similarly, the offcuts of the rushes used for making the Brigid's Crosses were placed in currachs to protect from drowning.

It is common to see little pieces of cloth and ribbons hanging from thorn bushes at holy wells, many dedicated to Brigid and, indeed, Gobnait. Equally, at many of those sites, such as Brigid's Well in Castlemagner and at Gobnait's in Baile Bhuirne, both in County Cork, there are examples of sheela-na-gigs, the extraordinary medieval carvings that display older women in a squatting position, often with their hands on their genitalia exposing the birth canal. Some wear a ribbon or cord around their midriff while others can be seen to give birth to the amniotic sac. Scholars like Barbera Freitag suggest the sheela-na-gigs operated as folk deities; icons of wise women who imbued positive, life-giving powers at birth, a point in the cycle of life, often sadly characterised by death. In a time before modern medicine and medical procedures, complications in

The Rituals of the Cycles of Life

childbirth led to high incidences of mortality – and the death of the newborn, the mother or, in many cases, both.

On a saint's feast day, more commonly known as a pattern day, women would visit and perform rituals at the holy wells dedicated to both Brigid and Gobnait and other local saints. Perhaps cognisant of such impending potential mortality, women did everything they could to empower and safeguard themselves. They would spend the day 'paying the round', moving in a sunwise direction and stopping at various stations, either leaving a votive rag or ribbon, partaking of the sacred waters and placing their hand on the sheela-na-gig.

Birthing in the Straw

Another custom associated with St Brigid's Eve was to make a small bed of rushes or straw in the corner of the kitchen, in case Brigid decided to stop in and rest. This *leaba Bríd* (Brigid's bed) was directly linked with older birthing practices, when women would give birth, not in a bed, but in a kneeling or standing position onto a bed of soft straw. This practice is borne out by such old Irish expressions as *'Ón oiche a tháinig mé ar an tsop'* ('Since the night I landed on the straw'), meaning 'since the night I was born'.

When a woman went into labour, the expression was that so and so was 'in the sop' or 'in the straw' in the same way that, for example, when a sow was about to farrow, she would make a soft birthing bed of straw for herself. There was an immediate need to call the local *bean ghluine* (kneeling woman), who had the accumulated experience of having helped many women to give birth. Her skill and knowledge were matched by the important belief people had in her; that she had a certain otherworldliness that would bring good luck and guard against ill fortune.

It was the custom that two people should always go to fetch the midwife and there was general relief, almost working as a placebo, when she was seen arriving, sitting at the back of the cart. Country midwives, given the size of families and the demand for their services, were jokingly nicknamed 'rabbit-catchers'. Nevertheless, in isolated rural areas, trained midwifes or nurses were few and far between. If a doctor had to be called, it was seen as a precursor to a lost cause and imminent death.

There were important medical advancements that included the training of midwives of the mid-nineteenth century, which culminated in the *Rules for Midwives* organised by the Central Midwives Board, which was established in 1918.

Whether a midwife was available or not, trust was placed in the older, wise women in the locality who would have overseen the medical and magical needs of a community. Often, given their advanced age and, being close to death themselves, they were deemed to be between worlds and thus insulated against the evil forces that were present at the critical times of birth and death. These older women operated as the *bean leighis* (the herbalist), who prepared and administered cures, and the *bean feasa* (the wise woman), who offered diagnostic and prophetic counsel. Often, they were one and the same person.

Her role as the *bean ghlúine* in bringing new life into the world operated in a different system of understanding the cosmos, which was outside of, and contrary to, that of the ever-increasing, pragmatic medical and scientific orthodoxies of the nineteenth and early twentieth centuries. Birth, like death, was the ultimate liminal time and it was dominated by fear of fairy interference and portends and superstitions about the health, future and character of the newborn. The *bean ghlúine* had much to consider.

Childbirth was a predominantly female affair and, in the days and weeks before and after, the women in the community would convene to bolster the expectant mother. They took over the everyday household chores of feeding the family – milking, cleaning, fetching water, minding fowl, tending the fire and baking. This lifecycle gathering of women attending a birth was ritually played out every Brigid's Eve with the arrival of the *Brideóg* (the Biddy Boys). When people went out 'on the biddy', they disguised themselves in straw costume and went from house to house carrying with them a *brideóg*, an effigy of Brigid in the form of a small straw doll. They would sing and dance, and their visit was seen to bring luck and good fortune to each household.

Irish and Scottish folk records suggest that the so-called 'Biddy Boys' were, at one point, predominantly made up of girls. Their straw *brideóg* doll was not only Brigid, but in size, shape and form, it was reminiscent of a newborn baby. It was fashioned from the last sheaf of the harvest, known as the *cailleach* (the old hag), and represented the regeneration of the life force that comes in the New Year.

The occasional time when men were actively involved in childbirth was in the sporadic practice of *couvade*, when men were called upon to indirectly lessen a woman's labour pains. The folklorist Séamus Ó Catháin records an account from County Mayo that tells of a woman who, when she was about to give birth, knelt in the middle of the straw-strewn floor, wearing her husband's *báinín* (woollen jacket) with her husband standing behind her, his hands on her shoulders, imparting his strength and encouragement. If the husband was away or not available, his position at birth was taken up by another man from the locality to the same end but, in all cases, he was under the watchful eye of the midwife.

Whether the men were present or not, it was common practice for the woman to wear something belonging to her husband – a jacket, a tie or a waistcoat – turned inside out, not only to magically give her extra strength but to protect her from abduction. If the pregnant woman prepared a big pot of potatoes or porridge and gave them to her husband who then ate it with gusto, this was one way of transferring to him some of her impending pain. Sometimes, the man would load up a heavy creel of turf, carry it on his back, and walk around the house a number of times, his physical exertion and effort operating as a type of sympathetic magic for his wife. However, it seems most times, the midwife decided to get husbands out of the way and directed them to carry out meaningless tasks, such as picking stray wisps of straw from the thatch or fetching buckets of water from distant wells, simply to occupy them and let her continue with her work unhindered.

The first thing that the handywoman would do was to open all doors and windows in the house and make sure everything that was locked was unlocked, including the undoing of any ties or knots on the clothes of the woman in labour. There are early accounts of special protective birth charms, written in Latin on little pieces of vellum, folded up and attached by a cord around the expectant mother's abdomen. Such protective birth charms or birthing girdles in the form of a *ribín Bríd* or a St Joseph's Cord of chastity and protection, with its seven knots, were undone and removed to make sure nothing would symbolically block or inhibit the birth.

The mere presence of the handywoman provided immediate succour to the woman in labour and the placebo effect of various magical activities reinforced the event as her dominion. The handywoman's shawl was, in itself, a type of *brat Bríde* and she would shake it three times over the woman while also bringing an extra-efficacious *brat Bríde* that, when placed on the woman's forehead in the throes of labour, had the effect of offering immediate relief. In addition to the magical, the handywomen possessed practical skills that were the result of hard-won or handed-down experience.

One of the most difficult births for the handywoman to manage was a breech birth where a baby was born feet first, as this often led to suffocation. If a breech baby survived, they were much in demand as a certain cure for rheumatic pain and lumbago. They would be asked, especially when they were children, to walk on the backs of the affected person.

Many children were born with birth defects and birthmarks. Such manifestations were always attributed to some activity undertaken when the mother was pregnant. Any children born with dark or red birthmarks were said to come from the woman, who, when she was with child, picked blackberries or blackcurrants for making jam. One woman whose child had a large birthmark on her face put it down to the fact that she had been making black puddings after the pig was killed.

If a pregnant woman ended up by some accident with a burn or a bruise, the newborn child would have a birthmark in the same part of the body as their mother had been injured. Some sought a cure for the birthmarks and for this the handywoman used to rub the placenta on the mark, before burying the afterbirth. Equally, a child with a birthmark would be taken to a wake and

The Rituals of the Cycles of Life

the dead person's hand was placed on the mark. It was thought that as the dead body decayed, the birthmark would fade.

When a hare, long associated with the shape-shifting *cailleach*, crossed the path of a pregnant woman there was a danger that the child would be born with a 'harelip' (cleft lip). To offset any such likelihood it was necessary for the woman to immediately make a small tear in one of her petticoats.

Birth, bringing with it such prospective complications and the potential of death, was underpinned by these deeply inherited beliefs and observances. The rituals and practice were overseen by the wise women who interpreted the lore and facilitated the passage from womb to life.

⁓ Fairy Changelings ⌒

The belief in abduction by the fairies and the replacement of the mother or child with a changeling was widely held and was a matter of profound distress throughout the nineteenth and early twentieth centuries.

In Irish tradition, fairies were an invisible otherworld community who occupied remote locations, such as hilltops, islands and ringforts. They incorporated a complex mix of otherworldly entities, including mythological ancestors and the dead. One prevalent belief was that they were fallen angels who had been expelled from heaven for following Lucifer.

Fairies had white blood and evidence of their activities was often ascribed to any white substance, such as cuckoo spit or bird droppings, that appeared in conspicuous places. As such, the fairies took it upon themselves to abduct newborn male children into their world as a mechanism to reintroduce red blood and so regain access to heaven.

The changeling – *malartán* or *síofradh* in Irish – was an old fairy who magically took the form of the human child placed in the cradle after the original child had been taken by fairies. This changeling caused no end of anguish for the parents, refusing to take food and vomiting up anything that was given to it. Parents would guard against this fate by placing the iron tongs from the fire across the cradle and never leaving the baby unattended until it had been baptised.

Our folklore record, dating from the eighteenth century to the near present, contains numerous accounts of how fairy

changelings were discovered. A journeyman tailor whose experience of the world made him wise is often the figure who uncovers the changeling's identity.

One story goes that a young couple were delighted with their new baby, even though it was wizened and possessed a strange and menacing stare. The baby refused to latch on and suckle from the mother, and any food it did take immediately came back up. The couple got no sleep and their hours were tormented by the incessant shrill crying of the baby. The parents were very quickly at their wits' end. Unknown to them, their baby had been 'swept' – as the expression goes – and replaced with a changeling by the fairies. As the days and nights went on, things went from bad to worse. In those days, it was usual that journeyman tailors would travel the countryside, stopping into houses to ply their craft. A tailor would bring his bag of needles and threads and turn a coat, make a suit of clothes and mend the frayed hems of skirts, whatever was required. On the arrival of this tailor, he looked at the bedraggled parents and assured them that he would look after their ailing child while they tried to get some sleep. The tailor knew by the look of the infant in the cradle that he was nothing but an old fairy pretending to be a baby and purposefully causing the mayhem for the parents. It now fell to him to reveal the true identity of the changeling.

The tailor began several actions designed to tease the changeling into exposing its true nature. He started by taking some plug tobacco, paring it with his penknife and rubbing it between the palms of his hands into a flake. He filled his *dúidín* (clay-pipe), lit it and blew the sweet-smelling tobacco smoke into the cradle. The fairy was gasping for a smoke and was tempted to grab the pipe for a smoke himself. Next, the tailor secured a bottle of *poitín* and using a large empty goose egg as a glass, poured a generous measure for himself. He sniffed and sipped the fiery whiskey while the eyes were popping out of the head of the parched and on-edge changeling. Next, the tailor took a fiddle down from the wall and played a few bars of a lively polka but, purposely, at the sweetest part of the tune, hit a few flat notes. Frustrated by the careless botching of the tune, the changeling forgot himself and shouted out, 'Hand me that fiddle and I'll show you how to play it!', and, in so doing, revealed his true identity. With the changeling revealed, it now fell to the tailor to put things right and secure the return of the natural child.

The litany of items used to foil the fairies were well known and included iron, fire, salt, blood, running water, dirt, a black-handled knife and a pure black dog with no white hairs. On this occasion, the tailor took out his longest, sharpest iron darning needle and heated it red-hot in the fire. He held it aloft as he approached the cradle, and this was enough to frighten the changeling who scampered out the door never to be seen again.

Other versions of this tale recount that the tailor gathered a few buckets of black *caoráns* (small nuggets of hard turf) and lit a huge bellowing fire. When the fire was at its hottest, he made a hollow in its centre with the tongs, turned to the changeling and said, 'Come on now, I have a nice new warm bed for you.'

In both accounts, the fairy ran out the door and the normal child was discovered crying outside and was brought back in. When the parents woke up, they found the tailor rocking the low wooden cradle with his foot and their baby safe and sleeping contentedly within.

This tale is an example of the wider spectrum of fairy lore but it belies a very sinister side of Irish life in the eighteenth, nineteenth and early twentieth centuries. If a baby was born with any physical or mental deformity, it was potentially looked upon as a *síofradh*. This often led to intense fear and neglect, and the baby could be left to die. Given that it might have been a changeling and that it was not baptised, it would not be buried in consecrated ground. This gave rise to unofficial burial grounds called *cillíns* and every hinterland in the country had its place to accommodate such burials.

The taboo of contamination by connection with the fairy otherworld was offset by setting these burial places in obscure locations. They were often on a small patch of land at a crossroads – *croisín na leanbh* (the crossroads of the children) – an area of no man's land, between townlands.

The folktale of the tailor and the changeling, of iron needles and disposing of changelings in the fire, speaks metaphorically of practices of infanticide.

There was a strong belief that nursing mothers who had given birth could also abducted by the fairies because they were needed to nurse the children who had been taken. There was also a belief that human breast milk could render the fairies mortal.

One account of a man whose wife was taken on the 1 May, the most auspicious day for fairy abduction, tells how he took to the drink, heading to the pub each day. He drank their savings and neglected the household and farm. One night, his wife came to him in a dream and told him that she was not dead at all, but that she had been taken by the fairies who tormented her by tying her on the back of a white horse. Every night, she formed part of the *slua sidh* (the fairy host), her set horse galloping wildly and sweeping her night after night through the countryside. The *slua sidh* were invisible to the human community, their presence only detectable as the *sidh gaoithe* (the fairy wind) as it flattened crops and tore limbs from trees.

Her legs were fixed by a belly band under the horse and, as they galloped at breakneck speed, she was greatly distressed by being jostled and flung in all directions. However, she told her husband that she had not eaten any of the fairies' food and because of that, she could be brought back. She told him that she would be at the crossroads at midnight on the next full moon and that he was to take his sharpest black-handled knife, cut the tie and take her from the horse and she would be back with him again.

When the man woke up from the dream, he decided to stop drinking and return to the farm, putting everything in order before the next full moon. Every night, he took out his black-handled knife and sharpened it on the leather strap until it was gleaming. On the night of the full moon, he arrived in the village early. While waiting at the crossroads, he grew more and more anxious. He decided he would go into the pub for a shot of whiskey to calm his nerves. One glass of whiskey turned into four or five along with a half-gallon of porter and, as the night slipped by, he ended up hopelessly drunk.

As midnight approached, he staggered out the door and, with the light of the moon and the dust rising from the road, he could see the outline of the *slua sidh* and his wife on the horse coming towards him. In his stuporous state, he could not locate his knife and the opportunity was lost; his wife passed by looking incredulously at her fool of a husband who had succumbed to the dangers of drink.

The overarchingly superstitious and often malignant practices of fairy belief and lore that were still current in some places up to the 1950s and 1960s have now entirely dissipated. The Irish have moved from a medieval perspective of magic and folk belief to one of extraordinary modernity. While some may lament the loss of a belief in fairies, I, for one, feel that the practices that stemmed from these beliefs, including infanticide and the ritual degradation of women, are best confined to the annals of our past.

LOVE AND MARRIAGE

'Would you like to be buried with my people?'

By St Brigid's Day, 1 February, both the wild and domestic world start to reawaken. The small songbirds are gathering sticks and soft linings for their nests, while the bees have re-emerged from their winter hibernation and are busy collecting the first dandelion pollens. As far as the eye can see, in countless straw-lined farmers' sheds, the ongoing miracle of new life is everywhere, with the next generation of calves and lambs being born.

In this timely milieu of seed-sowing, birth and new life, we sometimes forget that we too are part of this natural cycle of procreation. This is the reason why, in the observations and traditions of our folk year, we put such emphasis on love and marriage at this time. From women's Little Christmas on 6 January until the beginning of the moveable feast of Lent, there is a tight window of time that was expressly dedicated to arranging unions for marriage. This was the season for matchmaking and, all going well, it culminated in ceremonies on Shrove Tuesday, the luckiest day to get married.

Matchmaking

The various progressive Land Acts of the late nineteenth and early twentieth centuries witnessed the transfer of land from landlord to tenants. In 1903, the Wyndham Act ultimately finished the landlord system and helped finance the widespread repurchase of land by its occupiers. Following a long history of being dispossessed, the main concern of matchmaking at this time centred on land, rights to land, and the provision of a dowry or fortune. Essentially, the family house, farm or holding was passed down to the eldest son and, when he married, his bride had to bring with her money, farm livestock, house essentials, and maybe a few heirlooms and ornaments.

This seems a simple matter, but such a transaction was governed by a firm contract arranged by a matchmaker and agreed between the fathers of the betrothed couple. The matchmaker was a well-regarded individual in the locality who had tact and practical experience in settling deals. His prime function was to ensure that fairness prevailed and to smooth over any potential obstacles to a union, which was often organised, arranged and negotiated with little or no input from the couple to be married.

This negotiation was supported by the strong belief that it was unlucky to have a woman present when the matchmaking was undertaken. The usual scenario was that the matchmaker and groom's father would meet the father of the bride at a fair, or they might travel over to his farm with a proposal. The prospective groom would be brought along and, notwithstanding the prohibition of women being present, this might be the first time that he and his bride-to-be would meet. A bottle of *poitín* or whiskey was always carried and placed unopened on the table while negotiations took place. There would be an account of all belonging to the farm into which the girl would marry and, equally, the value of what the girl would bring with her into the union. The negotiations often became heated and many a perfect match was ruined over the difference of a paltry sum of money or a quarrel over a right-of-way.

If a tentative agreement was made, it was marked by opening the bottle and sealing the deal with the whiskey. When the matchmaking transaction took place in the home, it was traditional to cook a goose, and the agreed union and the fine detail of the match was celebrated in style, while 'picking over the gander'.

It was then arranged that the bride's father and the matchmaker would visit the groom's farm, to make sure all was in order. They would inspect all the livestock, the fences, the outhouses and the quality of the land. Sometimes, the holding would not necessarily match up to what had been promised at the match, and a host of well-known ploys could be resorted to in order to make everything look prosperous for the inspection. Some might temporarily borrow some heads of cattle and fowl from other family members or neighbours. The house would be whitewashed and dollied up with flowers. Fresh linen was put on the bed, extra holy pictures hung on the walls, a long mirror in the bedroom, flitches of bacon hanging from the ceiling and extra delph on the dresser.

The prospective groom would have to look his best, attired in a borrowed suit, and scrubbed and washed to within an inch of his life, with his face shaved and his hair cut. If he was ageing, a mixture of soot and hair oil was applied to hide his grey hair. Those without teeth used to borrow a pair of 'grinders' (false teeth) for the day, but not being used to them were advised that it was best to not speak or smile for the duration of the negotiations. Similarly, if they had a limp or a bad hip, the prospective groom would avoid walking around and elect simply to stand still in a corner, lest he scupper their future at the last hurdle. Many a bride returned to her new home after the wedding to find it sparser and more destitute than had been described by her father and, similarly, her new husband could be older, half-crippled and toothless.

The reverse might also occur. There is an account of the prospective groom who had a match made for him in a household full of available women. Their father was at his wit's end trying to find husbands for his daughters and paying out their fortunes. While the matchmaker was agreeing terms, the young man set his sights on the youngest and most attractive of the women but, as time was short, he had only a few moments to speak to her. The next time he met her was at the altar but, when she lifted her veil, it was not her, but her much older sister who was presented to him. He had no choice but to follow through, lest he be seen as a fool before the gathered congregation.

However, it happened such matches and supposed mismatches often worked out for both parties.

Fortunes and Dowries

When the match was settled, half of the agreed dowry would be paid over, usually in hard cash, a wad of notes of anything from £50 to £500. Being a large sum of money, it was referred to as 'the fortune'. It also represented the knock-on future fortune of so many others who relied on it. This fortune of money that came into a household was the ticket out for the next girl on the farm who could use it as a means to secure her own exit. The fortune itself might never be touched – it just continually did the rounds, perpetually changing hands as an integral part of the matchmaking process.

If you had the fortune, you became an attractive prospect and were next in line for the picking. In circumstances where a woman was widowed and had a daughter, the fortune was used as an enticement by the widow for a man to marry her daughter and gain a foothold into the farm. In this arrangement, he was known as a *cliamhain isteach*, literally 'married in', a term that had negative connotations and marked him as a kept man, as the control over the farm often remained with the widow until she died.

On top of the fortune, the bride's parents would gift a cow, a feather mattress and sometimes a dowry chest with bed linen and a patchwork quilt that had been safeguarded for the daughter. If the match was supported by prosperous families and the couple were moving into a new home, the wedding gift might be a new dresser made by the local carpenter who would pierce their initials and the year of the marriage into its top lintel. He would

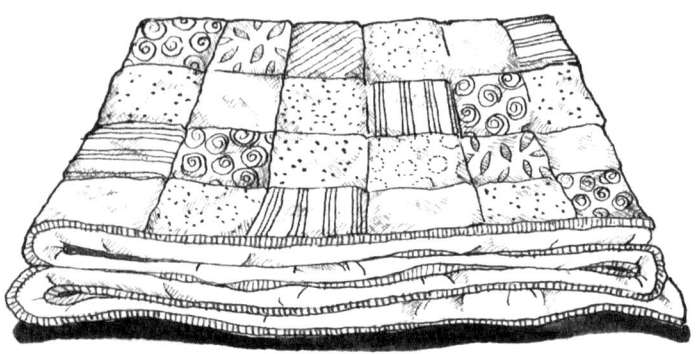

also pierce a heart, the most common decorative motif in the Irish vernacular, and one can deduce that many items decorated with hearts marked the occasion of marriage.

With the arrival of Irish independence, the nationalist fervour bolstered the notion that owning your farm might be viewed as winning back Irish soil from the oppressor. This new-found ownership of property and farms created a deep covetousness, and a rabid fear of the diminution or disinheritance of the land. Such was this fetishisation, it led to insurmountable problems of farm inheritance that greatly complicated marriage. The farm was left to the eldest son, but he had to wait until the 'boss' (his father) died or decided to give up his authority. When this did eventually occur, the son might well be fifty or sixty years of age and he would then look to marry a much younger woman who could bear him a son, who, in turn, would inherit the farm. Such unions were never founded on love but on practicality and lack of choice. A memorable line in Ciaran Cassidy's 2024 television documentary *Housewife of the Year* used by a woman to rationalise such an age discrepancy ran: 'I'd rather be an old man's darling, than a young man's slave!'

In circumstances where the family was without a male heir, the eldest daughter could only marry a man with the same surname as herself, so the farm could continue in the family name. When hampered by such restrictions the idea of two young people falling in love and living happily ever was more a fantasy than a reality.

Outside of these eldest sons and daughters, the younger brothers and sisters were left without a farm of land and had little prospect of marriage without a fortune or dowry of their own. If they did not move to the city or emigrate, they were generally destined to live out their single lives as bachelors and spinsters, living in the house or working on the farm in a subservient role. Despite contributing productively to everyday life in professions, such as teachers, dressmakers or farm labourers, there was a distinct view that, outside the married state, they were somehow unfulfilled and second-class citizens.

Some elected, as a status-saving option, to embrace religious life and became priests, Christian Brothers or nuns, but such pathways were not open to all and were hampered by the demands of education and the payment of a spiritual dowry. An unmarried middle-aged man, working on the family farm was still referred to as a 'boy' while terms like 'old maid' or 'spinster' for women, carried with them a profound sense of social stigma for the multitudes that did not have the wherewithal or inclination to marry.

In this closed, church-ridden and morally policed 'valley of the squinting windows' rural Ireland, honest, emotional and sexually positive human relationships were near impossible. Catholic guilt and a suffocating culture of shame and disgrace hindered healthy and positive unions. Any natural display of intimacy was openly condemned and regulated by the harsh castigations of priests, nuns and Christian Brothers. The moralistic episcopal letters read from the altar each week and the all-knowing confessional of the parish priest condemned the natural human inclination for love and sexual pleasure to something dirty and sinful.

The extent of such negativity was institutionalised in the Magdalene laundries and mother and baby homes. Intimate relationships went underground. Enamoured couples were confined to ill-managed, pathetic fumblings in fields and alleyways for their confused expressions and guilt-ridden experience of love. With such lack of opportunity and suffocating oppression, it seemed preferable for many to move to the anonymity and freedom of the big city or to hop on the boat to Glasgow, Liverpool or even to America. Nevertheless, the cities of Dublin, Limerick and Cork and the Irish ghettos of Britain and the USA provided little by the way of new prospects, such was the sense of guilt ingrained in those who emigrated.

Skellicking

There are a number of junctures in the Irish year that exhibit the extraordinary features of carnival. Carnival, deriving from the Latin *carne*, meaning 'meat,' is evident, for example, at the times of animal slaughter and meat-eating at both Halloween and Christmas. It is characterised by excessive feasting and drinking, along with dressing in disguise, resulting in a period of abandon, chaos and open social criticism.

This tradition of dressing in straw costumes – as Halloween Guisers or Wren Boys – to gain anonymity and then being fuelled with drink was a ripe catalyst for communal disorder. The long-lived, medieval tradition of carnival centred on the period before Lent with boisterous, anti-establishment, open-air processions though towns. The strict dietary constraints of Lent as a period free from meat and animal produce established the day before the fast began as a day of over-indulgent excess, known in many parts of the world as *Mardi Gras* (Fat Tuesday). In Ireland, it manifested as Shrove Tuesday – Pancake Tuesday – when the large stocks of eggs were gluttonously consumed in an excessive feast of sweet confection.

There are numerous examples of riotous carnival on Shrove Tuesday in different parts of Ireland. The forty days of Lent that followed was a time of stasis and transformation, dedicated to culling the infertile and non-productive animals and, in doing so, promoting the fecundity of the new stocks. In this way, it clearly demarcated the timing of Irish marriage.

SALTING, PUNCHING AND CHALKING

In Ireland, the religious restrictions imposed on sexual union during Lent meant no marriages took place over those forty days, so it followed that the most popular day for marriage was Shrove Tuesday. The churches were literally laden with couples getting married on that day. There is an extraordinary account of the importance of being married on Shrove Tuesday in William Richard Le Fanu's 1893 autobiography, *Seventy Years of Irish Life*. He recounts that on Tory Island, County Donegal, the weather was so stormy one Shrove, that the boat was not able to bring the priest to the island to conduct the marriages. Such was the dismay of the intended who did not wish to wait another year, that an ingenious solution was found. The couples assembled on the eastern side of the island and the priest, on the mainland opposite, read the marriage ceremony across the water.

Shrove became the make-or-break-it day for marriage and, if you were not married by the end of it, you were open to all manner of ridicule and social bullying. The day had a host of different names. It was called Salting Day, as people used to throw salt on the unmarried, so that they would be preserved until the following year. It was called Punching Day, when marriageable single girls would disguise themselves in straw costumes and attack their fathers demanding to know why he had not let them marry that year. The first Sunday in Lent was known as Chalk Sunday, when those who were unmarried were singled out and had the backs of their overcoats chalked by young blackguards as they came out of Mass. Some of the young boys would make up bags of soot and flour, stand at street corners and, when the bachelors and maidens came along, they would liberally pillory them with the bags.

On the Sunday after Shrove, the church would be full of newly married couples and this day was also known as Puss Sunday, as the young unmarried women, jealous of their sisters and friends who were now wed, would have had a miserable, envious puss (sulky expression) on their faces. In Cork and Kerry, Shrove Tuesday was known as Skellicking Day, when the open mockery of those who were unmarried was fully elaborated. The name derives from the magnificent medieval monastic island of Skellig Michael that had a reputation for calculating the date of Easter differently from the rest of Christendom. Shrove and Lent came later there, and it became inextricably linked with those who wished to get married. Throughout the nineteenth century, the monastic island became a place of Lenten pilgrimage associated exclusively with bachelors and eligible females. Instead of being a place of pious prayer, it gained a reputation as a sort of free-for-all singles club. In 1888, Lady Wilde wrote in *Ancient Legends, Mystic Charms and Superstitions of Ireland*:

> *As marriages were not allowed in Lent, it became the custom for the young people of both sexes to make a pilgrimage to the Skellig Rocks during the last Lenten week. A procession was formed of the young girls and bachelors, and tar-barrels were lighted to guide them on the dangerous paths. The idea was to spend a week in prayer, penance and lamentation; the girls praying for good husbands, the bachelors repenting for their sins. But the proceedings gradually degenerated into such a mad carnival of dancing, drinking and fun, that the priests denounced the pilgrimage and forbade the annual migration to the Skelligs.*

The Skellig Lists

It was out of such a mix of associations and traditions that the infamous 'Skellig Lists' emerged. These were anonymous printed broadsheets of song or verse that paired various men and women from a locality, who supposedly had designs to go to Skellig Michael on pilgrimage or to be married. The descriptions of the individuals were scurrilous, casting the men as lecherous womanisers and the women as insincere money-grabbers. This was the private made public, and while some verses stopped at simple mockery, others outed clandestine relationships, or exposed blatant philanderers and flagrant infidelities.

All over Munster these extraordinarily libellous poems were printed and sold by street vendors in their thousands in the build-up to Shrove Tuesday. The printed broadsheet bridged the traditions of orality and literacy, with the scandalous content being read out or sung to an eager and attentive audience in the pubs or at home around the hearth. They were given whimsical and enticing titles such as 'The Corkscrew', 'The Hours of Idleness', 'The Lads of the Whip', 'The Virgins of the Sun' and 'Roll the Old Barrel Along'. Their outrageous assertions were dreaded by the unmarried and yet eagerly consumed by everyone in the community.

There was no ambiguity, and certainly no mercy, in the Skellig Lists, and they were vehicles of acute social ridicule. Those singled out in them were identified by the street where they lived, their dress sense, their profession or their appearance. One such list from nineteenth-century Cork City includes a poem entitled 'The Satirist', where there is no holding back and the character assassination is pure vitriol:

> *Next comes Maurice Egan, dat man wot the tail,*
> *Which protrudes from its nest like the head of a snail,*
> *With Nancy Drinan he'll go if he can,*
> *But Nancy won't have him because he's no man.*
> *Miss Puffmuffin Callaghan goes next for the shore,*
> *With her waxbottom neighbour, the cordwainer Hoare,*
> *While Kate Lynch comes on after, decked out in black silk,*
> *On the bleak rocks of Skellig to skim her sour milk.*

The men fared little better. They were lampooned for their drinking, their lack of morals and usually cast as miserable leeches looking to marry wealthy widows.

> *Jack Re--en comes next, like a Laplander bear,*
> *His strawberry phiz all enveloped in hair,*
> *While he growls out a something in shape of a song*
> *To the braw Widow H—g-es, whom he hugs all along.*

There were numerous letters published in the newspapers by fathers threatening legal action if their daughters' names were included in the lists. Equally, the accounts of the Petty Court Sessions detail the regular arrest of street vendors and the fines imposed on the local printers who profited from producing the broadsheets. The establishment's outrage concerning these lists and its determination to outlaw them and similar publications culminated in the introduction of the 1889 Indecent Advertisements Act. However, the lists continued to be printed well into the twentieth century while the tradition of composing and singing them continued unabated. The following verse from 'Cúil Aodha' in 1944 is a good example.

> *I'll start with this lassie, the pride of our isle*
> *She's only a shoemaker's daughter.*
> *She has two bandy collops like the Banks of the Nile*
> *And a very short fall from her water!*
> *She's seen every Sunday going down to first mass*
> *She goes rather fast with a wag in her ass*
> *And I'm told that she paid a few rounds in the grass,*
> *With Paddy the Stal' from Grian Álainn*

The clandestine appearance of the Skellig Lists was a regular Shrove activity in towns and villages like Inchigeelagh, Skibbereen, Listowel, Castlegregory, Cahirsiveen and Portmagee, and many others in counties Cork and Kerry until well into the 1960s. Their anonymous authors often included scathing and salacious remarks about themselves to deflect the community's suspicions as to their authorship. The handwritten verses were typed and pinned to the window of a local shop or passed around in the pub, where the insinuating content was eagerly consumed by all and sundry.

The Skellig Lists were social dynamite and their once-a-year publication had serious consequences for the reputations of many individuals. The lists branded people, often unfairly, for their supposed short-comings and failings, and mocked them for their idiosyncrasies of dress and behaviour. Whether justified or not, such caustic stereotyping stuck and it was the verse in the Skellig List that characterised a person, to the point where it could scupper their chance of a relationship and even marriage.

Skellicking Day

The Skellig Lists were only one part of the Shrovetide humiliation for those who were not married. In the towns of Blarney and Cobh, an extraordinary remnant of a long-lived tradition continued up to very recently. On Shrove Tuesday the girls were left out of school earlier than the boys to give them a chance to get home because on Skellicking Day, the boys had the right to chase the girls with a rope, tie them up and sometimes dunk them in the horse trough. Often, this was benign good fun and, if a girl fancied a boy, she would let him catch her and he might even get a kiss. I interviewed some residents of Blarney about their memories of the tradition, and remember one account of a teenage girl who was teasing her would-be catcher because she was able to outrun him with ease. She ran a good few rounds of the square, exhausting her pursuer, by keeping just out of reach, before running in the door of her house and upstairs, leaving the chaser panting and frustrated at the threshold. Her mother came out to see what the young boy, standing at her doorway wanted, to which he replied, 'Please, mam, please, can I come in I want to skellig your daughter?'

In Cobh, the carry-on was more boisterous. Where the boys used to corral the girls with a rope and drag them to Jude's Well and dunk them in the horse trough. This raucous commotion

continued well within the living memory of the many residents that I have interviewed.

The practice has a long history – the same activity is clearly depicted in several nineteenth-century paintings, such as *Skellig Night on the South Mall, Cork*, when various older, unmarried citizens are depicted being forced to partake in a parade of mockery through the city. Some are set on the backs of donkeys, others on carts, while the frailer and more decrepit are propelled in wheelbarrows.

An account from Killarney tells that wheelbarrows all over the town were in great demand for similar parades there. In the paintings, the night-time is illuminated by flaming tar barrels, and unmarried men and women are being physically taunted and manhandled in the direction of the water-pump under which they are eventually doused. Boys are shown blowing horns and hitting kettles and drums to create a ran-tan cacophony of chaos. There are lads goading and riding backwards on a pig, others playing run-away-knock and older figures are falling over from an excess of drink. This wild abandon of Skellicking Day incorporates the core features of carnival that was a steadfast feature of life on this day, the last day of abandon before the severe restrictions of the controlled and stark Lenten period.

We may think that all these traditions and customs are long behind us, but many of them are still current, but under a modern guise. The Skellicking Day customs that survived in Cork and Kerry strongly resemble the excessive drinking, tying up and sexual humiliation associated with some of the wilder activities of the present-day stag and hen parties that precede marriage.

During the twentieth century, the role of the matchmaker was taken over by personal ads in *Ireland's Own*, and has now moved to the myriad of dating apps. The same exaggerations and misrepresentations of looks, means and interests pertain there as they did in the time of Dan Paddy Andy O'Sullivan, the famous matchmaker from Lyreacrompane in the Stack Mountains of north Kerry.

We might even congratulate ourselves that the character assassinations in the Skellig Lists are a phenomenon that we have left firmly in the past, but today it is far worse. The universality of mobile phones and the anonymous trolling and bullying of individuals on the many social-media platforms has a level of vitriol that has taken it to an all-time low. Regardless of such depressing observations, the opportunity and circumstances of relationships and positive marital unions in Ireland is now extremely progressive. The controlling cultural and social factors have changed, and people are generally free to marry whom they want. Younger siblings, without the farm or land are no longer left on the shelf and those who find themselves in failed unions have the opportunity to divorce and move on. We led the world in terms of major social change in 2015, when Ireland was the first country to legalise marriage equality through a popular vote.

Future Loves

Moon moon tell unto me
When my true love I shall see?
What fine clothes am I to wear?
How many children shall I bear?
For if my love comes not to me
Dark and dismal my life will be.

These words, spoken as part of a now-forgotten love charm, encapsulate the vain hope and unknowing fate of women in the matters of love and relationships in the not-too-distant past. Negotiated matches were practical marriages of convenience that secured the family name, land and money, and were rarely founded on romantic love.

This preoccupation of finding a life partner that would result in happiness and security was ever-present. Given the complex circumstances of inheritance and economics that regularly orchestrated arranged marriages, the practice of love divination and the invocation of love charms would have been employed partly in jest amongst women – yet, in private, their aspirations would have been in earnest. Such magical prognostications and charms demanded the words be spoken in the light of the first full moon of the new year. Equally, such activities were undertaken at Halloween, which was understood to be the most auspicious time for love divination and magic.

～ LOVE DIVINATION AND CHARMS ～

Halloween – 31 October – marked the end of the fertile year and was the age-old point of transition from harvest into the cold winter months. This was Samhain, the ancient junction of the old and new year.

It has long been the most auspicious time to foretell the future. Many of the folk rituals that make up the revelry of Halloween centre on the notions of prosperity or otherwise that might come with or without marriage. The charms that were hidden in the communal dish of colcannon or the celebratory *bárín breac*, 'speckled cake', all pertained to a person's prospects. Today, the only charm in commercially produced barm bracks is the ring, which, traditionally, was the portent of an impending marriage.

In earlier times, the bracks had many more charms: the pea meant no marriage that year; the rag indicated poverty; the coin indicated wealth; the button was for bachelorhood; the thimble for spinsterhood; the stick meant you would be beaten by your spouse; and the holy medal was a call to religious life. Whether a courting couple were compatible or not was established by the pair taking two hazelnuts and placing them on the stone hearth in front of the blazing Halloween fire. The shells of the hazelnuts would heat up and when they cracked, it caused them to jump. There was great fun and mirth watching to see whose nut jumped first or if both jumped together, and much was read into which direction they went in or if both ended up in the fire. Reading a deck of playing cards or the pattern of tea leaves at the bottom of a cup, or interpreting the shapes formed by pouring melted lead through a door key into a bowl of cold water, offered other well-established means of telling the future.

Many unmarried girls, anxious to know their romantic prospects enacted secret rituals at Halloween. If they were brave enough, they would sneak out alone into the dark night carrying with them a special, black-handled knife that would protect them while they dealt in magic. The destination was an out-of-the-way place, somewhere considered to have special power, such as a grave, the mouth of a ringfort or a crossroads of three townlands. Here, she cut three pieces of clay from a sod while reciting a specific charm. When back at home, she might add in some extra magical ingredients, such as the last spoon of colcannon, a few sprigs of yarrow, nine ivy leaves, some nail clippings or a pinch of hen dung. She would then tie the magic mixture in her left stocking with her right garter and place this parcel under her pillow – then she might dream of her true love whom she would marry and of her future fate.

A sure way to dream of your future lover was to go to bed fasting, having eaten nothing but a concoction earlier to bring on a great thirst. A dish of salted herring or a bowl of porridge laden with salt usually did the trick. These foods were scoffed in three bites and the girls went to bed without speaking to anyone, anticipating that their true love would come to them in a dream and offer them a drink of water to quench their thirst. There are also accounts of taking a spoonful of a mixture of flour, salt and soot. In the case of soot, it was considered to have special magical properties if scraped from nine different irons in the hearth.

A more elaborate charm involved the girl going to the riverbank, taking her shift (her most intimate and private garment), and dragging it against the stream three times before placing it out on the riverbank to dry. The belief here was that when she did this, while alone and somewhat vulnerable, she might catch a glimpse of her true lover fondly regarding her from the opposite bank of the river or she might see his face as a reflection in the water. The various versions of the charms contained elements of intimate female fantasies where their dream suitor would come and handle her shift, turning it while it was drying in front of the fire.

Likewise, if a girl went to bed without drying her face, her love would appear at the end of her bed, with a towel to dry her wet face while she slept. To ensure the desired machismo of her wished-for lover, and in a decidedly coquettish action, the girls placed in or under their beds, a selection of everyday objects that were strongly symbolic of male sexuality. Items such as an iron spade, a stout-handled wooden flail used for threshing corn, an overflowing distaff spindle covered in raw unkempt wool or a long, hairy cabbage root were all very clear symbols of the strong, virile male. Sleeping with such tokens under your pillow, bolster or bed augmented the chances of a girl finding a potent and well-endowed man.

COAX-EE-ORUMS

However, some people were not content with such vague prognostications and, instead, resorted to more direct folk magic to capture their future love by making what used to be called 'coax-ee-orums'. It was often the young woman or her mother or aunt who prepared and stealthily administered the love philtres. The local *bean feasa* (wise woman), with her in-depth knowledge of herbs and folk medicine, might also be called upon in matters of love. The preparations spanned from the benign to the bizarre to the near fatal, and involved the most unusual ingredients.

Boiling the excrement of a white gander or that of a black chicken or administering the juice of a boiled mouse were all thought to establish instant attraction. The dried and powdered liver of a black cat with white paws was also thought to be particularly effective. Leaving pins to go rusty in a dead mouse, before rubbing them on unusual fungi and fixing them into people's clothes was a common method.

An elaborate charm from Roscommon demanded capturing a frog and confining him in a little box until he died. The box was left unopened for six or seven months until the skeleton was clear of all flesh so the sought-after 'wishbone' of the frog could then be extracted. When the opportunity arose, perhaps in the church or at a crowded gathering, the frog wishbone was stuck unbeknownst into the coat or some other article of clothing of the beloved. Seemingly, this method was particularly powerful, the affection of the person sought was immediately won and it was difficult for anyone to dissuade them otherwise. In such cases, antidotes to the love charms could also be called into play. Secretly cutting one of the tassels from the charm-administering girl's shawl or a little strip from her fraying petticoat and then using these as countercharms turned the false love to feelings of pure dislike. Equally a snip of the girl's hair might be taken, again surreptitiously, burned and its ashes drunk in a cup of tea by the apparently besotted young man to restore him to his everyday senses.

Hair and nails were regular players in magic, given that it was thought that both continue to grow after death and were seen as containing something of the lifeforce of the person. It was thought that if a man took a clipping from the nail of his middle finger, the finger representing his manhood, and dropped it into a drink given to a woman, she would become besotted with him. Equally, if a woman was fed up with the advances of an overzealous lover, she would file her nails to create nail dust, which is a proven emetic, and this would cause him to vomit and withdraw his attentions. The implicit difficulty in acquiring or administering such intimate items of hair and nails for charms and countercharms afforded them their supposed potency and efficacy. There were, however, even more serious methods of love entrapment.

There are accounts of sinister and dangerous concoctions, many of which backfired badly. The early purple orchid *Magairlín meidhreach*, the tormented root, grows in bogs and marshy places and has long been used as a potent love charm and aphrodisiac. Its shape, with an erect head rising from two round tubers, is directly associated with male virility. There are always two tubers: one of which is large and the root for the following year, while the smaller one is the source for the flowering stem and withers away. Those involved in the love charm would dig up the tubers, which were white with a pink centre, and boil the larger of the two in milk in a little black tin. Otherwise, they would dry the larger tuber before grinding it into a powder and then secretly put some of this powder into a drink or food of the man they wished to fall in love with them. As always, it was vital to do this while speaking a charm, and Lady Wilde gives us an example that was incanted three times while preparing the beverage:

You for me
And I for thee
And for none else.
Your face to mine
And your head turned away
From all others.

If the magic was not conducted exactly as prescribed – for example, using the small, withered tuber rather than the large one – it caused the man to go out of his mind. The same bewildered madness was said to be the result of the wind changing direction within twenty-four hours of the consumption of the charm.

In truth, such advanced love charms, which included the use of hemlock and deadly nightshade, were no more than severe poisonous toxins that sedated and often rendered the recipient a deranged fool for the rest of time.

It has been said that the well-known figure of Biddy Early, (1798–1894) who lived in Feakle in County Clare, had no fewer than four husbands, all of whom died prematurely, as did her son. Her last husband came to her when he was in his thirties to look for a cure. She was in her seventies and she told him that if she cured him, he would have to marry her, which he did. All of her husbands seemed to be under some sort of bewildered and drugged state, most likely a result of a concoction that Biddy administered.

These mind-altering love philtres along with accounts of extraordinarily bizarre items including wishbones from de-fleshed frogs, plaits of skin from corpses, and nail and hair clippings, reference a time when belief in magical charms was paramount. That they would be used in the surreptitious provocation of love and entrapment tells of desperation and the lengths that some people would go to in their search for a relationship.

Runaway Weddings and Wedding Rituals

Regardless of the complications of dowries or Skellig Lists, as has been the way of the world through the ages, most people found each other and fell madly in love without the aid of any magic potions. In defiance of the complications of land inheritance and organised matches, there were plenty who wished to marry for love and, as a great family friend of mine, Teresa Barry, always used to say, 'If it is meant to be, wild horses won't keep them apart.'

Parental advice and common sense often held no sway in the face of passionate love and infatuated fervent lovers who resorted to ingenious strategies to stay together.

In the nineteenth century, a popular method of getting out of an unwished-for prearranged match was to have a 'runaway marriage'. For this, the loved-up couple, contrary to their parents' wishes, would sneak out and spend the night in a friend's house where a big party was arranged. The party attracted a large crowd of local people and revelries would carry on right through until dawn. In this way, the couple would have been seen to have 'spent the night together' in plain sight of all. Wakes were the ideal opportunity for such a couple to publicly declare their love before the community, and such unions were further consolidated by the fun of the mock weddings performed at these gatherings. After such an overt, voluntary and public exposition of love, any prearranged match was totally scuppered with the matched party openly humiliated and unhappy to play second fiddle. The only thing now for those in love was to arrange the day for the wedding.

There were no weddings during Lent and the adage, 'Marry in May and you'll rue the day', secured Shrove Tuesday as the most popular day to get married. When not at Shrove, it was unlucky to marry on the thirteenth of the month, while people also put great store in the day of the week for the wedding.

Monday for wealth
Tuesday for health
Wednesday the best day of all
Thursday for losses
Friday for crosses
And Saturday no day at all.

Similar rhymes specified the luck and fortunes of the married couple, and much was made of the colour of the wedding dress.

Marry in the blue, he is sure to be true.
Marry in grey, you will be far away.
Marry in red, you are sure to be fed.
Marry in green, he will always be mean.
Married in pink, your spirits will sink.
Married in black you'll wish yourself back.
Married in white, you have chosen all right.

One of the great customs from times past that still survives today, is that the groom should not see the bride on the day before the wedding and should only see her in her dress when they are at the altar. The bride was never to make her own dress and, when it was made, she should only try it on once for the fitting – it was unlucky for her to try it on again until the day of the wedding. On the day, she should wear 'something old, something new, something borrowed and something blue'.

It was considered bad luck for any man to kiss the bride on the morning of the wedding and that extended to keeping the dog locked in, lest he give her an affectionate lick. If the bride forgot anything as she left for the church, she was counselled not to turn back for it, while it was also a bad omen if, en-route to the church, the wedding party met a funeral. It was deemed lucky if the bride should first see a man, rather than a woman, as she went to the church, and sometimes spiteful girls would wait close to the house to be seen to dampen a bride's joy.

The weather was an important portent: 'Happy the bride the sun shines on and happy the corpse the rain falls on.' When leaving their houses for the church, the fire tongs and an old shoe or boot were flung after the groom and the bride for luck as they went out the doors of their respective homes. It was customary that a full assembly, not just close friends and neighbours, but the entire community, attend the wedding ceremony. The bride's side were on the left of the church and the groom's on the right, a tradition spanning from the time when the right-handed groom might have had to unsheathe his sword to protect himself without hurting his bride. In the past, the boys and girls of the village would run up and down the streets in excitement.

As the ceremony proceeded, everyone watched out for certain omens of the union.

Much was made of the wedding ring, if there was one. Some were forced to borrow a ring for the ceremony and it was considered very bad luck for a married woman to refuse a request of such a loan. There are accounts of some using the loop on a large door key in the place of the ring. It was unlucky for the bride to try on her wedding ring before the ceremony itself and, instead, it was measured with a piece of thread in advance. If the groom had difficulty fitting the ring on her finger and she had to help him, this was a sign that he would be under her control from then on. If the ring fell during the ceremony, bad fortune and death were said to follow.

People would watch out to see who would kneel first at the altar rail and, in particular, who was the first to step out of the church, as these represented who was to be the dominant partner and who was to have most trouble in the relationship. One tradition that may have it roots in the antiquated privilege of *droit du seigneur*, the right of a king or lord to sleep with his female subjects, was the scramble, often in the church before the ceremony was over, to be the first man to kiss the bride. It was often the best man who, being next closest to the bride, snatched the privilege but it was deeply frowned upon, even if it was done in jest.

The married couple were showered with handfuls of rice as they left the church to ensure prosperity. Sometimes, it was flung with such ferocity that it stung, ostensibly to remind them that not all married life would be so full of bliss. There were those looking on who would smile wryly recounting the old Irish witticism, 'The cure for love? Marriage!'

The Newest of Food and the Oldest of Drink

The processions to and from the church were a major part of the wedding day's festivities and a spectacle in themselves. The bride would be accompanied to the church by her father and, in the days before cars, she travelled by horse-drawn trap. In even earlier times, she rode *cúlóg* (pillion) behind her father.

Once married, it was highly symbolic that she would then ride *cúlóg* with her husband on their way back to the house where the wedding feast was taking place. The latter was the circumstance for a much-anticipated feature of the Irish wedding, which was 'the race for the bottle'. There was a hectic and often reckless horse race from the church to the house, with the winner gaining great adulation. It was often a ferocious competition and there are accounts of the bride being dislodged from her *cúlóg* position with the groom carrying on without her. There are also heartbreaking reports of fatalities during such wedding races.

Whoever got to the destination first would win the bottle and was rewarded with the all-important kiss from the bride. The winner opened the bottle, took a swig from it and passed it around to all who had raced. When nearly empty, it was given to the groom who would ceremoniously break the bottle. This action, like the breaking of the wedding cake later, was symbolic of the consummation of the marriage. The bottle was hit off a large rock or thrown high up into the air to break when hitting the road. If it smashed to pieces, it was a good sign, but if it failed to break after three attempts the marriage would be

troubled. The small pieces of glass were eagerly picked up by the unmarried women and used to foretell their own future love prospects.

Circumstances varied, but the wedding feast usually took place in the barn of the house into which the woman was marrying. When all the guests had arrived from the church, it was time for the wedding-cake ritual. This took place at the threshold of the house, where the bride would kneel at the front door. Her mother-in-law, or sometimes the priest, took the wedding cake, which was an oatcake or enriched soda bread, and, holding it over the bride's head, broke it in two. As with the pieces of the broken bottle, the little crumbs and morsels of the wedding cake were eagerly gathered by the unmarried girls. Later, they would ask the bride to pass the little pieces of cake through her wedding ring so by sleeping with the crumbs under their pillows, they would dream of their husbands to be.

When the bride was entering her new home, it was considered very bad luck if she stumbled, and she always had to step in with her right foot first. When the wedding feast took place in the groom's home, her mother-in-law would present the bride, the new woman of the house, with the fire tongs, symbolising her new authority in the home.

As in the case of the Irish wake, there was no expense spared for the provision of the wedding feast and, if the cost was exorbitant, the social memory of a lavish, *flaithiúil*, feast was more important. 'The newest of food and the oldest of drink' was the recipe for a good wedding. Even if scarce at other times, no wedding was considered complete without plenty of meat, and while home-cured bacon and cabbage was the usual, a bullock, sheep or fowl might be killed specially for the day, and beef, mutton and goose flesh were a rare and special treat.

While the typical and easiest method of cooking was to boil the meats in big pots, the well-to-do farmhouses would have had long spits that allowed the extra relish that came with roasting the meats by a fire. The wooden frame fixed to the wall that held the spits was called the clevy, and this also displayed the large blue willow-pattern platters that were put to use on the wedding day to serve the meat. There would always be a surfeit of potatoes, along with cabbage and rice, and these were a popular food for weddings. For the afters, there was plenty of home-baking with sweet cakes, buns and pancakes, all of which were complemented with shop-bought baker's bread and rich fruit cakes.

The major preoccupation was to provide a surfeit of drink. Porter came by the barrel, each holding 280 pints, and these were supplied, along with bottles of port wine, sherry, whiskey and *poitín*.

~ STRAWING ~

The fun of the evening was augmented by the visitation of the straw boys, who were made up of groups of young men who had not been invited to the wedding. Around the country, these disguised wedding visitors were known by a whole variety of names, including 'collickers', 'buck-cocks', '*cleamairí*', 'soppers', '*buachaillí bréige*' and 'ban-beggars'. They wore full-length costumes made of straw or they dressed in old clothes with their coats turned inside out, with some sporting long, ragged petticoats. They blackened their faces and their heads were covered with the traditional *sopiní*, the tall, conical straw hats that came down over their faces. They were purveyors of music, dancing and mischief and were led by a captain and a sergeant who both carried sticks and whose orders were carried out without question. Musicians were in their ranks with melodeons, fiddles and mouth organs at the ready once they gained entry to the wedding.

The captain would knock on the door and ask if the straw boys could enter. When they had received permission – it was considered bad luck to refuse them – the sergeant, who had numbered his troop, called them in one by one and the music and dancing began. The captain danced with the bride while the 'captain's lady', dressed in a skirt, danced with the groom. The centrepiece of their activities was a pageant, where the bashful bride was encouraged to kiss the groom in front of everyone. Being shy, she would refuse on three occasions before conceding. In turn, each of the straw boys would then get a kiss from the bride.

When there were many weddings taking place on Shrove Tuesday, there were numerous groups of different straw boys doing the rounds and, given local rivalries and fuelled by drink, sometimes their visits ended up in discord and fighting. To counter such unsavoury carry-on, some groups bore little signs on their hats declaring 'no food or drink' and they made their visits short and sweet, being rewarded with money as they departed. In the past, the 'strawing' of a wedding was an integral part of the marriage ritual and was considered vital for future good luck and prosperity of the newlyweds.

~ The Hauling Home ~

In the nineteenth century, amongst the wealthy and elite, the custom of the 'Bridal Tour' involved the married couple visiting different relatives and staying as guests in country estates or hotels. This was the forerunner of the honeymoon. As time moved into the twentieth century, the honeymoon became more popular in the general population, though not everyone could afford it.

The married couple would usually, depending on finances, 'take a room' at a seaside bed and breakfast or small hotel in

Bundoran or Bray, or in a big town such as Killarney or Galway. Some would travel by train to Dublin and enjoy a visit to the zoo and botanical gardens. They stayed for about two weeks before returning home and then there was another big party called the 'hauling home' or the 'dragging home'.

Whatever the circumstances, the party was preceded by the bride's flitting, when all her possessions and the wedding presents were loaded up and transported to her new home. If this was done by horse and cart, it was considered essential that an older married woman sat on the cart to bring the couple luck. This older woman might be a mother or an aunt or a close neighbour of the bride, and she would have the job of unpacking the collection of bed linen and quilts and directing where the new items of furniture would be placed. All would be in readiness before the newlyweds arrived and nosey neighbours in wait for the party would have a chance to cast their critical eyes over the contents of the flitting, remarking on its quality or its lack thereof.

In the rural countryside of the nineteenth century, the hauling home usually took place at night, with a line of sidecars starting from the bride's family home, the newlyweds in front, and the whole cavalcade being driven at helter-skelter speed to the new home. There was great noise and hullabaloo as the manic convoy galloped though the townlands, and well-wishers lit bonfires at crossroads and straw on hilltops to guide them on their way. The night of the hauling home was, on occasion, every bit full of fun and elaborate as the wedding itself and attracted a great crowd who revelled into the early hours.

When a widow or a widower married for the second time, the couple tried to keep their union low key and with no hauling home, their cheap-skating and union was subject to a continuous mocking taunt of 'horning' or 'kettling'. Bands of young blackguards would congregate around their house, blowing on cow horns. When the horns were hard to come by, they would knock the base off large bottles and blow across the top making a loud, deep, reverberating noise. Others would make their racket by clattering old kettles and pots or hitting tins with sticks while shouting and roaring and jeering at the top of their voices.

Regardless of circumstances, traditional weddings in rural Ireland were regularly riotous affairs that were enjoyed and witnessed by the entire community, made up of both invited and uninvited guests. Its celebration, demarcated by its varied customs and observances defined it as a distraction from the everyday, making it an anticipated occasion of wild fun and abandon to be enjoyed by all.

DEATH

Stopping the Clock

After birth and marriage, the absolute liminal point of transition is death. The spontaneous communal gathering in the face of death is a cultural reflex that is deeply ingrained in the Irish psyche. Even though our present response to death is usually managed by professional undertakers who embalm the dead and lay them out in funeral parlours, the removals are characterised by huge congregations of sympathisers who wait in long lines for a quick word with the bereaved.

Such is the pressure of time, the traditional exhortations of 'sorry for your troubles', 'he was great age' or 'she's at peace now' are as much as can be expressed. Despite the best of intentions, the nature of time-constrained removals make them somewhat soulless and metronomic. As such, Irish people are, more and more, returning to an older, more intimate approach and waking their loved ones at home. The wakes of old, however, were radically different from those of today. Such were the sheer excesses and outlandish funerary practices of earlier times, the Church succeeded in condemning and fully eradicating most of their distinctive features by excommunicating all who supported these rituals. What pertains in the wakes of today is but a distant echo of those extraordinary traditions.

The Time of Passing

In the nineteenth and twentieth centuries, when someone died, it was routine to stop the clock. Arresting its loud ticking and continual chiming created an air of silence and solemnity that suited the occasion of death. It also aided the doctor who would later register the official time of death. Stopping the clock pendulum meant symbolically stopping ordinary time and opening up the 'out-of-time' period of transition and ritual that was to be carefully observed over the next few days and nights.

People opened the windows, closed any curtains and turned pictures and photographs towards the wall. Similarly, any mirrors were covered because it was thought that the otherworld became visible in any glass reflection.

If a person died on a straw bed, it was taken outside and burned. Even if they had been in a feather bed in their last few days, the dying person was taken from that bed and placed onto a bed of straw beside it. They were sometimes placed on the bare earth to help them to pass. The burning of the straw was a way of protecting everyone from any disease or malady of the dead person, but it also gave notice to the locality that a death had taken place. In a rural setting, the dense plume of smoke that comes from burning straw would have been visible at a great distance and, if burned at night, the bright flames would signal to the community to gather.

Women and the Rituals of Death

Women were the prime managers of death. It was forbidden for anyone in the family to touch the corpse, and anything that had been in contact with the dead person was contaminated and was also a major taboo. It fell to one of the older and experienced women in the locality to wash and dress the body. This woman was known as the *bean bhán* (the corpse washer) and being elderly and close to death herself, she was thought to be insulated against any ill-fortune arising from touching the corpse.

Her first job was to wash the corpse and make it look presentable. Another man would be permitted to shave a dead man under her watchful eye. The hair was combed and when all this was done the water and soap that had been used was carefully stashed away, usually under the bed. The corpse water was guarded throughout the wake as it was used to mark the end of the wake. When the body was taken from the house and everyone had left, the *bean bhán* would throw the water away from the house in the direction of the funeral and in a place where nobody would walk on it.

Any towel, comb or soap that had touched the corpse was buried in the same spot. All the trappings of the wake and death were removed immediately, and nothing was left in the house when the family returned; for if they remained, these things would pre-empt another death before the next full moon.

In laying out the corpse, the *bean bhán* would dress the body in their best clothes or a long black or brown habit that the deceased had already invested in and had blessed by the priest. This habit was often seen airing on the line, a premonition of the death of an ailing older person. She would put a bandage around the jaw of the dead person to close the open mouth and put coins on the eyelids to keep them shut. She tied the two big toes together or pinned the two stockinged feet with a safety pin so the body would be properly aligned for the coffin. Crucially, before the corpse was placed in the coffin, she had the important job of removing any pins and undoing any tyings, in the exact reverse order that she had made them, lest they were seen as an obstacle for the deceased to get to the next life.

The dead person's rosary beads and a small crucifix were placed in their hands and a prayer book was placed directly under the chin to maintain the closed mouth and prop up the head. Men were never buried in their best suit of clothes. Instead, a son or a brother would wear the good suit to Mass on the next three Sundays. There were never any alterations made to the suit, regardless of how ill-fitting it might have been. This was to fool any malevolent forces, such as the devil or the fairies, and allow time for the soul of the dead to get to the next life without any interference.

Special white wake sheets – usually five in number – were kept in each locality, and when they were brought to the wake house, they were placed under and over the corpse and also pinned to the wall and hung from ropes to form a small enclosing tent, or *cabán*, around the body. Green laurel leaves in the shape of a cross were sometimes sown into the sheets. Depending on the circumstances of the household and the size of the wake, the body might be laid out in a bedroom, in the kitchen or in the parlour. The difficulty of laying out a body on a small bed or short kitchen table was met by taking the main door off the hinges and placing it on the bed or table.

In the past, pre-made coffins were not available and the family would buy the wooden boards and the local carpenter would make the coffin over the few days of the wake. When it was ready, the body would be placed in the coffin on the last day of the wake. If the crowd was big, the wake would take place in a large barn or outhouse rather than the house, with the body laid out on the door and temporary seating put in place. It was vital to surround the corpse with as many candles as possible. People often received a pair of brass candlesticks as a wedding present and these anticipated the need for them in the future at both the Station Mass and the wake. Neighbours would loan their pair of candlesticks for the wake.

As a counter measure against death, it was vital to have an uneven, rather than an even number of candles lit and, in addition to the pairs of borrowed candlesticks, an extra candle was fixed in an old bottle to make it three, five, seven and so on. Certain households, cognisant of the inevitability of death, had prepared chests or suitcases carefully packed with clean sheets, rosary beads, blessed candles and holy oils, ready to be called into action. It was the women of the older generation who amassed and curated these hallowed components, and in lending them, they set the scene and operated as the overseers of the sacred aspect of the wake.

～ THE MERRY WAKE AND GAMES ～

The customs of the wake demanded that luxuriant items of hospitality, in the form of tobacco, snuff and drink, were always amply provisioned. Their abundant supply, allowing free and unfettered indulgence, added to the celebration of the life of the deceased. Such communal consumption served the role of uniting and incorporating all involved.

It was absolutely vital, regardless of the expense, to provide plenty of tobacco and clay pipes for the wake. A box of new chalk pipes would be bought, along with a good quantity of plug tobacco. The tobacco was cut and rubbed and filled into the long-stemmed pipes and a plate of the tobacco-filled pipes was placed on the chest of the deceased. On entering the wake house, each person would take a pipe, light it and say, 'May the Lord have mercy on the souls of the dead.' Throughout the night, new pipes of tobacco were continually passed around and people often had a great supply going home. When an elderly person was not strong enough to attend the wake, the 'Lord have mercy' pipe, as it was called, was brought home to them, and they lit it and said a prayer.

The story is told that the watchers overseeing the tomb of Christ through the night were finding it hard to stay awake and were starting to doze off, when, miraculously and out of nowhere, a new plant appeared in the ground near them with a pipe alongside it. One of them plucked a leaf and started to smoke it, and it helped them to stay awake – ever since, tobacco has been smoked at wakes. The pipes that had been smoked at the wake were often placed in the coffin while, at other times, when the grave was backfilled, many would place their wake pipes on top of the grave soil as a mark of respect.

In addition to tobacco, a plate of snuff was passed around specifically for the women, who all took a pinch and murmured the unvarying refrain, 'The Lord have mercy on the dead.' Snuff was an expensive item but its presence at the wake, along with the wafts of pungent tobacco smoke, were both necessary and practical to help to mask the putrid smell of death in a time before embalming.

The other costly and indispensable component of the wake provisioning was drink. The obsession with providing a plentiful supply of tea, wine, whiskey and porter for the huge assembly was often the cause of penury while alive. People stashed away small fortunes, depriving themselves and their children of many of life's necessities, only to have the money lavished at their wakes, mostly on alcohol, so that they might be remembered as being *flaithiúilach*.

According to William Carleton, writing in the 1830s, such were the numbers drinking at wakes, the shortage of glasses and cups was met with people drinking from eggshells, pistol barrels, tobacco boxes and, in extreme cases, scooped-out potatoes.

The consumption of alcohol was the catalyst for the communal anarchy of the wake, releasing the assembly from their normal everyday social constraints. In the face of death, alcohol was the shared narcotic that promoted the cathartic discharge of emotion and fuelled the communal sense of abandon and chaos that characterised the wake as a liminal time.

Chief amongst the consumers of the free-flowing wine and whiskey were the *mná caointe* (keening women) who, along with the *bean bhán*, were always the first to be served drink by way of acknowledgment of their special role and to sustain them in their activities. The professional keening women were a remnant of a very ancient Irish tradition of extemporised eulogies for the deceased. They were integral to the ritual of the wake, leading the other women in a concert of open, vociferous grief. Their continual sobbing and *olagóning*, moving between soft murmuring to loud passionate wailing, set the emotive tenor and tone of the wake.

Certain older keeners held great prestige, and it would have been unthinkable and disrespectful to the dead not to have them perform at the wake. It was usual to have four keening women present. The central role and high status of these women became the direct focus of resolute opposition from the patriarchal Church. For example, in 1800, Dr Thomas Bray, the Archbishop of Cashel, wrote: 'We also condemn and reprobate in the strongest terms, all unnatural screams and shrieks, and fictitious tuneful cries and elegies, together with the savage custom of howling and bawling at funerals.'

As overseers of the wake, these female figures would have been seen as having something approaching the prowess of otherworldly priestesses, with their authority and actions stemming from, and incorporating, an ancestral heritage that was non-Christian. The characteristic loud crying of the keening women connects them to the figure of the *bean sidh* (banshee), the Irish death messenger. The *bean sidh* was a lone, dangerous, otherworldly figure in Irish popular belief, often encountered combing her hair, and it was best to steer well clear of her. She was said to follow certain families and when they heard her cry during the night, it was taken as a certain portent of death.

The presence of keening women at the wake was far from the only concern of the outraged Church, seeking to assert its dominion over the rituals of death. More worrying from their moralistic perspective was the sheer frivolity of indecent behaviour that became synonymous with, and came to characterise, the so-called 'merry wake'.

Such merry wakes followed deaths that were considered natural and timely and when the deeper emotions of tragedy were absent. They were a spectacle of fun and frolic, complete with wild pranks and licentious parlour games. They were greatly looked forward to by all, especially the young men, who, as soon as they arrived and giddy for sport and mischief, were at horseplay, competing with one another, arm-wrestling, scrapping and lifting barrels of porter over their heads. The licence for amusement was tangible, with card-games (a hand was often dealt for the corpse) and a wake pipe placed in their mouth. A regime of dares and forfeits permeated the night's activities, which could become more and more outrageous.

Anyone who dozed off during the night might wake up minus their moustache or have their face blackened with a mixture of butter and soot. Tying shoelaces together or sewing the two ends of a swallowtail coat into the back of a chair caused no end of chaos when the unfortunate was awakened suddenly and fell over. A popular prank was to climb up on to the roof and cover the chimney with a large sod of turf, filling the house below with smoke.

Wake pipes were sabotaged by filling them with pepper or unstruck matches and they would unexpectedly explode to the delight of all. Throwing little missiles from a distance and hitting an unsuspecting victim was also very popular. The long stems of the wake pipes were broken into little pieces and pegged at someone who might then pick up a piece of turf and return fire. Before long, the pot of boiling potatoes was raided and these, along with everything from the still-burning bowls of chalk pipes, to eggs from the hen coop, were sent flying in an all-out battle.

The more organised and even more boisterous games of the night were overseen by a prominent male figure known as the 'borekeen', a name that derives from *bórachán*, a bow-legged person and which was also the name given to the joker in a pack of cards. He was a recognised figure of authority and might also on other occasions have been the captain of the Mummers or Wren Boys. He picked out a few other men as his helpers and, together, they set in motion a whole host of unruly games and cruel tricks that were embraced with both fear and joy by the assembly.

Games could take full advantage of the naivety of some participants and were relished by those who knew what was coming. The popular game of 'Bees and Honey', for example, picked out a person who had never been to a wake and had never seen the game before. The borekeen called out a group of men and women to be the bees and designated the unsuspecting person to be duped as the hive, putting them sitting in the centre of the kitchen on a stool. He told the others to start gathering the honey and they set off circling around the hive, making the buzzing sounds of bees. This scenario was great fun and the person who was the hive looked around with a smile on their face. The borekeen suggested that there was more honey outside the house and the bees went outside where, unknown to the hive, they filled their mouths with water. They returned inside, still making their comical buzzing noises and when the borekeen gave them the word that it was time to put the honey in the hive, in unison, they jettisoned their mouthfuls of water drenching the poor unfortunate hive.

Many of the wake games provided an occasion for sexual intimacy, with games where girls were put sitting on different boys' knees and free-for-all kissing was common. In the game of Frimsey Framsey, the borekeen sat on a chair in the centre of the wake house and called a young woman to him, sitting her on his knee and kissing her. He then asked 'Frimsey Framsey, who's your fancy?', and she called the name of the boy that she would like to kiss, who had to come, sit her on his knee and kiss her.

He, in turn, was asked the same question and the kissing game continued all night.

A variation of this game involved a type of mock marriage by the borekeen, and this often functioned as a form of unofficial matchmaking. To designate his function, he wore a makeshift priest's stole made from a string of small potatoes. The boys were put outside the door and the girls were asked what kind of husband they would like and, with their answers, they were paired off. Sometimes, the match was comical, with a younger man placed with an old widow, or a tall girl coupled with a short boy. More often, it was based on some mutual, but as yet unfulfilled attraction, and the obligatory coupling of the wake game provided a welcome introduction. The mock priest would get them to put a ring on each other's fingers or jump over a broom, and with some words of gibberish, supposedly solemnise their union. Even though these casual, yet intimate, encounters were made in jest, many couples put great store in wake marriages. Their public courtship fell under the watchful eye of the onlooking community and having spent a night in each other's company, such an open display of intimacy cemented many a long-term relationship.

BURIAL

The wakes ran over two nights then, on the morning of the third day, the body was placed in the coffin, along with some wake pipes and whiskey and the family said their goodbyes with a funeral Mass celebrated in the house. The body was brought directly from the house for burial then, in later years, it was customary to bring the coffin to the church to rest overnight before the funeral.

The coffin was taken feet first through the doorway and rested on some chairs outside for a while, where the near final and most vociferous performance of keening and mourning took place. If the death was of a young married woman, which was often the case resulting from complications in childbirth, she would be buried with her own people, in her own family's grave, as the man would likely wish to marry again. The coffin was carried by four men who bore the same surname as the deceased, and it was a mark of respect to shoulder the coffin all the way to the graveyard. There were ready relays of relations and neighbours who were honoured to take their turn at shouldering along the route. If the distance to the graveyard was long, there were specific stones or resting places, often at crossroads or at the boundary of certain townlands, where the coffin was let down and a decade of the rosary was said. Nothing should interfere with the passage of the funeral and if anyone walking the road in the opposite direction met a funeral, they would always turn and walk three steps with it in its direction.

The longest route to the graveyard was always observed and when everyone arrived at the graveyard, it was the deceased's four closest relatives who carried the coffin again, being careful to take the longest path, always moving in a sunwise direction to the grave. Digging a grave was considered a great honour, with friends and neighbours almost competing to take on the task. If the person was to be buried on a Monday, people often 'scratched' the surface of the grave on the Sunday, as opening a grave on a Monday was seen to court death. The usual salutation, 'God bless the work', traditionally said when meeting anyone engaged at hard work, was never uttered when a grave was being dug.

While the days of the keening women and the raucous games of the borekeen are long since passed, there are still certain inherited aspects of the older rituals of death that are vividly manifest in Ireland. I remember when my own father died, my sister, who was pregnant, observed the old custom that a pregnant woman should not enter a graveyard. With all sorts of trip hazards from uneven surfaces around flat grave slabs and over-leaning headstones, Irish graveyards are veritable danger zones and there is a great risk of falling. Any pregnant woman who did enter the graveyard and who fell or tripped was putting their baby at risk of being born *bachachdaig* (bandy-legged), an affliction known as *cam reilig*, the crookedness of the graveyard.

The ninety-four-year-old mother of a farming neighbour of mine died recently and the family waked her in her house. It was a monumental undertaking with friends and neighbours, old and young, in hi-vis vests directing cars into fields and muddy yards, doing their best to manage the multitudes who came to pay their respects. The kitchen was chock-a-block with women making pots of tea and sandwiches, and others went around with plates of sweet cake, offering them to those who had sympathised with the family and who were sitting down.

There were men in huddles, whispering and laughing, while drinking beer and glasses of whiskey. The long line of people, waiting to shake hands and offer their condolences to the family moved slowly, as tender reminiscences were recounted and appreciated. The deceased lady was laid out in an open coffin, dressed in her favourite rig-out, with her hands in prayer, clasping her rosary beads. Everyone filed past, paused and smiled and placed their hand on the coffin as a mark of respect. I had never met the lady, but I was there, part of a huge unprompted congregation, made up of everyone in the hinterland and the countless others, distant relations, friends and simply casual acquaintances, all of whom had taken time out to travel from near and far to pay their respects.

When I was young, I remember seeing men handing out cigarettes at the gate of a graveyard in Sneem, County Kerry. I have watched relatives spilling whiskey on the ground and half a bottle of *poitín* into an open grave following a burial. The haunting notes of the slow air 'An Chúalainn' played on the accordion by my first cousins, Jimmy Daly and John Crummy, with genuine grief at my father's graveside and at other family funerals still resonates profoundly in the depths of my ancestral soul, like the piercing cries of the keening women.

The carefully wrought words of a thoughtfully composed, well-delivered, emotive eulogy can live on in one's mind for the rest of your life. In Ireland, through the process of waking our dead in our homes, we reclaim our ability to stop the clock, allocating time to death, and celebrate with sincerity the personality and life of the deceased.

PART TWO

Folk Life: The Extraordinary in the Everyday

The razzamatazz of the overseas holiday soon wears off. It doesn't matter how exotically sunny it was or how enticing the gourmet food was, after a few weeks, most Irish people have a secret craving for home. They have survived their brief exodus from their homely comforts by carrying with them vital supplies from their everyday lives: teabags, their own pillow, slippers, a few packets of Taytos and the last copy of their local newspaper bought before departure.

When away from our homeland, the Irish are often like fish out of water, our cultural disposition of openness miscued and frequently misunderstood. The sunburned Paddy on tour in his socks and sandals, saluting everyone he meets on his walk down the palm tree-lined boulevard in search of a pot of tea and a scone is lovingly known to us all. The modern, more cosmopolitan Irish traveller may disagree, yet they too default to the comfort of the familiar when they are away from home.

It is the subtleties and peculiar nuances of the inherited ordinary of the everyday that define our cultural identity. We may aspire to the sophisticated consumption of the confections of a master pâtissier with a tiny cup of intense espresso, yet, at home, our private solace and pleasure is a slice of hot buttered toast, maybe a rasher, a pot of tea, a sit down with the paper with the radio on in the background.

We recognise and embrace a materiality and character in our environments with an intimacy that firmly roots this sense of home. Our Irishness is manifested in cultural signifiers that resonate within us, hidden and unseen by outsiders: the Padre Pio sticker on the car window, the multicoloured sheep on a

mountain pass, an old lad on a Honda 50, a hand-painted sign advertising 'spuds for sale', the Angelus bell on the radio, a herd of cows going home for milking or the couple enjoying a 99 on a cold February afternoon. Irish people get the deep yet subtle nuances of the Saw Doctors' lyrics, the characters in *Father Ted* or the *D'Unbelievables* in a way that cannot be explained. The depth of context takes a lifetime to accumulate. Like stage sets for a John B. Keane play, there are kitchens all over the country with lino on the floor, the Sacred Heart light adorning the wall, and knitted tea-cosies and brown bread sitting on an oilcloth-covered table. There are tinny sheds, smoke-stained pubs, pine-pewed churches, dusty sweetshops and old schoolhouses that are ubiquitous in their accumulations of remnants from our past.

These are the locations with character, with a sense of knowing and a sense of where we belong, that we fully recognise and where we feel at home.

Apart from the materiality of culture, there is the non-material side of our sense of self that manifests itself in our addiction to conversation. The ever-popular enquiring Irish greetings, 'Any news?' or 'What's the story?' reflect our insatiable desire for topical and entertaining banter.

Like Beckett's characters who are waiting for Godot, we indulge in talk to fill time and space with narratives of realities of our own making. We extend invitations, not only for general talk, but as an opening to partake in the crafted finesse of expression. We share an insatiable need for conversation, for the exchange of words that is often parsed in wild, vivid and exaggerated detail. An example of such verbal amusement is a remark made about the man who outstays his welcome, 'If that fella went to a wedding, he'd stay for the christening!' or the jibe at the boy with the bucktoothed smile, 'He wasn't behind the door when the teeth were being given out.'

We are a people of consummate storytellers, who weave fantastical and highly entertaining stories drawn from scraps of the everyday. The lyrical orality of Irish expression – our pronunciations, idioms, phraseology and choice of words in English – stem directly from the roots of our native language. Those who are not avid talkers function as careful listeners, as the discriminating audience, soaking into their minds the wonder of the oratory and fine detail of the description. Their contributions might be more concentrated, often having the wit to sum something up in one or two words.

Irish understatement is an art form in itself. I love the aphoristic wit of the farm labourer who, after a hard day's work, sat down to the table and was presented with a miserable, dry piece of bread accompanied by the very smallest spoonful of honey on the side of the plate. He paused, staring at the tiny morsel of honey for a minute or two before wryly remarking to the *bean an tí*, 'I see, missus, you keep a bee.'

There were a series of places in Ireland's past where the joy of such speech and blather used to be fully elaborated: the blacksmith's forge, the pub, the creamery, the village water pump or outside the church on a Sunday were all convivial social settings for talk. It was talk that allowed us to pass the time and talk that made our worlds what they were. There were no external stimuli and little by way of extraneous diversions, and it was the internal imagination and individual's skill with words that manifested the distraction and entertainment of life.

The catalyst for talk was tea and putting the kettle boiling for a quick cuppa had nothing to do with thirst or need for sustenance; it was the mechanism for allocated time for quality human interaction. When meeting someone for the first time, the conventional conversation opener was an up-to-date pronouncement on the weather that could lead off into a lengthy meteorological treatise. In these ways, our everyday ordinary becomes fantastically extraordinary.

AT HOME

Dead From Tea and Dead Without It

When I makes tea, I makes tea, as Old Mother Grogan said. And when I makes water, I makes water.

Although Old Mother Grogan's stern declaration in James Joyce's *Ulysses* is a comical jibe on urination, it may equally be read as an admonishment against weak tea. It captures the sense of pride and attention to detail that a properly made cup of tea holds in the Irish psyche.

As Ireland's stalwart domestic beverage for numerous generations, tea has integrated itself into every social and cultural aspect of Irish life. A cup before going to bed, a bottle of tea in the bog, sweet tea after a shock or a big stainless-steel kettle of tea at a party are everyday settings that demonstrate its once-unarguable indispensability. However, with the changes in our modern lifestyles and the rise of outdoor coffee culture, our once-great tea-making tradition – long a core cultural unifier – could well be on the cusp of demise.

～◎ THE EARLY DAYS OF TEA ◎～

Tea only became popular in Ireland in the early nineteenth century and, given that it was imported from China, it was exotic and expensive and remained the preserve of the upper classes. In the big houses of the landed gentry, tea was so valuable and rare that it was kept under lock and key in small wooden tea caddies. Significantly, it was wholeheartedly adopted by female gentry who used the ritual of making tea, along with the sophisticated paraphernalia of silver kettles, bone-china teacups and sugar tongs as the context for social interaction.

According to the nineteenth-century etiquette manuals that sought to guide society away from what was thought improper and vulgar, it was instructed that tea should never be consumed before midday. Instead, invited guests should come between a quarter-past four and six o'clock to partake of a single cup of tea, poured with ceremony by the hostess herself. Such precise timing is the origin of the everyday use of 'tea' and 'teatime' that have been used ever since in Ireland for the meal taken in and around six o'clock.

In the nineteenth century, tea houses and tea rooms became popular in urban centres, serving afternoon teas accompanied by scones and sweet confections for the aspiring middle classes.

Tea-drinking was actively promoted as a healthy alternative to the excesses and harm of over-indulgence in alcohol by the temperance movement from the 1820s onwards. Fr Theobald Matthew, its chief motivator in Ireland, established the Cork Total Abstinence Society in 1838, and had some 2,400 members within a year. By 1845, over 3 million people in Ireland had taken the pledge and such national sobriety was facilitated by the accentuated lauding of tea. The society set up special reading rooms and organised social gatherings facilitated by free newspapers and lashings of tea. Special temperance meetings and parties centred on tea as a non-alcoholic beverage were organised by women. 'Teetotalism' – the term coined at this time to describe someone's total abstinence from alcohol – has often quite logically been confused with the idea that someone was a 'tea-totaller', a person who drank only tea.

At first, the rural poor knew very little of this exotic drink and were entirely ignorant of how to prepare and serve it. There is the story of the woman, conscious of the new trend, who bought in a pound of tea to serve to the priest at the Station Mass. She boiled up the tea in the pot over the fire, strained out the water and served up the wet tea leaves on a plate to the priest like it was a feed of cabbage. In a gentle rebuke, the priest suggested that the next time she might also serve up the soup of the leaves in a cup to him.

The fine detail of the gentrified tea-making process was absent in the poorer rural households of the post-famine period where tea-drinking was, nevertheless, becoming increasingly common. Most often a pot with the tea leaves was left stewing over the fire, ever ready to offer in hospitality to anyone who called. The strong tea was poured into bowls, or a teapot if they had one, and then the woman of the house would wet the tea by pouring more water on the old leaves into the pot for another brew.

The Tay-Man

By the early twentieth century, the now widespread nature and social status of tea-drinking made it a must-have commodity. In those early days, there emerged a figure in Irish life known as 'the tay-man'. The tay-man made a living by travelling around the poorer districts peddling tea to those who aspired to tea-drinking. He had a pony and trap and, like a drug-dealer, he would give a few ounces of tea on tick and come calling for the money later.

His favourite trick was to leave a bag of tea on a windowsill and, of course, people took it and drank it, only to be immediately in his debt. He had a small weighing scales and he made a ceremony of carefully weighing out the exact amount of the precious tea while proclaiming its many merits. In reality, his tea was usually of an inferior quality, sometimes mixed with dried turf mould from the bogs. Nevertheless, he was the main source for a lot of people and would call regularly with a continual supply.

People came to despise the tay-man as they seldom had the money to pay him, and when they saw him coming, doors were locked and the dog left out. There was one woman who had let her tea bill mount up and she was in dread because many of the tay-men had a reputation for coaxing those in their debt into a clandestine arrangement to settle their affairs. This woman was on final notice and at her wit's end wondering how she could escape the tay-man's advances. It was her cousins from over the hill who came up with the solution. Taking the door off the hinges and whitening her face with flour, they covered her with white sheets and laid her out as if she was dead. They put seven candles lighting all around her and when the tay-man came calling, he was met with loud keening and *olagóning* at the wake within. He took one look in the door to see the spectacle before her cousin informed him that the poor woman had died suddenly having suffered severely from a contagious fever. The tay-man turned on his heel, away with him as quick as he could, and was never seen again.

People were not so much addicted to tea but more habituated to it and it became firmly embedded into their lives: '*Marbh le tae agus marbh gan é*' ('We're dead from tea but we'd be dead without it!') When people ran out of tea, in desperation they would dispatch a child to beg an eggcup of tea from their neighbours until the tay-man would come again.

In time, displays of tea-associated accoutrements filled the dressers and sideboards of Irish houses: tin teapots made by the travelling tinsmiths, heavy delph teapots, enamel teapots and, of course, a lifetime collection of all manner of mugs, ponnies, cups and saucers, milk jugs and sugar bowls. Anything from decorative spongeware blackberry designs on slip pottery to blue-band earthenware mugs, willow pattern delph and fine bone china were called into action to present the sup of tae.

Even though your status in the household was expressed in the nature of the cup you were presented with, it was not at all special to be offered both a cup and a saucer for tea. For some early initiates to tea-drinking, the saucer was a confusing non-functional addition, but they soon put it to work, pouring the hot tea from the cup and slurping the cooled contents from the corner of the saucer. The Indian black tea to which the Irish became inextricably attached had such high tannins and an astringent nature that, to offset its harsh nature, it was necessary to add large amounts of milk and sugar. In fact, it might be considered that the Irish obsession with tea is only an excuse for consuming vast quantities of sugary, milky, hot water.

Everyone took sugar in their tea, loading each cup with two, three or, if they could get away with it, four, heavily laden spoonfuls of white granulated sugar. Part of the ritual was stirring the sugar into the tea and with an air of sophisticated panache some would tap the spoon with a tinkle on the edge of the cup before placing it back on the saucer. The stirring of tea in the cup was a habitual, almost meditative, comfort. When the tea was drunk, the extra treat was to scoop out the half-dissolved warm milky sugar dregs at the bottom of the cup with the spoon.

There were numerous occasions when such sweet milky tea found its way into vessels other than cups or mugs. When heading off to a football match or spending a day in the bog, very hot tea was carefully poured into empty, glass pint porter bottles and plugged tightly with a well-fitted bung of newspaper. Each was then slipped into a thick woollen sock and from there carried in the deep pockets of overcoats. Such insulation managed to keep the tea tolerably warm and palatable for when it was needed. Tea was also regularly presented in a bucket, especially when men were working together in a *meitheal* (group) in the fields, saving hay or stooking sheaves of oats. The long day's work would pause when the women and girls would arrive with a steaming bucket of sweet milky tea. In the corner of the field, cushioned on the dry, soft hay, each person sat around the bucket dipping in and filling their cups, slaking their thirst with the ample servings of revitalising tea.

Although despised by the real tea connoisseurs, the invention of the now ubiquitous teabag is attributed to an Irishman, Thomas Sullivan, who was a tea salesman in New York in 1908. He used to pack choice samples of his tea into small silk bags and people began using them as infusions. Before the ubiquitous takeover of the teabag in the latter decades of the twentieth century, all tea was loose leaf tea and dealing with mouthfuls of tea leaves was a part of everyday life. Some employed a small handheld sieve or tea strainer over the cup as the tea was poured from the tea pot to capture any floating leaves, while most simply waited for the tea to sink to the bottom of the pot.

In folklore, a stray tea leaf floating on your tea indicated that 'a visitor would come calling' – and if, on further examination, the tea leaf was hard the visitor would be a man; if it was soft, a woman. Reading the tea leaves was a favourite pastime. My grand-aunt, Auntie Kitty, used to read the tea leaves for us when we were children and her prognostications of 'a surprise', 'a letter in the post', 'you will go on a journey' or 'there's money coming your way', filled us with excitement, as they somehow always came true.

A Cup Out of Your Hand

It is still the case that when anyone calls to a house, the cup of tea is the core instrument of hospitality. It is around the cup of tea and its making, that conversation and the passing of time is most regularly attached. In Ireland, it is essential to offer a guest a cup of tea and equally essential for the visitor to refuse it, making sure the hosts are not put to any bother.

The visitor is confronted with the offer of tea in a direct statement. 'You'll have a cup of tea!'

This is met with the necessary standard response of refusal, 'Ah, no thanks, I'm fine', regardless of the visitor's earnest wish for a cup of tea.

The host will continue. 'Ah, sure, I have the kettle on. Have one out of your hand.'

A second automatic refusal is called for. 'No thanks, I'm grand, sure I only had one before I called down.'

The host will parry this with a complete dismissal. 'Have one anyway. I was just about to make one for myself.'

When the tea is made and the visitor presented with the cup, even though they had been witness to its preparation, they have to feign surprise. 'Ah, now, you shouldn't have gone to any trouble', and then, taking a sip declare, 'That's a lovely cup of tea! Thank you.'

In times gone by, it was considered not only bad manners, but a source of bad luck to refuse a cup of tea. There is the story of a man who was visiting his cousins late one night and, after a night of chatting, he got up to head for home. The woman of the house asked him to have a cup of tea before he left to warm him up, but he was anxious to get going and refused. Despite her protestations, he left and headed into the night but whatever the cause, he found it hard to find his way and, eventually, he came back to the house and sat down and had the tea. When he headed out again, he had no problem finding the road home and from that night on, he never refused a cup of tea nor ever got lost on the road home again.

Famously, the Chinese have a highly stylised tea ceremony, but the Irish also have their very own. When it comes to tea, it is all about heat – the kettle of steaming, boiling water had to be hopping off the range. There were large earthenware pots and, later on, voluminous stainless-steel teapots, big enough to accommodate a large family plus any number of visitors.

Firstly, the teapot had to be scalded by swirling boiling water around it, feeling the exterior of the pot until it was hot through. Next, the lid of the black and gilded rectangular tin tea caddy holding the loose tea was flipped open to access the dedicated teaspoon that always remained within. With the aid of this utensil, an unspecified number of variously heaped and non-heaped teaspoons of tea were carefully added to the steaming teapot. This process was pure alchemy as the tea could be neither too weak nor too strong, and the formula of a spoon for each person and one for the pot had to be carefully tempered with a mixture of experience and luck.

The boiling water was then added, leading to the next stumbling block in the tea-making challenge – the amount of time you had to leave the tea to draw. Importantly, while it was drawing, the brewing tea had to be kept warm, and many covered the teapot with a tight-fitting knitted tea cosy, usually the product of one of the children's domestic-science classes.

When gas cookers came in, the stainless-steel teapots were placed against a very low gas flame on the hob. This practice gave rise to a distinctive black streak running up the side of the pot, but it also ran the risk of the tea being stewed and duly rejected by the awaiting connoisseurs.

Many Irish people love strong tea – 'Strong enough that a mouse could trot on it.' However, tea that was stewed – 'You could stand your spoon in it' – or too weak – 'Dish water' – was, on a few occasions, the trigger for public ridicule. With a disbelieving kerfuffle and a shaming loud accusation of 'Who made that tea?', the tea was officially declared undrinkable by the experienced tea-drinker. The contents were ceremonially jettisoned and the novice tea-maker was chastened when the whole tea-making process had to be restarted and repeated slowly, step-by-step, in a lesson of instruction and humiliation by an elder in the family.

The next time you made the tea, probably an hour or so later, as people used to drink anything up to ten pots of tea per day, you made it carefully and without any short cuts in the hope of positive affirmation.

Each family in Ireland has a distinct loyalty to their own brand and blend of tea and while there has long been a cultural schism between the likes of Lyons and Barry's, when Irish people go abroad, such rivalries are quickly forgotten and all their own black teas are cherished. Being faced with the prospect of having to drink the insipid teas of other countries for a fortnight is almost enough to spoil an entire holiday. The first item shoved into the corner of most suitcases when packing for any excursion is a plastic bag full of teabags.

The desire and taste for tea may well come from the fact that most Irish people, when they were babies, were comforted with a bottle of sweet, lukewarm, milky tea. When the tea was being made, the child was not left out of the comfort and social enjoyment that tea-drinking represented. It is a notable phenomenon that, in Irish hospitals, following the most serious of operations or, indeed, the lengthy birth of a baby, the first thing presented to the patient or mother is a cup of tea.

It may not be an exaggeration to declare that the Irish were born to tea and whatever about being dead from it – *marbh le tae* – our cultural identity might not be the same without it – *marbh gan é*.

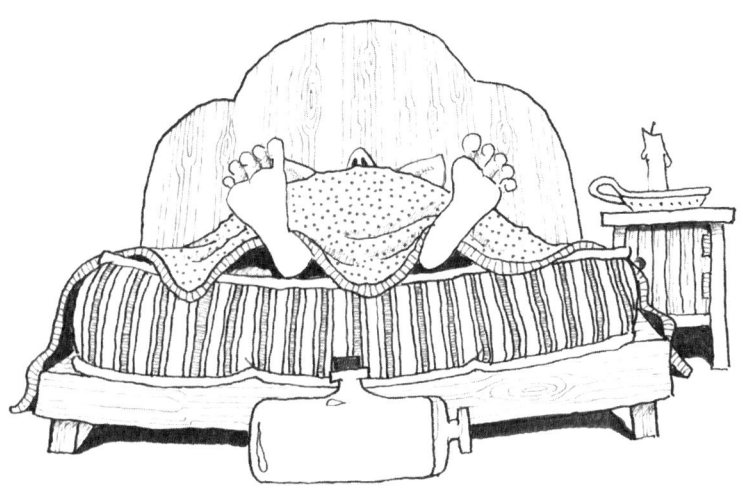

A Place to Sleep

The bed has always been the warmest place in the house and, in the deep cold winter, with only the solace of a damp turf fire, there was little point in getting out of it. In harmony with Irish badgers who do not hibernate but undergo what is termed 'winter lethargy', in the absence of heating, many people back in the day took to the bed for the winter months.

Cocooned under the sheets and woollen blankets and the quilted eiderdown and heavy overcoats, they slept through the inclemency of the season. A man in my own locality was known as 'Wake Mick', and, come November and the cold weather, he used to bid good luck to the neighbours and the lads in the pub, take to the bed and would not reappear again until the spring.

Even if not as given to the 'scratcher' as much as Mick, each person spends on average one-third or more of their lives in bed, and much can be gleaned about the characteristic nuances of everyday Irish culture by exploring the traditions of beds and sleeping.

STRAW AND RUSHES

Some of the earliest accounts of beds in Ireland, from the seventeenth century onwards, indicate that, amongst the rural poor, the bed was literally like a bird's nest and consisted of little more than a *sráideóg* (bundle of straw) that was set up each night on the bare kitchen floor in front of the fire. The priority of this 'shakedown' was to keep everyone cosy and warm.

By contrast, in the summertime, rushes were the preferred bedding material and were thought to keep people cool. An initial layer made of bent branches of bogwood or a bundle of burnt furze was first set down to create an insulating gap against the cold floor. Some would criss-cross lengths of hazel and willow, intertwined into a robust hurdle and on top of this, the straw or rushes and any other soft materials like hay, fern, moss or heather were placed. A long length of bogwood or a few stones defined the bedding area and kept the arrangement together. A large heavy woollen blanket was placed on top and then wrapped around the occupants.

From earliest times until the early nineteenth century, the modern concept of the bed was absent in homes of Ireland's rural poor. As time went by, it was more practical to keep the bedding together and hay, ferns, rushes and straw were sown into large sacks. A sack filled with newly thrashed straw was known as *leaba cocháin* (sack of newly thrashed straw) and some placed a *leaba chabh* (sack of chaff) on top of this for comfort and support. In addition, there was a widespread technique of knotting and plaiting straw into thick mats or mattresses.

Everyone in a family slept together – the man and his wife in the middle and their children, in decreasing order of age, outwards. At the other end, top to toe, there were the grandparents and older children, while any visitor was confined to the edge, perhaps bolstered by the warm body of the pig, with other animals, such as the cow and goat, close by. An early account of the joy of sleeping with animals is provided in the letters of English traveller John Dunton when he was the guest of an Irish family in their rural home in Connemara in 1698.

> *I had but just compos'd my self to sleep when I was strangley surprised to hear the cows and sheep all coming into my bed chamber ... I found the beasts lay down soone after they had enter'd ... and truly if the nastiness of theire excrements did not cause an aversion hereto, the sweetness of their breath which I never was sensible of before, and the pleasing noyse they made in ruminating or chawing the cud, would lull a body to sleep as soon as the noyse of a murmuring brook and the fragancy of a bed [of] roses.*

In the wintertime, everything was about heat, and all manner of blankets and extra coverings, such as heavy overcoats, were employed to insulate the combined body heat of the family and company.

By the early nineteenth century, as well as sleeping on straw and rushes, a number of interesting beds emerged in the traditional Irish house. In the lithographs of the nineteenth century pictorial newspapers, there are illustrations of long beds and benches close to the fire made from scraw, the soft top layer of the bog. The fibrous nature of this top turf layer holds the root material that supports the living plants of the bog and, when cut and dried, it provided a soft, yet firm, spongy material ideal for sitting upon by day and sleeping upon by night.

Sleeping close to the fire was one of the reasons that, in the northwest of the country, a special extension to the traditional Irish house was accommodated. This small extended alcove or outshot, about six feet long and three and a half feet wide, was placed right beside the open hearth and was known as the *cúilteach* (back of the house). Some people punned this name with *cailleach* (hag) as this was often where the more bed-confined older inhabitants slept. In the evening time, when the talk of the day, storytelling and general banter was going on around the fireplace, the older family members snug in their bed could still be part of the fun.

The ubiquitous sow, always present in the house, would often make its sty under this bed and the extra warmth wafting upwards was fully appreciated. This bed outshot is an architectural peculiarity that has its own discrete geographical distribution, confined in Ireland generally to the coastal counties of Galway, Mayo, Sligo, Leitrim, Donegal, Derry and Antrim. This feature is also found along the west coast of Scotland and in the Nordic countries of Norway, Sweden, Denmark and Iceland.

In addition to this intramural bed, a variety of wooden beds also featured in the Irish house, including the tester, or four-poster, bed and the canopy bed. Essentially, these were like small rooms within rooms, enclosed with wood and coverings, designed to keep the occupants warm and offer some privacy for moments of intimacy.

Perhaps the best remembered bed in Ireland is the settle bed, a multifunctioning item of furniture that operated as a high, long, deep seat during the day and transformed into a sizeable rectangular box that functioned as a bed at night. The bottom of the settle had two big hinges at floor level and when the flat wooden panels of the seat were pulled down to a vertical position to form the side of the bed, its occupants had a low wooden box bed where they cosily sheltered from draughts. Sleeping in the settle bed was the next step on from sleeping on straw in front of the fire. In the mornings, the hinged box of the open settle bed would be lifted back into its seat position, conveniently freeing up much needed floor space in the kitchen for the activities of the day.

As time moved on, more recognisable bedsteads came into being, with wooden frames supporting the mattresses. Some of these wooden beds had a clever method of providing extra comfort – their base consisted of a tight-knit, interwoven cord or rope fed through holes at the top, bottom and sides of the bed frame. Over time, with the weight of the occupants, these ropes inevitably stretched and sagged, and it was necessary to re-establish a comfortable tension. This was accomplished by taking a short piece of wood, fitting it into one of the loops of rope at the side of the bedframe and twisting in a tourniquet fashion until the bed cords returned flat and taut. This gave rise to the well-known wish at bedtime to 'sleep tight'.

At the turn of the twentieth century, metal became the chief component of bed frames, with ornate brass-topped iron bedsteads, woven sprung bed bases, and coiled and box springs incorporated into mattresses.

For children, their parents' big beds were an early incarnation of as yet unheard-of trampolines, and bouncing and playing on the bed was a real treat. Such abuse coupled with the general ravages of time made flitters of the mattresses and their springs, and, as the beds were handed down, going to bed became a dangerous affair.

Toss the Feathers

The settle bed was the ideal set-up for the most luxuriant and revered of all bedding: the feather-filled tick mattress. The goose-down mattress was regularly part of the dowry that the woman brought with her to the marriage. People not only kept geese for their eggs, meat and fat, but also for their feathers. There was a whole industry of feather merchants who encouraged the keeping of geese, specifically as these stubble geese fattened on the fallen grain following harvest.

Either the housewives themselves would pluck the geese or teams of goose-pluckers would visit farms in the weeks coming up to *Fomhar na nGéan* (Harvest of the Geese) on 29 September, when the geese were killed. The agronomist, Arthur Young, visiting Ballynough County Leitrim in 1779, outlines that every goose yielded feathers worth three farthings or a halfpenny each year. The goose-pluckers came on two occasions, once in early July and again at Michaelmas, to harvest their supplies, which promoted the practice of plucking the geese while they were still alive. An account from the 1839 by Martin Doyle in his *Cyclopaedia of Practical Husbandry* outlines the barbarity of the practice.

> *They pull out the feathers in the most rough and rapid manner to save time, without paying the slightest attention to the tortured birds ... After this operation, geese are sick and thin, and in reality and appearance, especially in cold weather, very miserable until the new feathers cover them, when the same barbarities are repeated.*

Young remarked that such defeathered birds 'make a dreadful ragged figure' – the old Irish seanfhocal, '*Chomh lom le gé bhearrtha*' ('As naked as a plucked goose') describes this plight.

The tick mattress was so called because the fabric ticking was a very tightly woven cotton or linen, which stopped the sharp end points of the feathers poking through. The ticking was made into a bag and then some fifty or sixty pounds of light, downy feathers were sown into it. The goose-down tick mattress was of such value that it became a cherished heirloom and there are numerous accounts of people leaving their bedding and mattress in their wills.

Another heirloom, often provided as a wedding present from a mother to her daughter at marriage, was a patchwork quilt. Old clothes were cut up to provide the material while others resorted to getting off-cuts and scraps of material that had to be bought by weight from dressmakers, tailors or textile shops.

Heavy materials such as tweed, serge and flannel were the favourites used to make a large heavy quilt, known in places as a beggarman's quilt. The small scraps of material were carefully cut into geometric shapes, hexagons, squares and triangles, and, as each was diligently sown together, the women took great pride in the magnificent kaleidoscopic patterns that they created.

In turn, this delicate patchwork had to be reinforced by sewing or quilting it to a back sheet. This sheet was provided by repurposing some old flour sacks that had first had their printed labels soaked and blanched in the sun. The quilting demanded a special large quilting frame that kept the patchwork, its padded interlining and bottom sheet tight, while a quilting party of half a dozen or more women worked together sewing from the outside inwards. Such quilting was far from an easy task, and was a time-consuming, precise undertaking. Nevertheless, the resulting quilt, representing the combined enterprise of family, neighbours and friends, was a manifestation of the communal best wishes directed towards newlyweds.

～ Hot Jars and Bri-Nylon ～

My memory of the beds of my childhood are of nothing but discomfort. Our beds were hand-me-downs from previous generations that had already passed their best years. The depressing mahogany tops and bottoms, sloping inwards, were, in turn, poorly attached to two metal rails and the slightest of movements resulted in the whole bed creaking and rattling in an endless clamour. It is small wonder that we got any sleep at all.

The patched mattress had collapsed corners, deep hollows and sharp, protruding metal spring ends, demanding that you had to be something of a contortionist to get through a night's sleep unscathed. The bed board sitting upon its two metal rails was tentatively held in place by two pendular metal stops and these were regularly booby-trapped by my older brothers. Lifting the stops up, it was possible to perch the bed board on the very edge of the rail and as I unsuspectingly launched myself into the bed, the whole thing would spectacularly collapse and I was unmercifully wedged between the iron rail and mattress to the great hilarity of all. The bed-falling-down trick was an at least once-a-week distraction.

We grew up in the era before duvets and in the era when one had to 'make the bed', a preoccupation that took a great deal of time and was the focus of many a family argument. The bed clothes consisted of striped flannel sheets and blankets and perhaps a candlewick bedspread. The trickiest sheet to get right was the under sheet because it could easily come loose. This changed in the 1970s with the introduction of fitted sheets that wrapped around the mattress. As wonderful as this sounds, it had a major downside as it came in a new fabric – Bri-Nylon. Not only did these sheets of artificial plastic fibre come in headache-inducing powder blue, baby pink and luminous green, the build-up of static electricity was also such that you literally got electrocuted getting in and out of bed. This was in addition to friction burns as you struggled to get warm and the danger of having your toenail ripped off as its sharp edge got caught in the microfibres. Bri-Nylon sheets were impermeable and brought everyone out in streams of sweat and, as their presence overlapped with the introduction of the electric blanket in the 1980s, bed was perhaps the most unsafe and least appealing place to find one's rest.

Before the electric blanket, cold beds were warmed with hot-water bottles made of pink or blue rubber, called 'hot-water jars' by many because their predecessors were large ceramic crocks. At nine o'clock at night, after the cup of tea and a biscuit for supper, the kettle was boiled and the hot-water bottles were filled at the kitchen sink. You had to make sure you didn't scald yourself by overfilling the bottle or when battling the boiling overflow as you twisted the black bung back into position.

In the post-war years, large Irish families of eight to twelve children or more were common, and such numbers made sleeping arrangements complicated. If you were lucky, your parents invested in the very popular bunk beds and clambering up the ladder to the top bunk made bed a plaything as well as a place of status for whoever got to sleep on top.

There were others who had to share a double bed and this arrangement had a whole set of unwritten rules. There was an imaginary line running down the centre of the bed, the policing of which would keep you awake into the small hours. There could be no incursion into enemy territory as it was instantly punished with a thump or a dead arm and could escalate into an all-out kicking war. In large families, there was often four in the bed, sleeping top to toe as in the *sráideóg* tradition. After much rummaging for space, contending with bony knees and smelly feet, like a litter of newborn puppies, the communal heat sent everyone off to a night of contented slumber.

In the present era, as family sizes have decreased, many children have their own beds – and, indeed, their own rooms, with a few even having their own en-suite bathrooms. Beds have grown in size with doubles, queens, kings, superkings and beyond. There are Japanese futons, orthopaedically adjusted bedsteads, memory-foam mattresses, hypoallergenic duvets and pillows. The world of the bed has had the full technological makeover yet regardless of modernisation, it remains a timeless place, the great leveller, where whether king or pauper, each and every one of us repairs to our otherworld, the land of dreams and lullabies, the place that my father affectionately called 'Seoithín-seo'.

The Fear of God

The remarkable Irish obsession with religious fetishes might have its origins in the era of the Penal Laws of the seventeenth and eighteenth centuries when no manifestation of Catholic identity was permitted. This was the time when Mass had to be celebrated secretly in the open air at Mass Rocks, and priests were in danger of being put to death.

In my own parish of Matehy, the memory of such times is kept alive by how the area got its name – *Magh Teithe* (plain of the fleeing). It recalls how the priest who was secretly celebrating Mass was surprised and struck down by the redcoat, Captain Fox. In a triumphant display, the captain galloped off with the decapitated priest's head paraded atop the captain's sword. However, his cavalcade of glory was short-lived. On riding down a steep hill near the Shournagh river, the captain was thrown from his horse and broke his neck. In fear of reprisals from the locals, his comrades quickly dug a grave and in haste interred him in the nearby old graveyard at Loughane. However, that night, it is said, that all of the Catholic dead, their place of rest now contaminated by the presence of the priest murderer, climbed out of their graves and, carrying their headstones, crawled their way across the steep plain to Matehy graveyard, where they reinterred themselves. To this day, there is but one headstone in Loughane graveyard.

A Rebounding Faith

This local, living memory serves to bridge the present to a seminal moment in our historic past and, for many, such past persecution is the very root of their religious faith and identity. The severity of religious suppression in Ireland made the substantial rebound of the divested majority an inevitability.

The mutual tie between the re-emerging Catholic religion and what was to develop into nationalism and independence was now afoot. Towards the latter end of the eighteenth century, the Penal Laws were no longer valid and, by 1789, Catholics were granted freedom to worship. This led the way for the liberator – Kerry barrister Daniel O'Connell – to launch his campaign of emancipation in the early years of the nineteenth century.

In 1823, he founded the Catholic Association, which eventually registered over 3 million members from all strata of Irish society. Ingeniously, he organised a Catholic census in 1825 to highlight the numerical disparity between Catholics and Protestants and, with monster meetings and clever legal and political arguments, enabled him to win Catholic emancipation in 1829.

What followed throughout the nineteenth century, despite widespread deprivation, poverty and famine, was a fanatical financing and mushrooming of Catholic churches, cathedrals, schools, hospitals and colleges all over the country. This was an extraordinary cultural phenomenon of the dispossessed Catholic majority who were on the rebound and wished their faith to be made as physically manifest as possible.

By 1850, Maynooth had become the largest seminary in the world and, along with the plethora of other seminaries, religious houses and orders of Christian Brothers and missionary nuns, Irish Catholicism became a defining cultural phenomenon both at home and throughout the world. The overarching position of ultimate power of the Catholic Church in the new Ireland of the twentieth century was cemented when religion became the pacifying context that held authority in uniting the different factions of the Civil War in the 1920s.

In June 1932, the Eucharistic Congress was a snapshot of how holistically the Church had incorporated itself into Irish life and how it had become the beacon of national pride and identity. Close to one quarter of the entire population of Ireland attended the Mass in the Phoenix Park, and the setting-up of the new radio transmitter in Athlone enabled Ireland's devout evangelism to be broadcast around the world. At the offertory of the Mass, to everyone's great pride, Ireland's internationally renowned tenor, Count John McCormack, fully captured the mood and status of the occasion with his powerful rendition of 'Panis Angelicus'.

In 1950, Pope Pius XII decided on a major campaign of Catholic fervour, establishing the so-called Holy Year, where devotees could partake in impassioned plenary indulgences, such as extra prayer, pilgrimage and acts of devotion, designed to shorten a person's time in purgatory. In Ireland, the Holy Year was observed like nowhere else and, in addition to pilgrimages to Rome led by the President Seán T. Ó Ceallaigh, numerous crosses were erected on prominent hilltops all over the country.

Significantly, it was this incentive that started the broadcasting on the radio of the Angelus bell at noon and 6pm each day.

Four years later, in 1954, the pope doubled down on the success of the Holy Year and decided to dedicate it to the Blessed Virgin Mary. The Marian Year saw every parish and every convenient nook and corner, whether in a garden or the end of a red-bricked terrace of houses, adorned with a statue of Mary or the construction of a grotto, a replica of Mary's apparition to Bernadette in Lourdes.

Any girl born in that year was invariably named Mary, Marie, Maria, Máire or Maureen, while boys too were given Mary as their second name. Obediently acceding moral and social authority to the Church by fully embracing and demonstrating one's Catholic identity, in name and action, was a way of cementing one's new-found status in this emerging independent Ireland.

～ SACRED HEARTS AND CHALKY GODS ～

Most houses boasted an impressive portrait gallery of holy pictures on their walls and often these were the only images in the home. Pictures of the Sacred Heart, the Immaculate Heart of Mary, the Madonna and Child, angels, children at prayer, a selection of favourite saints (such as St Patrick, St Francis of Assisi or the much-revered Padre Pio), along with the pope of the day, were hung in kitchens, hallways and bedrooms and displayed with pride. Sometimes, a few secularly beatified figures, such as Michael Collins, de Valera or JFK, were interwoven into the blessed gallery.

Pride of place was given to the Sacred Heart often hanging prominently in the kitchen, where the bearded, long-haired Jesus, his suffering heart exposed, was fully dramatised by a special, perpetual red electric light. If you made eye contact with the Sacred Heart, his eyes would follow you around and look disappointedly at you in a mournful gaze, topping up your Catholic guilt, especially when coming in late from a dance or a night on the town.

A friend of mine told me that their Sacred Heart was placed at the top of the stairs, but it had to be moved because his daughter was inconsolably terrified and traumatised by the open-heart image. She would refuse to look at it and would keep her eyes closed going up and down the stairs, placing herself in great danger.

Another stalwart display was a framed cream parchment with a picture of the pope, in the form of a papal apostolic blessing that marked the marriage of the couple. Pictures were often set off by the piece of withered, brown, palm branch from Palm Sunday and remained there the whole year.

In harmony with the many sanctified images, most houses had a haphazard assemblage of chalky gods, which were holy statues of all shapes and sizes made of plaster. Many would have inherited specimens from previous generations, while a new Our Lady of Fatima, Michael the Archangel or St Anthony made very popular wedding presents and were widely advertised as such in the newspapers. There were many shops and outlets specialising in imported holy statues, while several Italian craftsmen – such as Angelo Bernardi in Cork and Ter Bussoli in Limerick – moved to Ireland and made a living by servicing the constant demand. Their personally crafted cast and hand-painted plaster statues were considered original and authentic and innately more sacred than the imported mass-produced plastic impersonators that had begun to appear.

Statues sometimes fell from their plinths on to a hard tiled or terrazzo hall floor breaking into a thousand smithereens, but the resultant chalk fragments were happily reused by children marking out the squares to play pickey or hopscotch. More common damage to a statue – and, ironically, less severe – was a simple decapitation and poorly reattached heads. Indeed, headless statues were a common sight.

Ireland's most beloved headless statue was the Child of Prague, specifically because of its magical meteorological powers. Headless or not, the ornate Child of Prague statue was placed outside in the garden, sometimes buried upside down, before every wedding or important family occasion to guarantee fine weather. Brides-to-be would be fully reassured by aunts and neighbours the day before their wedding day with affirmations of, 'I have him out for ya' and 'He's out! 'Twill be glorious!'

When not managing the weather, the Child of Prague sat contentedly on a threepenny piece in the corner of the bedroom ensuring that there would be no sickness and no shortage of money in the house. Many years later, when the National Lottery scratch cards came in, these were placed under the statue overnight to affect a win.

Every house also had a small holy-water font inside the front door and everyone that crossed the threshold would, in a habitual reflex, dip their fingers in and make the sign of the cross to bless themselves. When we were heading out to dances, our father would splash us with Brut aftershave to bolster our romantic aspirations, while our mother doused us liberally with the holy water at the door as a sort of counter charm, quenching the fires of passion.

The constant draw on the holy water meant that it had to be restocked from the church and the best quality was that collected on Easter Saturday. This Easter water was especially important in the countryside where it was indispensable for ridding the crops, animals, fowl and family of all diseases and misfortune. In many households, the same container of Easter water had to be collected for over seven years to make it effective, being topped up each year to maintain its potency.

A popular container for holy water came in the clear plastic shape of Our Lady of Lourdes containers, the top of which was a blue crown that would twist off. These plastic Holy Marys were brought home in massive quantities from the various diocesan pilgrimages to Lourdes that became the first foreign holiday for many from the 1950s onwards. Mothers travelled by ferry from Ireland to Santander in northern Spain or by plane to Tarbes as part of well-organised five or seven-day religious pilgrimages. They brought home all manner of Spanish exotics from bottles of sweet muscatel wine, castanets, fans and dolls of Spanish dancers in frilly dresses. As expected, they brought a surfeit of miraculous medals and holy-water containers that were distributed to every neighbour, cousin and random passenger on the bus into town.

The larger plastic Lourdes Holy Marys were of real value as they were used by some as the most ingenious way of smuggling and distributing *poitín*. Nobody took a blind bit of notice as the holy statue of clear liquid was handed over to an appreciative uncle or neighbour. On a cold winter night, pouring a 'drop of holy water' straight from the head of the blue-crowned Virgin Mary to make a hot punch was a real miracle, fully appreciated by the chosen few.

There was a continuous brisk trade emanating from loving aunts in keeping young children safe from harm's way by providing endless supplies of holy medals, scapulars, rosary beads and prayer books. Fastened with a safety pin, a jangle of three or four miraculous medals were fixed to a baby's pram and cot, and, eventually, pinned on to a vest or underwear as they got older. All manner of religious items for protection was resorted to. One of my first girlfriends was fitted out by her mother with a tiny statue of the Virgin Mary concealed in her bra to act as a disincentive to any amorous advances.

More omnipresent were the red, brown and green scapulars, all belonging to different religious orders and each designed to keep you safe from fire and drowning and the malevolent activities of ghosts and devils. The scapular consisted of two little religious images with prayers sown onto two pieces of cloth, attached to a cord and worn around the neck. The extent of the personal, unseen and portable religious trappings only came into public focus when undressing for swimming or playing sport. The excess of such religious amulets attached to every child would not have been out of place on the ritual regalia of a shamanic medicine man.

The gifting and exchange of religious objects was never-ending, and the mass-accumulation soon became a problem. Such objects and symbols of devout religious observances could not be disposed of easily, unless, of course, you gave it to someone else, but sooner or later the excess had to be released. It would have been sacrilegious and a certain way of courting bad luck to dispose of them inappropriately and this is where the holy well came in. Each area had its own holy well dedicated to its local saint and bringing the old chalky gods turned a problem into an act of devotion. Likewise, the excess rosary beads, miraculous medals and scapulars found their way to the rag bushes and around the necks of the battalions of statues at the wells.

In our home, my mother's religiously zealous relations left her two over-sized chalky gods in their wills, a Sacred Heart and a

Holy Mary, that were so large and terrifying to us as children, they were eventually exiled to the attic. There they continued to terrorise us, covered in dust and spider's webs, staring at us from the dark corners when we came to collect the Christmas decorations.

Down on our Knees

The twice-daily recitation of the Angelus was one of the hallmarks of growing up in the all-pervasive Catholic Ireland from the 1950s to the 1990s. With the advent of television in the 1960s, the Angelus marked six o'clock just before the main evening news and was the watershed of the day. Often caught off-guard, the eighteen echoing bongs of the tolling bell, either at midday or teatime, would prompt a devout parent into the Pavlovian intoning of rhythmic responsorial prayer.

The first line: 'The Angel of the Lord declared unto Mary' was dutifully responded to by the rest of the family – halfway through their bowls of powdered oxtail soup or plates of fishfingers – who momentarily dropped everything and chanted, 'And she was conceived of the holy ghost.' Even though it was every day and sometimes twice a day, the Angelus was a relatively short and sharp affair. In contrast, the Rosary was a much more elaborate and time-consuming observation, especially when it became a nightly event during the months of October and May.

My aunt used to visit all the churches in the city and pick up the various combs and rosary beads that were left behind having fallen out of people's back pockets when kneeling in church. She would bring them down with her on her Monday-night visits, and we could have set up a shop with all the pouches of rosary beads in our collection. My favourite was a luminous glow-in-the dark set, and these would keep me distracted as we knelt down in the kitchen each night of the holy months to recite the Rosary.

We each took a stool or a chair and, on our knees, we leaned prostrate over our beads, all facing in different directions because it was an ordeal on such solemn adult occasions not to laugh. Anxious to go out kicking a football, sometimes you might get away with saying only nine Hail Marys in a decade and even when the long ordeal of the five sorrowful mysteries were said, you still had a litany of the lingering Hail Holy Queen and some extra prayers that your mother would tag on. For a household of young children, full of fun and manic energy, the Rosary was a real penitential chore.

During Lent, there was an even greater chore when my father got us up at the dawn and we were brought to early seven o'clock Mass over the forty days of Lent. In the 1970s, everybody attended Mass on a Sunday without exception and the churches were packed to the roof, with many standing at the back and along the side aisles. One of the developments of rural electrification in the 1950s prompted the installation of PA systems in churches so the priest might be better heard by the large congregations.

There is a story that in Adrigole, West Cork, the congregation were all excited to witness the newly installed sound system, but the priest was having trouble getting it to work. Unfamiliar with the new apparatus, he kept twiddling knobs and flicking switches while tapping the microphone at the lectern. Unknowingly, he got everything right and at full volume his under the breath frustrated comment, 'There's something wrong with this!' bellowed out all over the church. The brethren, thinking the Mass had started, responded immediately, 'And also with you!'

As we got older, the compulsory Sunday Mass became the weekly social occasion and opportunity to spot the talent. It was like a fashion show, a weekly occasion for the girls to wear their Saturday night rig-outs to church and the mini-skirted procession to Communion was watched with disapproving eyes by the devout, but with pure lust and excitement by the hormonally charged teenagers. The later the Mass, the bigger the crowd, with a large gathering outside the door, paying little attention to the ceremony. Some were already peeping through the pages of the risqué *Sunday World* newspaper that was first released in the middle of Lent in 1973.

Pope John Paul II came to Ireland in 1979 and while this was touted as a symbol of the constancy of Ireland's Catholic devotion, in reality, it marked the watershed – for the next twenty years the Church went into monumental decline. The fallout from the heated debates and referenda on contraception, abortion and divorce, as well as revelations concerning institutional abuse in mother and baby homes and Magdalene laundries, cover-ups of paedophile priests, prominent clergy fathering children, and the embezzling of parish funds, all contributed to lessening the moral authority of the Catholic Church.

Somewhat like a teenager coming of age, Ireland began to grow up and the widespread excessive display of Catholic paraphernalia started to disappear.

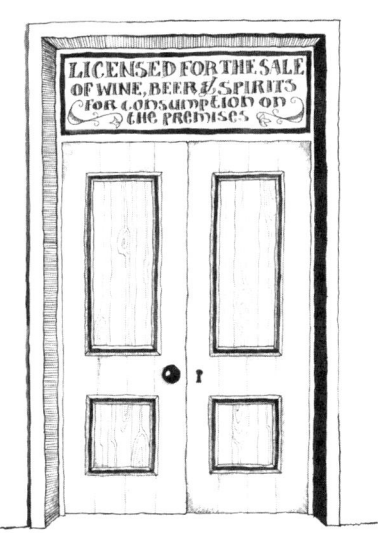

IN THE COMMUNITY

The Forge: Men's Sheds

There once was an old shopkeeper and he had to be the most miserable man who ever lived, for there was only one thing that ruled his life: money. He had swindled everyone in the village out of every penny they had, overcharging them for goods, making unfair bargains and calling in their debts without any mercy. Everyone in the village was poor and despaired for the future. The miser kept the fortune of gold coins that he had accumulated in a big pot under his bed and, every night, he'd take it out and count out the coins on the kitchen table. He used to make little golden towers of the coins that twinkled in the reflected light of his paltry fire and a small candle. He'd gaze on them for hours before tumbling them all back into the pot and hiding them under the bed.

He never spent any of his fortune and he had no friends for fear they would ask him to pay for something. He had no wife and no children, lest they cost him anything. His clothes were torn and ragged and his shoes were worn to the heel. He was skinny and wasted as he'd spend nothing on food. On top of all of that, he could never sleep soundly; he'd wake and sit bolt upright in the bed, listening, in case someone would sneak in during the night and try to rob him. He stayed wretched all his life and, when he came to old age and death was nearing, he wanted to take his pot of gold with him to ensure that nobody else would have the money.

In those times, the centre of life in all villages in Ireland was the local forge and at its helm was the strongest and most respected of all men – the blacksmith. The forge was the hub of all village activity with large groups of men staying well on into the night close to the heat of the fire enjoying the chat. One night, when he was on his last legs, the miser dragged himself down to the forge and waited outside for everyone to go home. Just as the blacksmith was about to close the big double doors, he presented himself with his predicament. 'I have all of this gold, but I don't want anyone else to have it. I'll give you a gold sovereign if you can work your magic and I can take it with me to the next life.'

The blacksmith knew the shopkeeper from over the years, for he had never paid any of his bills to him. In truth, he felt he would do him a favour by putting him out of his misery. 'Bring me the gold at cock crow,' said the blacksmith, 'and I will heat it in the fire and melt it down and, when it is ready, you can drink it and nobody can have it then.' The miser was perplexed but he knew that the blacksmith had special skills and, in any case, it was his only hope.

In the morning, the miser heaved his heavy crock down with him to the forge where the blacksmith was stoking a huge fire. The smith took the pot from the miser and went to put it up on the white-hot embers. The smith pushed hard on the big bellows and the forge fire became so fierce that the miser had to put his hand up to block the intense heat and, in that moment, when his eyes were covered, quick as a flash, didn't the blacksmith switch the pot of gold for one containing two pounds of fresh butter. In no time, the butter was melted and when the miser looked into the pot as it cooled all he could see was what looked like his melted golden fortune. When it was cool, he was so delighted with himself that he drank the whole thing back and such was its impact that he died on the spot.

The blacksmith took his one gold sovereign as agreed with the miser and then shared out the rest of the fortune to every house in the village by putting a little tower of gold outside each person's door. In no time, there were new clothes, food, drink, weddings and christenings and a smile on everyone's face. Everyone came to the forge to buy new tools and to have their ponies shod and, of course, they all paid the blacksmith in golden coins, and all was right with the world again.

The Heart of the Village

This folktale reminds us that the skilled blacksmith and his forge was once at the very core of Irish life. He was indispensable and universally respected as he was the one who made every tool both for the common labourer and the skilled tradesman. He made ploughs, harrows, rakes, spades, shovels, *sleáns*, axes, saws, adzes, hammers, nails, hinges, tongs, pot hooks, cranes, knives, gaffs and pikes: every tool for every job came from him. He mended kettles, pots and ovens and he also made and shod the iron shoes for donkeys, ponies and horses in addition to making bands for the wheels of carts: 'shoeing wheels' as it was called. The range and depth of his knowledge of his complex craft was accumulated from the depths of an ancient heritage spanning as far back as the Bronze Age.

Every village, town and district had a forge. Sometimes, the buildings were distinctive with an elaborate entrance in the shape of a horseshoe. Initially, most had a thatched roof but, with sparks flying and inevitable fires, they were replaced with roofs of tarred canvas on timber boards or slate and, later on, the ubiquitous corrugated iron.

The rule in the forge was first come, first served – and people in need of repairs or new tools would congregate at first light. You could be at the forge all day or even over a few days before the blacksmith got around to your specific need, such was the demand for his trade. The forge therefore became a kind of lad's club, full of men chatting and passing time. It was made even a more attractive venue given that the blacksmith was the one who made the all-important 'worm', the twist of coiled piping used to cool the distillate for the *poitín*-makers, and therefore was afforded a ready supply for himself and another for distribution.

Many blacksmiths were themselves skilled *poitín*-makers and in the snug heat of the forge fire there was storytelling, jokes, riddles, card-playing, gossip and convivial company. There was talk of politics and the state of the country and of injustices, and it was here that plans were hatched to right the wrongs of the oppressors. It was in the forges that the pikes for the rebellion of 1798 were made, and all kinds of covert activity – from the nineteenth century Land League insurrections and boycotts to the guerrilla warfare of the 1920s – were hatched in the forges.

It was never a place for women, and this was supported by the belief that it was unlucky for a woman to cross the threshold of the forge. The only exception to this was when the blacksmith declared the 'day of the women', which was a special day usually just before Christmas. All men's work was set aside on that day and instead he dedicated his time to repairing and patching all the pots and kettles and kitchen utensils that needed mending, all of which had been deposited to the forge in the weeks before. The blacksmith also took the large blue-and-white willow pattern ceramic platters that might be cracked and, by drilling two holes, he would reinforce the porcelain by inserting a wire staple tie in from behind, pulling the crack tight together.

Blacksmiths would not work on Good Friday, and it was deemed especially bad luck to drive any nail on that day.

The remarkable strength of the blacksmith was often demonstrated by their ability to handle the heavy sledgehammer. One almost impossible feat of strength was for the blacksmith to hold the sledgehammer (weighing anything from five to ten pounds) by the long handle and lift it outstretched in front of him, from the ground until it was over his head, with a fully extended unbending arm.

There are accounts of the exceptional blacksmith who was somehow able to sledge the hot iron on the anvil using two heavy hand-hammers simultaneously, one in each hand, normally the work of two men. The centrepiece of the forge was a solid wooden block, two and half feet high, on which was perched the iron anvil. Typical specimens weighed anything from three hundredweight (twenty-four stone) to seven hundredweight (fifty-six stone) and the blacksmiths could move and even lift these on and off the block as needed.

The story is told about the proud blacksmith, Paddy Creedon from Blarney, who was known countrywide for his incredible strength. On hearing that there was another blacksmith with strength equal to his own in Donegal, he set out one day on his horse to meet him. When he arrived at the forge, he shouted in the door for a light for his pipe. The Donegal blacksmith heard the Cork accent and, looking out the door, twigged immediately who it might be. Instead of taking the coal with the tongs, he placed it on the anvil and handed it out to the stranger in one hand. Paddy smiled at the incredible strength but took the anvil by the peak in one hand, lifted it up to his pipe and handed it back to the smith. 'Ah,' shouted the smith with glee and admiration, 'you must be Paddy Creedon from Blarney, the strongest man in Ireland!'

The blacksmith's skin was rendered perpetually dark from the dust and ash that seeped deep into his pores as he sweated over the hot coals and slack. In the evenings, he washed off the outer layer of grime with the forge water and many believed this is what afforded him his special strength and healthy complexion. With muscles and sinews more powerful than any wrestler or athlete, blacksmiths not only had to have incredible strength, but they also had to embody a sense of confidence, calm and control in the face of what were often dangerous and very difficult tasks. There was no room for fear or caution when deftly paring the hoof and burning on the hot shoe of unwieldy fillies or bad-tempered jennets as they were being shod.

Sometimes, hastiness and inexperience led to the blacksmith's young apprentice being killed by a kick from a horse. Ever since, it is said that the ghosts of such unfortunates can be heard sledging on the anvil in the forge after midnight.

Cures and Curses

It is little wonder that people turned to the blacksmith when they were in need of specific help. Long ago, when someone had a toothache, the blacksmith became the dentist, and his remedies were practical, if also a little magical. People often first treated themselves by various means, including placing a live frog in their mouth, filling any cavity with oatmeal or candle grease or, regardless of your age, smoking a pipe of tobacco. If the tooth became more painful, they would go to the forge and ask the blacksmith for three horse shoe nails and bless the aching tooth by making the sign of the cross over it with the three nails before hammering them into a thorn bush by way of a cure. The three nails corresponded to the three nails used to fix Christ on the cross and the blackthorn trees near forges were full of nails.

When a tooth was throbbing with pain and it had to come out, the blacksmith would use an awl to loosen it and then use a special set of pincers that he had made himself to extract it.

An alternative extraction method involved tying one end of a short cord securely around the affected tooth and the other around the anvil. The blacksmith would work away chatting to the unsuspecting patient for a time while taking a red-hot iron from the fire and working it on the anvil. All of a sudden, he would lunge at the man's face with the red-hot iron and the man would pull back with great force and the troublesome tooth was left dangling on the cord fixed to the anvil.

The blacksmith's craft involved continuously cooling the hot irons in a trough of cold water and this forge water was thought to be a sure cure for many kinds of ailments. It had a certain amount of iron in it and was taken as a sort of tonic for delicate children and those who were anaemic. It was a certain cure for warts, corns and the aforementioned toothache, while it was also used to cure ringworm, psoriasis and all manner of skin disorders, as well as open sores and infected cuts.

The forge water was the panacea for most everything and its efficacy was attributed to a folk account of what happened to the Virgin Mary when she was walked by a forge one stormy day. The wind and the rain were so strong that it blew her cloak open and she was drenched. She came upon the forge and asked a shepherd who was sheltering there if he could give her a wooden pin to fasten her cloak, but he said that he had only one for himself. She had no money but the blacksmith, seeing her plight, forged her a strong and beautiful iron pin and gave it to her as a gift. She smiled at the smith and declared that, as recompense for his kindness, the water in which the forged pin had been cooled would hold a cure for everyone. Consequently, the hard life of the shepherd, out in all weathers is the result of the selfishness shown to her.

The iron anvil, the focal point of the forge, was almost like an altar and was used in magic rituals undertaken by the blacksmith. When he was beating the red-hot iron and sparks flew out the door towards someone, they were convinced that they would come into money. The cure for rickets prescribed bringing the afflicted child to the forge between midnight and one o'clock so the blacksmith would carry him around the anvil before placing him on the anvil and making the sign of the cross with the sledge over him three times. This process had to be repeated on three different occasions with nine days between each visit.

Those who wished to get married used to go to the forge and if they could jump over the anvil three times without stumbling or a fall, all would go well for them in the future. It was also important that the blacksmith should be invited to a wedding, and any such occasion without the smith was said to bring bad luck.

In turn, people believed that the blacksmith could curse you by walking around the anvil three times, and the number of times he hit a hot iron was equal to the number of curses. People were terrified to take anything from the forge for fear of the blacksmith's curse, which was so virulent, it would follow down to the fourth generation. The item stolen would become red hot and the person would be burned until they brought it back. It is said that the blacksmith even had the power to cause death by taking soil or grass from a grave, placing it on the anvil and turning the peak of the anvil towards you.

Given such power, people always kept on the blacksmith's good side by bringing tobacco, fowl, eggs, butter and other provisions with them as gifts and part-payment for his work. Each person always gave the blacksmith a few stooks of corn when they were harvesting and a rail of turf when they were drawing home and, therefore, he never had to worry about providing for himself in any way.

When a horse or a pony was being shod for the first time, it was customary to bring a bottle of whiskey and when the blacksmith drove the first nail, everyone would shout, 'Whiskey, whiskey.' In an extension of a tradition that goes all the way back to the early medieval period, when a pig was killed, it was usual to gift the head to the blacksmith, perhaps because he was the one that often came to stick the pig or at least sharpened the knives used to cut it up.

One of the strongest beliefs was that the blacksmith had the wherewithal to banish rats. There were never any rats around the forge given the flying sparks, the constant clattering and noise from within and the great body of traffic of horses and carts coming and going. Others attributed their dislike of the forge to the sickeningly pungent smell of sulphur that came when the smith put a red-hot shoe against the horse's hoof, especially if the horse's hooves had thrush. When a house was plagued with rats, the ash from the forge fire and the forge water were mixed and poured in and around the rat's nests by the blacksmith. He also had a special anti-rat charm that he would recite while he walked around the anvil. There were certain blacksmiths who wrote a special charm on a piece of paper and placed it at the opening of the rats' burrow. The next day the rats scurried away from their homes, and it was said that one man saw their leader with the piece of paper in his mouth.

One of the first people I recorded was the blacksmith, Timmy Scully of Donoughmore Cross, County Cork. I was writing an academic paper on turf-cutting and Timmy was famous for making excellent *sleáns* (turf-cutting spades). He was a pure rogue with a big smile and bulging arms. When he saw my small tape-recorder he thought he would have some fun and gave me reams of information, great chunks of which were made up and completely farcical for his own amusement. When I asked him how he stopped turf-cutters blistering the palms of their hands when cutting, he told me with great sincerity that he used to spit on the top of the handle and that did the job. I still drive by Timmy's forge on a regular basis, though Timmy has passed away and the forge is long since locked up. Someone broke in and stole his anvil, plucking the heart, the blacksmith's altar, as Seamus Heaney called it, from its core. As technology moved on, the once-indispensable blacksmith and his forge became instantly redundant and now sadly resides mainly in memory.

'Have Ye No Homes to Go to?'

There was always bitter disappointment when, as an inquisitive child, your father consented to letting you take a sip from what looked like the creamiest and sweetest of all confections: the top of his pint of stout. The unexpected sharp sour tang was a body blow and offered no relief from the never-ending weariness of sitting with your father in a pub full of men drinking, smoking and talking endlessly. This was, however, part of the Irish acculturation process and, over time, that once-insipid sour taste turned into a relished nectar of pure Irishness, and the pub and all its carry-on established itself in our communal psyche as an ever-present familiar refuge.

Make no doubt about it, the pub is at the core of our being. Passing thorough the towns of Killorglin and Cahersiveen on our summer holidays, my father used to remark that both towns had a pub for every week of the year. The historian Elizabeth Malcolm tells us that at the turn of the last century, 50 per cent of the population of Dublin patronised a pub, while in Cork there was one pub for every for forty adults and in Limerick – nearly 20 per cent of all houses in the city were pubs. In my parents' era, every man I knew went to the pub each night and drank a half gallon of porter.

In stark contrast to activities and concerns of the Church, the pub became the convivial venue outside the home, an inviting sanctuary of distraction and companionship, promulgated by the sousing power of alcohol.

⌒◌ Shebeens and Ale Poles ◌⌒

The sheer number of pubs in Ireland stems from their development in the late medieval period. In the beginning, the sale of alcohol (mainly wine and brandy) was confined to the front rooms of merchants' houses. From the sixteenth century, in areas of English colonisation, drinkshops and alehouses fermented their own ales and beers, and were common in most towns, with customers moving from one alehouse to another as each brewing batch became available.

The late eighteenth century witnessed a huge increase in the consumption of whiskey and *poitín*, with everywhere from small grocer shops, dramshops and make-shift shebeens openly selling alcohol, most without licence. The term 'shebeen' (Irish illegal pub), which is now used all over the world, got its name from *séibín*, a small wooden mug used as a quart measure for ale and grain. In addition, *síbín* was used to describe bad or stale ale. Regardless of its quality it was cheap, and it attracted the hordes.

The official designation that a proprietor was legally licensed to sell alcohol came in the form of a wooden nameboard, but there were older forms of vernacular signage that catered to the illiterate. Each alehouse advertised the availability of a newly brewed batch of drink by hanging a sheaf of barley or wheat from a special ale pole placed outside their houses. It was understood that if the house also supplied wine, a bush of holly or laurel evergreens was tied to the pole. The licensed purveyors of alcohol did not wish to miss out on potential business at open-air events, such as horse-racing and fair days, and would set up a temporary tent to sell their produce. The distinctive tall ale pole was placed out the front brandishing the proprietor's nameboard along with various insignia that were understood by all. An old jug or bottle signified that drink was available, while a ribbon or an old boot indicated that there was also music and dancing on offer. A rusty saucepan or the broken lid of a pot was hung from the pole to indicate that food, usually in the form of a cut of tough boiled mutton, could also be had.

Throughout the nineteenth century, this unhindered consumption of alcohol in shebeens and at the open-air gatherings of fairs and pattern days led to the widespread drunkenness that regularly ended in reckless faction fighting.

In addition to such alcohol-fuelled anarchy, the authorities recognised that the illicit shebeen houses were hotbeds of insurrection and rebellion and, wishing to control the masses while also lining their own pockets, they doubled down on the system of licensing public houses. A licensed public house had to maintain standards and have certain features: it had to have two rooms each with a fireplace, hence the origin of what would become the lounge and the bar. The measures were standardised, along with the lawful sourcing of beers and spirits and the local magistrate could refuse the annual renewal of the licence if the rules were breached.

In 1872, following from the nameboard, each legal public house had to advertise their licence in the form of the proprietor's name 'licensed for the sale of wine, spirits and beer for consumption on the premises' painted in small letters on the window over the front door.

The customary abuse of official drink measures is at the root of the age-old Irish drinking ritual of *An Pota Phádraig* (St Patrick's Pot) when Irish people are obliged to 'drown their shamrock' and drink the health of the national saint on 17 March. According to the legend, one day as St Patrick was wandering around the country converting the population to Christianity, when he stopped into a shebeen and asked the landlady for a glass of whiskey. She began telling him of all her woes and her lack of money and the hard life she had trying to make ends meet. As she poured the whiskey, Patrick noticed that she only half-filled the measure and presented to him a miserable glass to drink. Patrick pulled her aside, grabbed a candle and brought her to the back room where the drink was stored. In the flickering candlelight, she was shocked to see a terrifying black dog, with a slobbering mouth and a big evil grin, living in amongst the barrels. Patrick told her that this black dog was a gluttonous devil that was thriving from all the savings she was making by half-filling measures. He made her promise that from that day on, each glass she poured out would be brimming and overflowing. He said he would check in with her a year later.

True to his word, he didn't forget to show up. On his return, he could hardly push in the door for the crowd that was inside, singing and dancing and full of merriment. The landlady took Patrick to the storeroom and there cowering down behind the barrels was the black dog, faded away to nothing, whimpering and miserable and on its last legs. She knew the saint's advice had changed her fortunes. Patrick tapped the black dog with his crozier and it vanished in puff of smoke.

This popular folktale was the necessary endorsement to partake of a least one drink in honour of the saint, even though St Patrick's Day always falls during the penitential period of Lent when many would abstain from alcohol. The ritual involved taking the shamrock from your hat or coat and dipping it in whiskey and loudly vociferating a toast such as 'low rent and long leases' and, with that, everyone took a drink. It was usual on the last drink to eat the shamrock from the glass.

Availing of a drink when you were not legally entitled to do so seems to be a great Irish obsession. Up to very recently, there were two days in the year – Good Friday and Christmas Day – when the pubs were obliged to close and nothing was more relished than a forbidden drink with a steady stream of locals always wangling their way into a premises.

In the early twentieth century, country pubs were also a grocery shop, selling the essentials of tea, tobacco, sugar, rashers and sausages, along with household cleaning products, drapery, boiled sweets and everything else from mousetraps to paraffin oil. These 'spirit-grocers' were born from the heydays of the temperance movement in the nineteenth century when sales of drink decreased and publicans had to diversify to stay in business.

The pubs and spirit-grocers were the centre of every community and often doubled-up supplying the services of undertaker, bicycle shop, petrol pumps and seed merchant. In an effort to curtail drinking, particularly on Sundays after Mass, the government introduced restricted opening hours with obligatory pub-closing in the afternoons. However, one exemption was introduced for so-called bona-fide travellers – if you had travelled a distance of more than three miles, you were entitled to a drink. A number of enterprising drinkers used to address letters to themselves at the home of a distant friend or relative more than three miles from the pub and produce the envelope as their drinking passport.

The bona-fide rule was abolished in 1967, but an earlier drinking loophole, introduced in 1927 that allowed a number of pubs in cities across the country to open at 7.00am to facilitate night workers, fishermen, market traders and dockworkers, is still in use. These were also a refuge for those seeking the hair of the dog, a cure from a night of over-consumption. A sure-fire remedy for those suffering from a combination of a hangover and drink-induced heartburn was a 'Paddy and Pep', a shot of Paddy Whiskey with a dash of peppermint cordial.

Pubs were almost an entirely male dominion in Ireland up to the 1960s, with the feminist critic Valerie Hey suggesting that, given the numbers of bachelors in Ireland, the pub could be viewed as a type of female substitute offering warmth, sustenance and companionship. It would not be unusual to walk into a pub in the middle of the day to find a dozen men sitting quietly, nursing their pints. To this end, many would only call for a half pint by day and others, conscious of pacing themselves and minding their money, would call for a 'may-dhum' (medium) where the publican would only fill the glass three-quarters of the way full.

The pubs were ill-equipped for women, specifically in respect of toilets where the men simply went out into the backyard. If there was need for an outhouse, they were handed the big key and a sheet of newspaper.

Any woman walking into a pub on her own would have been considered a loose woman, therefore, a woman had to be accompanied by a man. When they did frequent the pub, women were confined to the taproom, a small space at the end of the bar where the beer barrels were kept. This segregated private space was known as the snug and the occupants had a little bell that they could ring, with the publican passing the drink in through a small hatch. Women and children would also head straight to the snug to get the beer jug filled, which was then brought home and drunk in the evening while the man remained in the pub. This mug of mulled porter, heated by plunging a hot poker into the jug, was a favourite solace for both women and children before they went to bed.

○‿ The Pub Comes of Age ‿○

The 1960s and 1970s saw everything change and a cluster of Irish pubs rocketed themselves into the modern world. In the cities, the lounge bar developed with its open, sophisticated spaces adorned with modern stainless steel and leatherette furniture, colourful carpets and piped American music. No longer the sequestered refuge of the Irish male, the modern bars invited young couples and groups of single women, in their jaw-dropping mini-skirts and knee-high boots, to partake of a new range of classy drinks. In an expression of their chic worldliness, they partook of gins, martinis and wodkas (vodkas), mixed with ginger ale, tonic or soda water and embellished with a slice of lemon or orange served in fancy glasses. A great favourite for the ladies was a Babycham, a sparkling pear cider served in a swanky champagne coupe.

In addition to drinking, this was a time when smoking was highly fashionable and at its social zenith, and each table and alcove of the lounge bar was amply supplied with large ashtrays emblazoned with alcohol and tobacco enticements. There was table service with dicky-bowed floor-boys busily cleaning ashtrays and navigating trays of drink to tables, working their way through the dense fog of cigarette smoke.

It was also a time when people still smoked pipes and the complex heady aromas of rich pipe tobacco filled the air. Pubs with ceilings that were once white gloss were tanned to a sickly nicotine yellow. There was also the exoticism of cigars on offer with a choice of a Henri Winterman's half corona, a slender Hamlet or the ultracool flat tin of mild café crème mini cigars with their plastic tips. A special report on the RTÉ's *Seven Days* programme pointed out that, in 1970, Irish men spent £1 of every £5 they earned on alcohol and tobacco.

In smaller country pubs, the concept of the lounge was simply accommodated by carpeting one of the pub's two rooms. This dichotomy of space with the confirmed drinking regulars in the bar and everyone else – women, married couples or visitors – in the lounge is an enduring legacy of the pub experience.

The bar became a sort of daytime crèche for the single drinking male and, over time, a host of games and gimmicks were introduced to keep him entertained. In the 1950s and 1960s, there was the simple game of rings, while the 1970s witnessed the introduction of the dart board whose flying projectiles were considered highly dangerous by the older generation making their way to the toilet. Overnight, the green baize of the pervasive pool table with its finicky coin slot found its way into the backroom and annex of every pub. Some pubs had table soccer games and others brought in one-armed bandit machines, all designed to keep the clientele distracted and spending. In turn, the two-bob-a-play of the latest single records in the brightly lit jukebox became the soundtrack to long afternoons of smoking, drinking and just passing the time.

In the evening, the lounge was the venue for music and a balladeer with the guitar on the high stool became standard. A repertoire made up of a homage to the past and aspirations of the future included covering songs by Johnny Cash, the Clancy Brothers, Brendan Bower's version of the Hucklebuck, Doris Day, Frank Sinatra and Demis Roussos, as well as traditional songs, such as 'The Galway Shawl' and 'The Men Behind the Wire'. Each balladeer would finish his set with a rendition of the national anthem where everyone, regardless of their state of inebriation, would spring to their feet, chest out and sing with passion and pride.

Before ushering them out the door to bed, some pubs had a special finale with everyone joining in with gusto, last pints waving in the air. One universal favourite began with the opening lines, 'Once upon a time there was a tavern, where we used to raise a glass or two', from Mary Hopkins's 1968 classic 'Those Were the Days'. Then, the night ended and the lights were switched on, the pub was cleared with shouts of 'Time now, ladies and gents please' or, as was the case in a pub in Dingle, 'All aboard for Tokyo.'

Food never featured as a central tenet of the Irish pub, save perhaps to ply the clientele with as much salt as possible to increase their thirst. While some sustenance was always available, it was only enough to keep hunger at bay and maintain the uninterrupted drinking. Some pubs specialised in boiling up a big pot of pigs' crubeens and this free steaming gelatinous mass of feet was enough to dissuade many from heading home for their tea. The major problem with the crubeens is that you could never get the glasses clean after them.

Pubs even had their own version of Taytos, pub crisps with a distinct extra salty smoky-bacon flavour and, while we pestered him for them, my father always resisted, telling us that they were fried in horse fat. Children were accommodated in Irish pubs, especially as they were attached to the fathers who often simply used them as their excuse to get out of the house, usually on Sunday afternoon. A bottle of lemonade or fizzy orange in a dark brown bottle, complete with a straw, kept the children quiet for a period. When boredom set in, a further bribe for more time came in the form of a small packet of salted peanuts or a bar of Fry's chocolate cream.

In the 1960s and 1970s, the main staple food on offer in the pub was the toasted sandwich. Some establishments would boil a ham and buy in some tasty Irish cheddar and with fresh bread, this sandwich was of excellent quality. Over time, with the industrialisation of food, the ham became synthetic-like, and this was combined with a slice of processed cheese and sandwiched between two slices of insipid sliced pan. Astonishingly, this unappetising sandwich ensemble was enveloped in a plastic bag and toasted under the large grill, to be served with a stainless-steel bowl of oxtail soup, straight out of a packet. There was some improvement with initiatives like the cleverly named Pubuffet, where a consortium of pubs in the 1970s set out to offer quality hot food. The era of fine dining and the gastropub were far in the future.

At night, the most sought-after circumstance was to find oneself locked in after hours. The publican would give the nod when bolting the door before pulling down the blinds and turning off the lights, save for the small set of year-round, dim fairy lights behind the bar. This glimmering twinkle was enough to enable the drinking to continue and such an occasion was golden time when the cherished privilege of extra pints with a select few often led to memorable nights. The thrill of the illegal lock-in was the communal sense of mischievousness, and, on occasion, this wanton bravado was tested when the gardaí came knocking on the front door. There would be an immediate hush before everyone attempted to conceal themselves in the toilets or upstairs in the proprietor's home. I've heard of a large host of inebriated patrons who evaded being caught by hiding in wardrobes, standing still and silent in the family bathtub, a contingent under the beds of sleeping children, while others had manged to hoist a few dozen into the attic.

One brave getaway was foiled when, despite everyone tiptoeing out the backdoor in ordered silence, the enthusiastic leader of the escape party went to push open a gate made from a sheet of corrugated iron, only for it to fall over with an almighty clatter loudly proclaiming their location to the guards. When caught, it was usual to give a false name and address. A famous example given to a naive garda recruit was, 'John Mandeville,

The Square, Mitchelstown', and when the novice garda went to follow up, he was greeted with the imposing statue of John Mandeville, a leader of the Land League wars in the 1880s, standing on a plinth in the middle of the market square.

The unique cultural ambiance of the Irish pub has resulted in its mushrooming all over the world, everywhere from Chief O'Neill's in Chicago to Muddy Murphy's in Singapore. The local Irish pub has been relocated from the everyday and ordinary to a complex international commercial phenomenon. The convivial and homely atmosphere of the pub provides a familiar welcoming milieu, catering for both enchanted and disenchanted diaspora along with those who want to play at being Irish.

At home, whether occupied daily or only on special occasions, the local pub still holds a unique place in Irish life. It is our refuge to watch the match, to repair to after the funeral, to celebrate a twenty-first or eightieth birthday, or to settle in the corner on a cold day and enjoy a toasted sandwich and beverage of your choice. The special pub for me is the Long Valley in Cork, a timeless and welcoming home from home, full of memories, simplicity and friendliness, and a place that might be regarded as a venue for the eternal return.

The Fat of the Land

There is a deep, now-forgotten, sensuality that comes with the milking of a cow. I remember the smell and feel of the cow's warm rump against my innocent childish cheek as I sat upon the small stool in the cowhouse with my uncle as he taught us this ageless process. It took time to learn how to simultaneously squeeze and pull the teats to bring the milk but, as I improved, each short jet of milk slowly collected in the white enamel bucket, creating a bubbly froth on top. That familiar sweet smell of the cow, the warmth and feel of her body and the rhythmic sounds of the milk hitting the bucket are a vestige of a different time.

My uncle John Leary, known as 'the grocer', was one of the very last of the small farmers, working his small holding without mechanisation, save for a small pony and two donkeys. He had four cows that he milked morning and evening and, when his churns were full, he'd bring them on a donkey and cart to the creamery in Cahersiveen. The milk from the cows was his main source of income and the creamery was the economic and social hub of the whole community. Such creameries were first established in the late nineteenth century, following the widespread adoption of Swedish inventor Carl de Laval's steam-powered centrifugal machine that facilitated the large-scale separation of the milk from the cream. The cream from the creameries was sent to larger stations where it would be mechanically churned into the most valuable and important of all Irish commodities: butter.

Butter is to the Irish as olive oil is to the Italians. It is our manna. It has been the main luxury foodstuff that can be traced from our prehistoric and medieval past to the present day. For example, the English bookseller John Dunton, travelling in Iar-Connaught in the late 1690s had presented to him as an unpretentious gesture of hospitality 'oatcakes along with a greate roll of butter of three pound at least'. The cabin where he stayed was not a wealthy one, yet his landlady wished to provide fresh butter for him, despite not having a churn dash. Instead, she enthusiastically plunged her arm in and out of the churn to make the fresh butter.

An Irish table is not complete without a half-pound of butter at its centre. The intoxicating anticipation of a bowl of steaming new potatoes is unimaginable without glossing them with copious dollops of melting butter. A warm slice of bread fails without a thick lathering of creamy butter. The temptation of the proverbial 'lakes of melted butter' in the steaming mashed potatoes and colcannon invariably defy the GP's advice – we are a country of butter lovers.

Churn and Market

Before the widespread development of the creameries, each household produced its own butter and, in the rich grassy pastures of Munster, an active trade with butter was promoted by the development of the Butter Market in Cork City, which functioned between 1770 and 1924. Butter was salted and packed into fifty-six-pound barrels called firkins and transported to Cork to be sold. The firkins were slung over the backs of horses, secured by ropes of twisted straw and carried from as far away as Valentia Island to the market. Some men and women made the journey on foot, travelling incredible distances, carrying the barrels of butter on their backs or on their heads. When they got to Cork, an expert butter inspector checked the firkins, took a sample on his thumbnail, tasted it and declared its quality, grading it between first class and sixth. The standards were high but, such was the reputation of Cork butter, that the top grades fetched a very good price. When the quality was good, the long and often dangerous journey home, made hazardous by the threat of highway robbery, was deemed worthwhile.

The production of properly salted first- or second-class butter resulted not only in the wherewithal to pay the rent but also in the affordability of significant luxuries, such as a bolt of cloth, tobacco, tea, sugar and whiskey. The quantity and quality of butter was the lifeblood for multitudes.

In such a world of butter production, it would be difficult to find an item of everyday life more symbolic than the churn. The pasture and fodder on which the cows were fed gave fat-rich milk and, when left to settle in low wooden keelers, the cream was skimmed off and put into the dash churn. The woman took hold of the long dash and laboriously churned – or 'brashed' – the contents to yield the concentrated luscious storable and sellable butter.

Butter was literally the fat of the land, and the churn was the vessel, the key component, in the equation that transformed the natural milk into the radiant yellow essence of fertility.

Churning has always been women's work and the churn itself, with its classic hourglass female shape, took on something of a symbolic sense of womanhood. The Irish for the churn is *cuinneog* and is related to the Old Irish *cuiniu* (a woman) and the action of churning, with the dash plunging in and out of the vessel, would have connotations of sexual intercourse.

The repeated action of the dash in the churn resulted in the butter breaking or coming and the obvious sexual symbolism was well understood by all. For example, the folklorist Bríd Mahon mentions that a bachelor courting a woman should never lift the butter from the churn, as to do so would render him impotent. The process of churning butter was physically arduous and, depending on temperatures, air pressure and know-how, it took time, strength and skill to make the butter come.

It sometimes happened that the butter did not come, and this was seen as a clear reflection of the woman's own fertility, along with her ability to provide for her family.

As it would take too long for one single farm to fill a firkin for market, women, by agreement joined together, packing their individual rounds of butter into one barrel. This was the circumstance when varying quantities of butter resulted in various judgements being made and suspicions of magical interference were raised. The alchemy of butter was a mystery and when one woman with the same number of cows as another had a much greater quantity of butter, accusations of butter stealing were voiced. There existed a deeply ingrained system of belief that another woman could steal your 'butter profit' using different magical *piseogs* and charms.

Piseogs and Charms

The most important time for butter was the morning of 1 May, the pivot of the agricultural year when fertility and fortune were in the balance. In the ancient past, this was the festival of *Bealtaine*, marked by the ritual of driving the cattle between two bonfires before they were taken to the rich herbage of the booleys (summer mountain pastures). In more recent times, branches of the white blossoming May Bush, the hawthorn, were decorated with ribbons, the eggs from Easter and lighted candles. It was bad luck to bring the May Bush into the house so, instead, they were set up outside the door or on bridges and crossroads, and revered as markers of fertility with dances and merrymaking.

In the cowhouse, the dairy, the spring well and around the threshold of the house, people would gather all the yellow flowers that were in bloom – the primroses, cowslips, buttercups and furze – to bring the yellow butter to themselves. The malicious stealing of the butter profit was most usually attributed to a lone older woman, known as a *cailleach* (hag). To steal the butter, she would walk over the fields before sunrise on May morning, skimming the dew off the grass, as one skims the cream off the milk, using the hem of her long skirts or else a long briar or whitethorn branch. Very often she performed her charm using a *buarach* (a spancel) made from cow-hair, rush or straw. This was usually used to restrain the cow during milking by tethering its legs and, as such, was understood as something that caused restriction. On occasion, the old woman would tie knots in the spancel to represent the number of cows from whom she would profit.

If the cows were in the field, she would place the spancel on their backs or hit each of them with it as she passed by, to hamper the production of milk and take it for herself. Equally she might surreptitiously dip the hair spancel into a neighbour's churn or keeler of cream and with this the *cailleach* would let the milk drip into her churn. There are accounts that she was seen hanging it in the hearth in her home and milked the spancel as if milking a cow. There is the story of a *cailleach* who offered a golden sovereign to a servant boy to steal a spancel from the cowhouse and dip it in the cream. On advice from his master, he dipped it in the cesspool instead and the curses and lamentations of the old woman were heard far and wide as the filth flowed from the spancel into her churn.

To make good butter, it was vital to have a supply of cold fresh springwater to wash out the buttermilk, otherwise it would go rancid and spoil the butter. The spring well was often a place for *piseogs* (negative charms). *Piseogs* took the form of items that were dirty, negative and infertile, and the unadulterated waters of the spring well might be desecrated and contaminated with offensive taboo materials. These included human faeces, urine, dead animals or their entrails, glugger eggs that had failed to hatch, or soiled menstrual rags. Finding such items in the well or concealed in potato drills was the cause of huge psychological distress and perceived misfortune. Life invariably presents different people with varying levels of bad luck and good luck but, in the past, people made the association of an illness, an unexpected death, a poor harvest or the loss of butter to the casting of a *piseog*.

Before contaminating the well, the *piseog*-wielding hag would skim the water off the top and as part of the ritual, would incant a specific simple verbal charm such as: 'Come all to me, all to me …' The antiquarian William Wilde records an old woman at a spring well cutting the heads off the tops of the watercress with some scissors, muttering the names of people who had cows and reciting, *'Is liom-sa leath do choda-sa'* ('half of your portion is mine').

On another such an occasion, a young curate who was returning home in the early hours of the morning having given the last rites to one of the parishioners overheard the strange recitation coming from the roadside well. Not thinking too much of it, he shouted out, 'And half to me also.' When he got home, there was consternation. The servant girl, who only made the smallest quantity of butter for the parochial house, took him into the outhouse to reveal great swathes of butter, pouring out over the top of her small churn.

Conscious of the *cailleach* and the potential of her butter-stealing charms, people were fastidious in protecting and insulating themselves against her magic. In and around May Day, the Irish hedgerows are radiant with the white May blossoms of the hawthorn, the blackthorn and the rowan. The white blossoms of the rowan, also known as the mountain ash or 'quicken' tree, turn into thick clusters of vibrant red berries over the summer months. The May blossom and striking red berries identified it as a tree that offered protection against magical interference. Each May morning, it was common to head out and cut a rod or withy of the mountain ash and fix it around the churn as a sure form of protection. Salt, fire and iron were rudimentary in the preservation against evil and magic. Anything from the exactitude of three grains of salt to a pinch onto a fistful of salt was placed in the churn or on its lid to safeguard the churning. A lighted sod of turf was taken from the fire with the tongs and swung around the bottom of the churn three times, while saying a prayer and making the sign of the cross. In the same manner, a lighted coal was placed under the churn at each churning. A small iron horseshoe was also regularly fixed to the base of the staved churn or a number of blacksmith-made iron nails hammered into its wood. It is the combination of both fire and iron together that proved most efficacious as a counter-charm against the *cailleach* butter stealer.

On May Day, it was thought that anything that left the house would be missing for the rest of the year, so people were conscious of not lending or giving anything important away on that day.

If someone came into a house, took up the tongs and lit their pipes from the *griosach* of the fire and then left the house – especially while churning was taking place – they were seen to leave with the fire, which was seen as a clear act of butter stealing.

Everybody that came into a house during churning would have to take a hand at 'brashing' the churn dash and to neglect, forget or refuse to do so was met with great suspicion. Such occurrences might coincide with a difficult churning with the cream refusing to break. To counter the perceived magical stealing, the iron tongs or the iron sock of a plough was placed in the fire and reddened. The doors and windows were bolted and shut tight and then the red-hot iron implements were plunged into the churn. The burning heat was transferred to the butter-stealing women, who would be heard banging at the doors to get in and screaming outside in inexpressible torture from the iron in the churn. Such a process was enacted to get rid of the butter stealers and their magic but, equally, the rise in the temperature of the cream was enough to make the stubborn churning turn into butter.

THE BUTTER-STEALING HARE

One antiquated and popularly held belief was that the old butter-stealing hags changed themselves into hares, which gave them access to the cows and enabled them to take the milk and steal the butter profit. This belief was held far and wide all over Ireland and there are numerous accounts of it. The following is the version of the folktale that has always stuck in my head.

One May morning, a wise old farmer got up out of bed while it was still dark and took himself off up to the cowhouse. Full of fear of *piseogs*, he had kept his few cows inside overnight to make sure that nobody could interfere with them. He stood at the cowhouse door, his cows secure within, and he looked at the first light coming in the east, glimmering on the dew. He felt at ease, thinking everything was right. His intention was to enact a small ritual by taking a blessed candle and carefully singe the udders of the cows to protect his milk.

However, the sense of smugness soon left him when, as he approached the first cow in the stall, he heard a sound coming from under her and when he looked in, what did he see, but a hare suckling away. The russet-coloured hare fixed him with her eye for a moment and did not move. He blew out the candle and, in a fluster, all he could do was to grab an old pike that was leaning against the wall and, being careful not to hit his cow, he started stabbing at the hare who was cowering in the corner. In the darkness, he could not see what he was doing but, all of a sudden, a loud and terrifying yelp came when he managed to pierce the leg of the hare with the iron pike. With that, she darted out between his legs and straight out the door. He turned and watched. Despite her injury, the bleeding hare bolted down the lane, over the wall and up the side of the mountain.

Any other time, it would have been useless to go after the hare but given that she was injured and there was a trail of blood, the farmer set off after her. He could just make her out as she scurried upwards towards the old booley huts on top of the mountain that were used in times gone by. When he got to the top, he was sweating and panting but was full of determination, as the butter from the farm had been very scarce for the past few years and his poor wife was at her wit's end.

The droplets of blood led to the door of a small overgrown hut, half of it swallowed by the mountainside. When he went inside, it was pitch dark and dank. He got a bad feeling and wanted to leave but he paused for a short while to let his eyes adjust. What did he see? Not a hare but an old woman sitting shivering in the corner. He looked down at her long skirts and thought he saw some blood, so he went over and lifted her skirts and revealed the blood running down her leg. In that instant, he realised she was the hare. He knew that some old women had the power to change into the form of a hare to steal the milk, but now that she was marked and maimed, he knew she would not be able to do it again. He gave her a stern warning to quit the place and never to come back. From that day on, the farm had fine full firkins of rich creamy butter that they sold to the market, and all was good with the world.

It seems a little strange that the hare – such an inconspicuous and unthreatening animal – would end up being so maligned in Irish folklore. The Irish hare (*Lepus timidus hibernicus*) is Ireland's oldest endemic mammal and has been here since the Ice Age. In the Irish mind, the hare is almost always female and there is a long-held belief that the male hare could change its sex to bear young. The female hare is the archetype that represents the wild and free natural world. She is Mother Nature from which we steal fertility for the benefit of humankind, when we hunt, plant crops, harvest and make butter. We use all the advanced techniques of our civilisation – fire, salt and iron – in an attempt to subjugate the natural world for human advantage.

The ritual suppression of the hare in Irish folklore is one telling manifestation of how we as humans interact with our planet.

From the 1950s, the rise of the creameries and the development of the Irish co-operative movement, along with the introduction and marketing of the Kerrygold brand of butter into European and global markets, have made Irish butter a worldwide phenomenon. Ireland does a number of things well, and butter is certainly one of them.

However, it has always been somewhat perplexing to me that such a deeply ingrained part of our culture was so easily sidelined by the introduction of margarines and spreadable vegetable oil mixes in plastic tubs. The pastries of our youth, my sister Karen's apple tarts that she learned to make in home economics class at school, clearly called for Stork margarine rather than butter. With the introduction of electric refrigerators, butter became difficult to spread. A greater awareness of health, warning about heart attacks from clotted arteries, caused butter's position of primacy to be challenged for some time. The tide has started to turn again with many less than impressed with the artificially produced hydrogenated oils and their health claims over the natural butter.

Butter can be seen as a bit of a guilty pleasure, but for butter lovers there is no alternative. Butter is the essential accompaniment, transforming the dry and mundane into something perfectly irresistible.

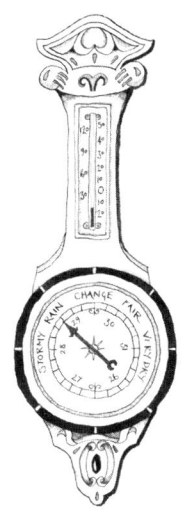

NATURAL EXPRESSION

'When Spiders From their Cobwebs Creep'

'Shocking!'

'Beyond a joke!'

'Did you ever see the like?'

'Will we ever forget last Thursday?'

'It's becoming ridiculous. I can't take much more!'

'Will we ever see the sun again?'

These are the eternal everyday expressions of a nation emphatically obsessed and communally consumed with one core concern: the weather. With deluded positivism and naivety, we are a country constantly hoping against hope for good weather. It is the unconscious perpetual anxiety of the Irish psyche.

From the moment we wake each day, we peer out the bedroom window, check weather apps or listen to the forecast on the radio. The bulletins following the news are often more important than the news itself. Weather apps show detailed satellite imagery and can predict accurate ten-day forecasts – it makes you think about how people in the past fed their need-to-know-weather addiction. When I was growing up, my mother inherited a large barometer from her family home and this was hung in the hall. It had a large circular face, like a clock, but with only one arrowed hand and, each time we went past, we would ritually knock on the glass to see which way the arrow would budge. Its face had a few settings displayed in fancy lettering, 'very dry', 'fair', 'change', 'rain' and 'stormy'. From memory, the hand was stuck mainly between 'change' and 'rain'. Looking out at the rain, we used to hammer on the glass in the vain hope that the barometer would effect a change in the inclement weather.

Vernacular Meteorology

The vestiges of weather-predicting proverbs, such as 'dew on the grass, no rain will come to pass', remind us that there was a time when there was no technology and mass-communication mechanisms to foretell the weather, and a different set of indicators were used. This vernacular meteorology was the product of a vast body of inherited knowledge, gleaned from untold lifetimes of closely observing such things as the activities of birds and animals, the shape of clouds, the visibility of the moon or the condition of the fire in the hearth. They were effective for immediate or short-term forecasts. In Kiskeam, County Cork, for example, they would simply look out the door at the mountains and pronounce, 'Mushera cloudy, Clara clear, that's a sign that rain is near.' If sheep were on the top of a mountain and they started to come down, it was a sign of rain; while if the cattle were seen on the top of a hill, it was a sign of good weather. Like the old barometer, the Irish weather was usually in that zone of change between the states of fair or rain.

The proximity of animals to the fire in the hearth, the smoke in the chimney and the colour of the flames were all major

portents of weather change. If the cat cleaned behind its ears, settled into the hearth and turned its back to the fire, it was a sure sign of cold and wet weather. On lighting a fresh fire in the morning, people would go out to see the direction of the wind. If it went straight up, it was a sign of fine weather, a wind blowing from the north to the south would indicate a day of fair weather, while winds from the west or east were met with unease, as this would mean a change in the weather.

A wind from the east was never good. My old friend, Rita Moynihan, from the Long Valley Bar in Cork, used to have all the old maxims and one of her favourites was, 'Wind from the east, good for neither man nor beast.'

When there was a downdraught and the smoke did not go up the chimney at all but filled the whole kitchen with dense smoke, it was an indicator of low pressure and cold temperatures. In the smaller fireplaces, temporarily blocking the large opening by holding a newspaper against the surround helped create an exaggerated draught to remedy this. In the large open hearths, lumps of soot often fell from the inside of the chimney, and this often occurred in advance of high humidity and rain. In the old houses with mud floors, with the high humidity of impending rain, the earth would start to weep and the salt in the hard salt cone or the salt box beside the hearth would go soft. When the soot that was stuck to the sides of the pots, pans and kettles in the open hearth would start burning, this was a sign of frost. A blue flame in the fire was a sure indicator of a storm with heavy rain.

In the west of Ireland, when raking the fire in the hearth at night, some of the *gríosach* embers were seen to burn bright blue and green, almost like glow-worms, and were known as *corrchogailt*, foretelling either frost or rain.

Everything from the cricket singing to the dog sleeping or the sight of spiders in their webs indicated wet weather: 'When soot falls down and spaniels sleep and spiders from their cobwebs creep, then we shall have rain.'

Watching the position and feeding habits of different birds and listening to them sing were also sure signs of changes in weather. If the companionable robin was singing atop a bush early in the morning, it was going to be a great day, while if she was on a low bush close to the house, it signified the opposite. The crane became extinct in Ireland in the seventeenth century, but Irish people still refer to the grey heron as the crane, and to see her fly upriver was a sure sign that the river was going to flood following rain. A flock of seagulls sitting in a field inland meant a storm at sea and bad weather, while a field full of starlings in the wintertime bespoke a spell of harsh, cold weather. The continual crying of the curlew and snipe meant there would be rain the following day.

The hens in the coop were a very clear indicator of rain. In the morning, if they all came out together and without any stragglers, it was a sure sign that the day was going to be good. If they were inclined to stay inside and stayed together pecking close to the coop, it was an indication of rain. It was thought that the hens could hear thunder better than people, and they would run into their coop and roost early when a storm was approaching. When the hens started pecking at themselves and dislodged a few feathers, heavy rain and snow were forecast.

The most direct way of telling what the weather was going to do was to look at the sky. A clear night, when the stars were seen to twinkle, was a sure sign of frost. Much was read into the 'hen's eye', which was what people called the ring around the moon. If there was a large circle around the moon, it was a sign of rain; a smaller circle was a sign of frost – 'near ring, far rain; far ring, near rain'. A bright full moon meant good weather for harvest, 'If the moon shows like a silver shield, be not afraid to reap your field. But if she rises halved round, soon we'll tread on deluged ground.'

Another version of the 'red sky at night' proverb is: 'The evening red and the morning grey are said to be signs of a very fine day. The evening grey and the morning red bring down rain on the traveller's head.' There is a solid rationale behind this observation. The vivid red of the evening sky is caused by high pressure that concentrates all the particles of dust and pollen in the air that in turn reflect and amplify the sinking sun's light. High pressure is associated with fine weather and given that it is in the west, it is coming our way the following day. The red sky in the morning means the high pressure is in the east and has passed over us leaving the likelihood of poor and inclement weather to follow.

People also read the clouds – their shape, colour and height – and could distinguish between heavy showers from dark clouds and continual rain from low grey skies. Thunder showers and snow had their own cloud formations, while long broken clouds stretched along the sky foretold high winds and storms: 'Mackerel sky and mare's tails, make lofty ships carry low sails.'

Gougane Barra in County Cork is my favourite place in all of Ireland. Its deep, dark lake is surrounded on all sides by tall and imposing rugged mountains. My good friends, Neil and Katie Lucy, who run the magnificent hotel there, have inherited a whole set of ways of reading the weather. When what they call the *sí gaoithe* (fairy wind) manifests as small crescent-type waves moving across the lake, it forecasts rain. Neil's father, Christy, used to observe the *snas* (shine) off the rocks on the mountain and that would bring rain.

Neil can smell the rain, and rain does have a particular smell. It comes in the form of petrichor, the dry dust of decayed organic matter that settles on rocks and soil that, when wetted, dissolves into the air, producing its own characteristic smell. A rise in temperature in Gougane can be seen visibly on the lake, when the extra warmth causes the grub at the base of the lake to hatch out and the fish on the surface enjoy a feeding frenzy. Following persistent rain, the steep and craggy mountainous terrain that envelopes the lake is broken by small cascading torrents that roar their way down into the lake.

Standing at the side of the lake, the sound of the waterfalls indicates the direction of the airflow and what weather might be expected. When the wind is westerly, the tumbling waterfalls at the very far end of the lake, the source of the River Lee, can be heard. When the wind changes to northwesterly, it is a different fall, humorously labelled *mún an tsean duine* (the old person's piss), that is clearly audible, while the northerly wind amplifies the water leaving the lake at the other end.

Neil looks to the leaves of the sycamore and ash trees turning inside out as a sign of rain. In the summer months, he knows if the air pressure is low or high by watching the swallows and martins as they soar high up, feeding on insects, or swooping low down to catch those on top of the lake.

Despite the wonders of scientific meteorological forecasting, many of Ireland's micro-environments, such as the off-shore islands or mountain oases like Gougane, can exhibit markedly different weather patterns than the rest of the country. In such remote locations, the ongoing intimate engagement with local weather lore draws from and feeds into a profound accumulated heritage of observation and experience. It reinforces a personal empowerment and control over the vagaries of the everyday and an invested connection to one's sense of place.

'It's Only a Shower'

The Irish fixation with weather centres on rain. On the west coast from Donegal to Cork in any one year, it rains on average 230 days, making it a feature of life on two out of every three days. It is no wonder that Irish people take so many sun holidays.

The very first map of Ireland was made by the Greek geographer, Ptolemy. He took detail from an earlier geographer Pytheas and combined this with the names of our rivers and tribal groups from Roman traders who visited here in the first century BCE. The name given to Ireland by the Romans was

'Hibernia', literally meaning 'the wintery place' – cold, wet and miserable where it is inclement all of the time. It is no small wonder then, that like the native Inuit cultures of the Arctic who have so many words for snow, Irish people have their own lexicon for rain.

It is not that we have so many nouns for rain in the forms such as mist or drizzle, but we tend to describe the rain by the degree, duration and the extent of its ferocity.

It often follows that you will be asked by someone in the house to look out and see what the day is like weatherwise, and to classify the state of the rain, if applicable. The first type of description covers very light rain which is often a kind of

denial of rain – as if by not naming it, it will go away or will not affect you. 'It's barely raining' or 'it's trying to rain' or 'it's just spitting' reduces the rain to minimal proportions and is a cause for optimism.

'It's damp', 'it's a fine soft day', 'it's misty' or 'it's drizzling' covers a sort of begrudging, but not fully committed, recognition that it is actually raining. This progresses to an ambiguous, but still non-committal state, deflected by 'it's only drops', 'little drips, no need for a coat' and 'it's on and off'.

When it is raining, the prospect of it stopping is immediately resorted to – 'It's very patchy' and 'It's only a shower, it might clear up. Give it a minute or two.' Nobody in Ireland takes this type of rain seriously and would be embarrassed if they were to, even for a moment, consider changing their plans. Bebhín O'Malley, one of my students from Clare Island, told me that her father would send her out to tend the sheep in the rain declaring, 'Sure, you're not made of sugar lumps!'

A majorly different attitude emerges when the rain turns wet. The profound declaration of 'that's wet rain' may well confuse a non-Irish person who might consider all rain to be wet. Wet rain differentiates the ordinary, indiscriminate, quotidian precipitation from the serious non-stop downpours. Here the lexicon becomes more animated and antagonistic. 'It's rotten out', 'it's miserable' and 'that's in for the day' all characterise the displeasure of the very wet day. Sometimes, it is summed up tersely with just one word: 'dirty'.

The volume and force of the rain is governed by different phrases: 'It's pouring out of the heavens' means it's very wet, while 'it's pelting rain' and 'it's pissing down' increases the intensity to a visible barrage of droplets 'hopping off the ground'.

'It's lashing rain' – where the 'lashing' is always said slowly and with gravitas – speaks of blankets and sheets of rain driven sideways by gusts of wind. 'Bucketing rain', 'teeming rain' and 'torrential rain' result in people being 'soaked' or 'drenched' or 'drowned wet', the latter often accentuated by the insertion of an extra elongating syllable as in, 'I was drown-de-ded.'

'It's coming down in stair-rods' likens the long thin shafts of rain to the long brass bars that used to keep the carpet fixed on the stairs. The Irish versions of 'it's raining cats and dogs' is *ag cur foirc agus scaena* (it's raining forks and knives), even more cutting is *tá sé ag caitheamh sceana gréasaí* (it's throwing down shoemaker's knives).

Of course, the Irish language has its own innumerable and extraordinary words and expressions for rain and weather. *Braon báistighe* (a little shower of rain) is distinguished from *braoille fearthana* (a heavy shower of rain), while expressions such as *tá sé ag clagarnaigh báirlighe* (it is pattering down rain) were collected by the great Fr Pádraig Ó Duinnín when compiling his *Foclóir*, an extraordinary Irish-English dictionary, in 1903.

Far more than a dictionary, Fr Ó Duinnín's work is a linguistic evocation of the lore, customs, crafts and traditions of Ireland's rich vernacular past. In 1927, he published the greatly expanded second edition, a chunky volume of 1,300 pages with more than 750,000 words. I inherited my copy of the Irish Texts Society's edition from my late father, and it is, by far, the single most important reference book in my library. In it, we find wonderful words such as *atal* explained as 'stillness, calmness after a storm, cessation from rain; cheerfulness, pleasantry'. There are words like *ceobhrán* (a heavy dew or a drizzling rain), *draghnánach* (drizzling of rain), *díleannta* (deluge-like), *spéachán* (a spit or kick of rain), *brádarnach* (a slight fall of rain or snow, hazy weather) and *bearradh caorach* (fleecy clouds, portending rain).

Given its frequency and our endless appellations and pronouncements on the nature of rain, Irish people consider themselves to have a monopoly on it and classify themselves as experts on precipitation. When abroad, we nonchalantly walk in the drizzle or light rain to proudly exclaim to the natives our familiarity with it and as a proud cultural signifier, we display our resultant defiant hardiness.

The Ash Before the Oak

My farming neighbour, Jerome Callaghan, is a fountain of wisdom and has great respect for nature. Conscious of conditions for ploughing or the best time for leaving cattle out into the fields, he remembers many of his father's expressions and observances. We were chatting one morning as he was moving his cows after milking, and he came out with a gem of an age-old maxim: 'The oak before the ash, splash. The ash before the oak, soak.' I love the idea that the sequence of leaves opening on the different trees in response to the temperature and moisture might be used as an indicator of wet weather.

However, even with the most sophisticated modern meteorological techniques, long-term weather prediction is complicated and unreliable. In the past, there were specific days of the year that represented diagnostic auguries of the weather to come. People always put great store in the weather on the auspicious ancient Celtic quarter days, such as Brigid's Day or *Lugnasadh*, and also the so-called 'crooked' days that marked the equinoxes and solstices.

The autumnal equinox was celebrated at Michaelmas on 29 September. An old saying observes that good weather on the day would forecast additional cold ahead: 'If Michaelmas Day be bright and clear, there will be two winters in the year.' The day was marked by feasting on the Michaelmas goose, one of the geese that had been fattened by gleaning the grain in the stubble following harvest. The carcass of the goose was a sure means of predicting the winter weather. The large breastbone was held up to the light and, if the light shone through, it foretold a mild winter. The left-hand side of the breastbone spoke of the period up to Christmas, while the right-hand side represented the period thereafter. Depending on how thin and transparent or thick and opaque the bone was in each segment, people would read the proportions of either as to the extent of good or bad weather. The thick and dark bone indicated rainstorms and heavy snow. Great store was placed in Michaelmas predictions for the winter ahead.

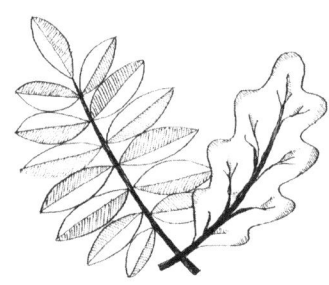

The last day of the twelve days of Christmas is the feast of Epiphany, when the three wise men eventually made their appearance beside the crib. This was also known as women's Little Christmas, greatly enjoyed by the women who got a rest after all their hard work over the Christmas. It was the last hurrah, a final day of feasting and merriment.

In the back of people's minds, given that the twelve days of Christmas corresponded to the twelve months of the year, there was also the long-held belief that 6 January was to be the day that the world was to come to an end. On 6 January 1839, many must have felt that this prediction had come true when the entire country was literally levelled by the biggest meteorological event ever recorded. This was *Oíche na Gaoithe Móire* (The Night of the Big Wind), an event etched deep into Irish folk memory. The day or two before had seen a scattering of snow and people had built snowmen, oblivious of what was to come. On the morning of the 6 January, the day became unnaturally warm and the air clammy with an unusual and confusing hollow calmness that had people rightly perplexed. The temperature rose to over twenty degrees and the snow melted. At mid-afternoon heavy rain began to fall. By teatime, it had developed into a raging storm with violent winds and continuous rain, forcing everyone inside to shelter. By 9pm however, the storm escalated to a full force 12 hurricane.

Right across the country, roofs of thatched houses, both the timber and the thatch, were blown clean off, while the sturdy leaded and slated roofs of the big houses suffered the same fate. The towering, noble old oak and beech trees of the walled demesnes of the gentry were uprooted and toppled, with an estimated 2 million trees being felled across the country. The sea rose so high, that the waves crashed over the Cliffs of Moher and the Aran Islands and there was flooding inland from the ingress of seawater. The wool of the sheep some fifty miles inland was covered in salt from the spray of the sea. The carefully made plump haystacks, storing the winter fodder for the cattle, were blown into oblivion. Church steeples were blown over and the windows and doors of houses were blown in, some causing fatalities. More lives were lost at sea and large vessels and small boats were smashed to smithereens. The official death toll was put at mere 300, but the devastation and hardship that followed was considerable.

The memory of the Night of the Big Wind came into focus in 1909, some seventy years later when in March of that year, the old-age pension for anyone older than seventy years was introduced. In the absence of official records of birth, those who could describe the events of the night in detail were awarded the pension.

~ THE WEATHER YEAR ~

The dark wet cold and raging storms of the winter months were a real trial for many, and the vestiges of the changing seasons were eagerly anticipated. The promise of the end of the winter weather and the beginning of spring following Brigid's Day on 1 February, was reckoned on Candlemas (2 February): 'If Candlemas be fair and bright, then winter will have another flight; if Candlemas brings clouds and rain, winter will not come again.' As with the now worldwide famous weather predictions of the groundhog at Punxsutawney in Pennsylvania, in Ireland the Candlemas assessment of the weather was judged by the enthusiasm, or lack of, displayed by the badger or hedgehog awakening from their winter slumbers. If the animals were to see their shadows at Candlemas, they would retreat back into their setts and nests for another six weeks, as they knew hard weather was coming.

For the farmers, a dry February was a disaster because it meant the crops did not germinate: 'If February brings no rain, there will be neither hay nor grain.'

As the equinox approaches, the month of March is characterised by harsh winds and blustery inclement weather. Most Irish people's memory of St Patrick's Day is watching the marching battalions of FCA troops and baton-twirling majorettes, sodden and frozen with the cold as they tried to keep their balance against the gusts of wind, parading past the equally miserable raincoated and umbrellaed crowds.

In the past, people understood that the winds would decrease as we moved past the equinox: 'If March comes in like a lion, it will go out like a lamb.' The transition into April and the prospect of fine weather was heeded in the salutary tale of *An tSean-Bó Riabhach* (*The Old Brindled Cow*). The first three days of April were known as the 'Borrowed Days' and the story is told that an old cow, with its distinctive tawny streaked coat, having made it through March and got to 1 April, confidently proclaimed that the severe weather was now gone. With grass growing again and the weather fine, she bellowed out that she would live yet another year. However, March, on hearing such audacity, asked April if she could borrow three days and inflicted such cold and blustery weather, that the old cow went hungry on the first day, died on the second and a sharp wind took the skin off her back on the third day.

When, at the start of April, such severe weather regularly occurred, the older generation took pride in passing the knowing remark 'they're skinning the old cow'. A similar bout with a severe cold wind at the end of April and the start of May, when the weather should be getting better, caused misery and was known as *Scairbhín na gCuach garbh í agus fuar* (the scaraveen of the cuckoo, rough and cold). Scaraveen is an anglicisation of the Irish *garbhsíon*, which literally means 'rough weather', and this southwest Ireland version of the French mistral wind brought total unpredictability: sudden drops in temperature, frosts, hail showers, violent gusts and storms. It played havoc with crops like oats that might have been planted late or the early potatoes that were just sprouting.

Given that the cuckoo arrives from South Africa in April, a lazy or ineffective farmer was known as a cuckoo farmer. One proverb tells of what farmers should do to get the best return, dependant on the time of the cuckoo's arrival: 'If a cuckoo sits on a bare thorn, you should sell your cow and buy corn, but if she sits on a green bough, you may sell your corn and buy a cow.'

The maxims of ancient weather lore are still current and ever-present in our lives today. As someone who likes to wear shorts as soon as I can each year, the sight of my bare legs is regularly greeted with the old nugget of wisdom: 'Ne'er cast a clout till May is out!' Remarking on a wet day as I sat down for a cup of tea in our local garden centre, the waitress remarked, 'a wet and windy May fills the haggard with corn and hay' and, in a flash she added another, 'a dry June makes the farmer whistle a merry tune'.

In the middle of a very wet summer, I got a text from one of my students on St Swithin's Day (15 July), quoting and questioning the validity of the rhyme: 'St Swithin's Day, if thou dost rain, for forty days it will remain; St Swithin's Day, if thou be fair, for forty days, twill rain nae mair.' Swithin was a ninth-century English bishop who, in a gesture of humility, requested that when he died, he was to be buried outside Winchester Cathedral with the commoners. Ignoring his request, the clergy placed him in the vault within the cathedral but, as soon as they did, it started to rain and continued to do so for thirty-nine days until on the fortieth day, they interred him outside and the rain stopped.

Most of us who have lived through the constant rain of the summer months in Ireland may be inclined to put credence in Swithin's revenge, so I set about contacting none other than Met Éireann's climatologist, Sandra Spillane, to see if there was any account of a continuous spell of forty days of rain. I fully expected the answer to be no, but Sandra informed me that there was one recorded incident. It occurred at Belmullet, County Mayo, and the rain (0.2mm or more per day) began on Wednesday, 15 July 2009 and continued for fifty-two consecutive days, totalling

262.5mm in all. This was an exceptional circumstance and as rare as it is, there is not one single account of it being continually dry for forty days.

The truism of Irish weather is that it changes by the minute and, as the expression goes, 'If you don't like the weather in Ireland, wait ten minutes!'

'English That for Me'

Over the years, I have managed to pick up a functional competency in French. I am not a great linguist, and my French rarely distinguishes between masculine and feminine nouns or past and present tenses, yet I am content to blather away to all who will endure my enthusiastic banter. When in full unconscious flow, often facilitated by a glass of wine, my mindset changes and I literally become a different person. Like a chameleon, I exhibit all the classic French shoulder shrugs and hand gestures, as if alternative brain pathways have been taken over to produce a system of communication that expresses meaning and enables a shared understanding.

Language is more than just a collection of words, it is a way of perceiving, conceptualising and manifesting our everyday reality. Through language, we articulate our distinct views of the world and, as such, it is the central component that encapsulates our ethnicity. The unique nuances and deep inheritances of the Irish language represent the major repository of our ancient culture. Pádraig Pearse captured this idea in his powerful aphorism, *'Tír gan teanga, tír gan anam'* ('a country without a language is a country without a soul').

The Irish language is at the very heart and soul of our cultural identity.

Beyond the Aboriginal

One consideration to keep in mind is that the Irish language has not always been the language spoken in Ireland – it was not native insofar as it was not the first language to be spoken here. When I was a student, the polymathic scholar Jim Mallory from Queen's University Belfast used to travel down to meet his old pal Peter Woodman in the Archaeology Department in University College Cork. As a class group, we would sit wide-eyed and open-mouthed as Mallory posed challenging questions, such as when did Irish first come to Ireland? With his far-reaching expertise in linguistics and archaeology, he introduced the concept of the Irish aboriginal language that was present in the early periods of the Mesolithic hunter-gatherer-fishers and the first farming communities of the Neolithic period (4000–2500 BCE). We would explore the different 'horizons' from the Bronze Age through to the Iron Age to judge points of entry for a new language that would match cultural shifts in the archaeological record and what we knew about Indo-European linguistic pedigree.

What was so interesting about these fascinating seminars was that Mallory suggested that the introduction of the language was not the result of a major invasion of Celtic-speaking people who wiped out the native population, but a set of circumstances where it became advantageous for the large population of aboriginal Irish to adopt the new Celtic language. Perhaps it was through the simple need for trading and economic well-being that the Irish language became important.

The literary record extant in the huge corpus of medieval manuscripts attests that Irish was well established as our language from long before the fifth century. It remained so until the conquest by the English-speaking Anglo-Normans in the twelfth century made English the official language of law and administration in the urban centres. By the fourteenth century, the Anglo-Norman influence had hybridised with the native Irish, and Irish was again the vernacular spoken tongue. The horrific extremes of the sixteenth and seventeenth centuries, not least the Elizabethan and Cromwellian plantations, began the process that decimated the old Gaelic order of native Irish society.

In this, the language was its symbolic identifier. From the 1690s right through much of the eighteenth century, the persecutory Penal Laws endeavoured to eliminate any power and influence of the Irish Catholic population. By 1800, it is estimated that half the population of Ireland were still monolingual Irish-speakers, with the majority living in the rural and impoverished areas of the west. These were the families that were wiped out by the ravages of the potato famine of 1845–51. With the colossal death-toll and the subsequent ongoing mass emigration, a major knock-on effect was the loss of the language.

In the subsequent years, Irish came to be seen as a badge of poverty and humiliation, as well as a mark of ineffectiveness.

The prospect of survival or advancement in Ireland – or on the streets of New York or Boston – was not helped by speaking only Irish. Parents took it upon themselves to empower their children. Their active encouragement of speaking English is exemplified by the accounts of the *bata scóir* (tally stick), that was hung around the necks of some children. If the child was heard speaking Irish in school, the stick was notched with a knife and, when they got home, they were punished by their parents. The decline in Irish speaking was rapid. In the census records of 1891, the respondents who identified themselves as having Irish as their only language had fallen to a remarkably low 1 per cent.

Nevertheless, the language has remained enshrined all around us; its magic and intrigue are fossilised into the placenames of every rock, river and antiquity of our landscape. The *loganimneacha* (placenames of the country), are anglicised so, while losing their pure Irish incarnation, their English form provides a starting point that makes the depth of our linguistic heritage tangible. Our landscape is invested in cultural associations that colour our hinterlands and bring them to life.

When I am travelling down to west Cork, I pass through the little hamlet of Lisavaird and think of its Irish name *Lios an Bhaird* (ringfort of the singing poet) and imagine the ancient singer of tales, accompanied by his harp, performing to the gathered assembly in the nearby ringfort. When close to Clonmel, I think of *Cluain Meala* (meadow of honey), an area full of scented apple blossom and still famed as the home of the native Irish black honeybee. In Cahersiveen (*Cathair Saidhbhín*), my mind fills with the mythological figure of Sadhbh who, after making love with Fionn, was magically changed from a beautiful woman to

a deer and, in that form, gives birth to the great hero Oisín (the little fawn). Oisín is immortalised in the nearby mountain pass of Ballaghisheen (*Beallach Oisín*, Oisín's/the fawn's pass). The island of Inisbofin, off the Connemara coast, derives its name from the goddess *Bó-Find* (white cow or cow wisdom), who also gives her name to the mighty River Boyne that envelops the great complex of Newgrange and other ancient megalithic tombs in County Meath. It is said that at certain times the river flows white as milk. Such imagined animations of the ancient lore preserved in the Irish language anchors our profound sense of place and identity.

While a number of the dispossessed and poor, through economic necessity, forsook their vernacular language, the very opposite took place amongst an influential group of the ascendency and literati. The nineteenth century was an era of pioneering scholarship in Irish antiquarian and philological interests. Archaeological studies were initiated by the likes of George Petrie, along with the magnificent scholarship on Irish placenames by the great scholars, John O'Donovan and Eugene O'Curry, as part of the Ordnance Survey of Ireland. They and other intellectuals such as Kuno Meyer, Standish O'Grady and Whitley Stokes were pivotal in making available the extraordinary texts contained within Ireland's magnificent collection of vernacular manuscripts. This was a window into an ancient past, something of a golden age for Ireland before English influence.

The heady mix of romanticism and antiquarian enquiry were the ideal ingredients for the Celtic Revival and, along with the Irish Arts and Crafts Movement, the emphasis on Irish spoken language was core. Central to this was *Conradh na Gaeilge* (The Gaelic League), founded in 1893 and headed by Douglas Hyde and Eóin MacNeill. It established an active philosophy of de-anglicising Ireland, emphasising what it regarded as indigenous cultural elements in music and dance and intertwining itself with the blossoming Gaelic Athletic Association, which had been founded in 1884. The countrywide setup of the GAA provided the perfect mechanism to assist the revival of the language by providing Irish-language classes. In 1904, the Gaelic League boasted 600 active centres around the country with over 50,000 attending members. Its publications included *An Claidheamh Soluis (The Sword of Light)*, which was a bilingual weekly newspaper (edited by Pádraig Pearse between 1903 and 1909). In halls and upstairs rooms in cities and in towns, clusters of middle-class men and women gathered for the social occasion of learning and speaking Irish along with dancing and singing and, in doing so, were active in shaping and redefining their cultural character.

The resurgence of the Irish language as a potent cultural identifier was central to the ideology of the fight for independence and the establishment of the Irish Free State in 1922. It was immediately declared the official language of the state and was taught in both primary and secondary schools, becoming mandatory for the matriculation examination to enter university.

～◈ The Gaeltacht ◈～

The fervour and excitement of the newly claimed Irish identity in the language was huge in my parent's generation. My father was born in 1922 and my mother in 1926 and, when they were courting during the war years, my father insisted that their courtship would be conducted through Irish. My mother told me that such was his fanaticism that for one full year he would only converse with her in Irish. They both loved nothing more than repairing to the beautiful hinterland of the Muskerry Gaeltacht of Cúil Aodha, Ballingeary and Gougane Barra where the isolating mountainous terrain had maintained an unbroken link with the living language.

When my father died in 1988 and we waked him at home in Cork, there was a steady stream of old Muskerry Gaeltacht friends that came to pay their respects in recognition of his deep love of Irish. Yet my father was also a modern, somewhat cosmopolitan and flamboyant individual, with a wider worldview than that which he had inherited from our tortured past. He plied his trade as a commercial artist and contributed to various Irish cultural events, such as *An Tostal*, a countrywide celebration of Irish life in the 1950s, and putting the Irish spin on *Féile Scannán Chorcaí* (Cork Film Festival). In that manner, he was bridging the new, emerging Ireland, where the language was not a fossilised relic of a backward-looking de Valerian idea, but one that was in tune with an open and progressive future. He broke with the stereotype of the purist, as did many of his friends, broadening their horizons and bringing the language with him.

My mind goes back to 'babies' – Junior Infants – and the first days in school in Miss Quill's class in St Anthony's in Ballinlough. I can still remember the very first sentence that we learned in the Irish language: *Tá eitleán sa spéir* (there is a plane in the sky). I often remark that this was an early sign of the new, progressive Ireland of the late 1960s, with something as modern as an aeroplane featuring in prime position in the development of a young child's Irish lexicon. The second sentence that we all learned, of course, was the functional bathroom request: *An bhfuil cead agam dul go dtí an leithreas?*

When we progressed on to Miss Lynch's class in 'high babies', and the years beyond, we were introduced to the extraordinary world of *Buntús Cainte*. In the 1970s, we were oblivious to the stereotyping of the social paradigms in our new sentences, *tá Mamaí sa cistin* (Mummy is in the kitchen) and *tá Dadaí ag obair* (Daddy is at work).

As we progressed through the world of national school, our teacher, Ger Scannell, a native of Baile Bhuirne, would tell us stories of Fionn and the Fianna and teach us the ubiquitous litany of songs in Irish. He would play a note on his melodica or strike his tuning fork against the table and the resulting note would set our childish voices off in the timeless cacophonies of *'Trasna na dTonnta'*, *'Beidh aonach amárach i gContae an Chláir'* and *'Oró, Sé do Bheatha 'bhaile'*. By Sixth Class and the first few years of secondary school, we were confronted by the idiosyncrasies of Irish grammar with the enigmas of the *Tuiseal Ginideach* and the dreaded *Modh Coinníollach*.

Such a confusing grammatical quagmire was offset by a wondrous coming-of-age summer in the idyllic surrounds of Cork's Muskerry Gaeltacht of Cúil Aodha, hidden away in the Derrynasaggart Mountains. I was packed off for three weeks to learn my Irish but was probably more adept at learning how to dance the 'Siege of Ennis', how to play ping-pong and how to appreciate the enchanting singing of the O'Riada Mass. My Irish failed somewhat as I experienced my first crush on a girl named Pádraigín. She was a real beauty with jet-black hair, perfect skin and red-rosy cheeks, and she had come to work for the summer to help the *bean an tí*. My naivety in our native tongue was clear when I presented her with two ping-pong balls that had been stood on and wanted her to put them in a pot of hot water so they would regain their shape. I remember the shocked look on her face as I asked shyly, *'Beir mo liathróidí le do thoil'*, a phrase that can be translated as either 'boil my balls' or 'grab my balls please'. She blushed but, from that moment on, we danced every dance at the weekend céilí and I managed to pluck up the courage to give her a kiss. In that moment, everything changed, it was as if, like in the great mythological tales, I had met the goddess and that embrace marked my initiation into a different world.

English Woven on a Gaelic Loom

Every child in Ireland learned Irish in school and many gained great proficiency in the language, only to lack any meaningful outlet for their expertise. Nevertheless, the language is still clearly manifest in the way the Irish speak English. The so-called Hiberno-English – the everyday, English vernacular spoken in Ireland – has firm roots in the idioms, pronunciation and syntactical forms of expression inherited from the Irish language. As sportswriter Con Houlihan coined it, this is English 'woven on a Gaelic loom'.

Following university, I ran away to Paris with my girlfriend and found employment as an English teacher only to find out that I knew nothing of English grammar. I felt like a complete imposter in the language and, not only was my English considered off-kilter but I was also at a total loss how to explain my inherited patterns of speech. I had no idea, nor could I explain, the difference between the simple past – 'I ate my dinner' – and the present perfect – 'I have eaten my dinner'. This was because the simple expression for me straight from the Irish language is, 'I'm after eating my dinner.'

In addition, the Irish accent and pronunciation may have its own charm, but non-conformity to the conventions of standard English has connotations of ignorance, poor education and inferiority. Our national inability to pronounce 'th', because it does not exist in Irish, is the classic example. In appreciation we will offer our 'tanks' and when we need to wash, we go to the 'batroom'. Try as we might, our inherited parlance is ingrained in us and attempts to modify our natural propensities can lead to confusion and uncertainty.

The insertion of extra syllables and the elongation of vowels is also an inheritance from Irish. There are frequent renderings of 'com-a-tee' for committee and 'cal-enn-dar' for calendar and 'tee-aa-ter' for theatre. In addition, there are the long rounded double vowels inserted into words like 'fil-um' and 'wor-um'. I was once trying to explain to a group of American students that in early medieval Irish-language literature, rather than a snake or serpent, a monster is a *peist* (worm). The puzzled, blank faces suggested that my pronunciation was confusing them. I attempted to clarify the word by slowly repeating and over-articulating it, 'wor-um, wor-um', but this left them even more flummoxed.

Our pronunciation is one issue, but our choice of words and their usage can cause further confusion. The Irish use of the word 'grand', for example. Outside Ireland it means 'magnificent' or 'imposing', we use it in everyday expressions like, 'We'll be grand' or 'I'm grand altogether', and simply means that all is ok. When we ask someone to 'show me that screwdriver', we are asking them to hand it to us. In England, to be bold means to be brave, to be confident and to take risks, while in Ireland, it is simply refers to misbehaviour.

Those of my students who were born in England tell me that they have been entirely at a loss when confronted with everyday Irish word usage. There was absolute bafflement when asked to put something in the 'hot press' (airing cupboard), while expressions like 'that's gas' (that's funny) and 'cop on to yourself' (be sensible) and 'I must get the messages' (buy groceries) had to be learned over time.

Confusingly for non-Irish people, 'I will, yeah!' said by an Irish person means the direct opposite, as in 'I will not!' This is related to the Irish expression *mar dhea*, which is delivered in a sceptical tone of voice meaning, 'Right, yeah, as if!' This, in turn, provides the basis for the adjective 'mocky-ah', which means something that is only pretend or false.

The active revival of our beautiful Irish language has had its ups and downs over the twentieth century, but there is a present resurgence that is far from 'mocky-ah'. Ireland now has a full-time body of academics and etymologists who meet once a month to agree on the Irish versions of new words that are emerging continuously. They accommodate some 3,000 new Irish words every year, hastened by the fact that, in 2022, the Irish language gained full status as an official language of the EU, so all EU documents must be translated into Irish. Equally, the language needs to reflect the modern world and, as there are so many new contraptions and situations that never existed in the past, the task is an onerous one. When looking at 'tweeting' on social media, the Irish word *giolc*, which is the sweet chirping sound made by a bird, was favoured, but the Gaelicised form *tuít* for the English 'tweet' is what is most popular. My favourite new word is *féinín*, the Irish for a 'selfie' taken on your mobile phone.

My four grandchildren all receive their primary education through Irish, attending a *Gaelscoil* (Irish school) that make up 10 per cent of Irish primary schools. They blather away to me in Irish as freely as in English, correcting my mistakes, and are so proud when they are regularly awarded the school prize of *Gaeilgeoir na seachtaine* (Irish speaker of the week).

Some of the best documentaries on Irish television are on TG4, the Irish-language channel, and, with the aid of subtitles, the rich depth of the language is tangible and readily comprehensible. The channel will soon be in existence for thirty years and the subliminal nature of the medium has modernised and reset the character of the language. Irish has become normalised for commentary on rugby matches, weather forecasts and cookery programmes. When the all-Irish film, *An Cailín Ciúin*, was nominated for an Oscar for Best International Film, there was sincere pride, not only in the story and cinematography, but more so at being represented in our native language.

PART THREE

Instruments of Change

A few weeks ago, I was driving to the Daniel O'Connell Summer School in Derrynane House to give a paper. The Google maps display on my dashboard was telling me there was traffic congestion ahead, so I decided to make good use of this delay by calling my brother, Barry, who lives in Perth in Australia. My mobile phone is connected to the car's handsfree system and I asked Siri to phone him using WhatsApp. He was eight hours ahead; he had just finished his day's work and was about to buy a coffee before he cycled home on his electric bike. He paused the chat momentarily while he paid for his flat white by tapping his watch against the card machine. We blathered about the Ireland rugby match that I had missed but I told him that I might watch it on my iPad when I got to the hotel.

When my lecture at the summer school, which was live-streamed over the internet, was over, I took a leisurely spin back over Coomakista to Waterville and on towards Coomanaspig where I stopped at St Finian's Bay, one of my favourite places. I stood on the white sands and paused for a moment of contemplation, watching the wild breaking waves and revelling in the magnificent spectacle of Skellig Michael in the distance. It is a beach we used to go to as children, a stimulus of many family memories. I smiled as I remembered my childish fervour in my choice of Finian as my confirmation name. I took out my phone to take a little video of the crashing waves and sent it to my brother, Anthony to warm his heart with familiar reminiscences. In that timeless place, I began to muse on the extent and the rapidity of technological change that has transformed Ireland and its people even in the past fifty years since my own childhood days.

This corner of Ireland's Atlantic coast has a scattering of modern holiday homes intermixed with semi-derelict and ruined houses. These latter abandoned architectural skeletons, stone relics of our past, were once vibrant homes – places where families ate and slept and lived out their time on our planet. Their way of life was hard, frugal and rudimentary, and relied on little by way of technical provision. Theirs was a tough subsistence, dependant on the resources and materials available locally, and inherited traditions and skills necessary to harness and exploit them for human survival. Turf was cut and saved and stacked for the winter to cook and to keep warm. Pigs were fattened, killed and cured, while boats were put out to sea to catch the shoals of mackerel that were gutted and salted in barrels as their stock of food. Life and living were arduous and, even as time moved on, the new forces of change, some which had been long established in the cities and towns, took that bit longer to get to such remote areas of the country.

Electricity – the major sweeping stimulus of modern transformation – only made it to the Black Valley in County Kerry in 1976, literally and figuratively plugging it into the wave of modernity. The subsequent years of unprecedented technological and social change have been rapid and colossal. As I looked around the south Kerry hinterland, the great adage 'the past is a foreign country' could not have resonated more.

The modern houses, with their triple-glazed panoramic windows, air-to-water heat-pumps, solar panels and satellite dishes, along with the people who live in them, seem as if they are from a different planet when compared to the world of their traditional predecessors. I saw a family parking their electric car in a pristine landscaped driveway, the children hopping out with an array of colourful beach paraphernalia. We now inhabit a world of hyper-technology: headphones, mobile phones, barbeques, robotic lawnmowers, microwaves, coffee-machines and social media. There are some who seek to return to some notion of the past as a refuge from such life noise. The trap of romanticisation and nostalgia regularly masks the stark realities of the past. It is wise to remember that life used to be brutally hard, both physically and mentally. On occasion, through lack of food and heat, it was life-threatening. Given the various social and cultural inheritances, it was far from being a time or place of great joy, but was, instead, frequently miserable.

Technological advancements in Ireland over the past two generations have profoundly changed people's lives for the better. Such has been the liberation of time and efficiencies brought about by the conveniences of new technologies, the older systems of survival, with their associated traditions and know-how, have been quickly put aside. However, traditional practices and knowledge still rest under the surface and re-emerge when the need arises. We repair to fundamental technologies when we need to be more connected to the world around us. A spin on a bicycle will transport us back to the pure joy and freedom of our youth. A home-made birthday cake, baked with love and affection, will always hold more weight that one conveniently bought in the supermarket. There is pleasure and solace to be found in the timeless occupations of walking, swimming or growing vegetables. Equally, we know the value in putting pen to paper when we wish to express our deepest emotions rather than texting a message. The traditional enables us to rejoice in the simple and primal.

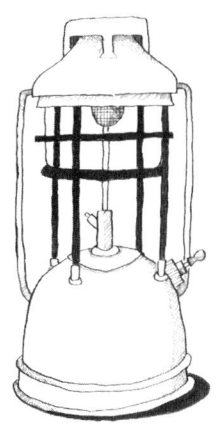

LIGHTING THE DARK

Illuminations

Not too long ago, say forty years or so, if there was a storm and the electricity went out plunging the house into darkness, you'd automatically feel your way to the kitchen drawer and rummage around in its corners until you found the end of an old candle stashed away for such an event. With a match struck from a box of Maguire & Patterson matches, the curled black wick would hiss and spatter itself into a radiant source of light. Once lit, you'd let the concave hollow of the top of the candle fill with the melting edges and then carefully drip the candle grease into a little puddle onto a saucer, before standing it upright in the hardening blob. In that instance of the candle-lighting, we were immediately transported, like unsuspecting time-travellers, into a previous time without the conveniences of electricity or the technologies of the modern world.

This little beacon of light in the middle of the kitchen table was enough to light the dark and conquer the suffocating and all-consuming blind-black night. Its soft, comforting, flickering yellow-sepia glow gathered us together and, while the power was out, we idled our time, laughing and joking, passing our fingers through the candle flame and messing with the amassing stalactites of candle grease dribbling down its side. This was time out, a temporary dreamlike escape from the stresses of the modern world. In the mellow glow of the candle, time stood still. Then with an abrupt clamour of the reconnecting electrical devices and the blinding white light of a flickering fluorescent tube, the magical time travel was over, and the calmness and joy of the candle was extinguished: blown out and thrown back into the corner of the kitchen drawer.

In the time before electricity, gas and paraffin oil, it was the candle that enabled people to light the black night: to see in the dark, so life could continue beyond the hours of daylight. Schoolwork, knitting, letter writing, card games and a host of social activities depended on the light of the humble candle. Tallow, the hard fat of cattle and sheep, was the chief ingredient of the many tallow chandlers who produced candles commercially. Over time, candles were made from a variety of different waxes and oils: everything from beeswax to paraffin wax and even spermaceti, a waxy oil found in the head cavity of the sperm whale.

In Cork, with its abundance of slaughterhouses, tallow from beef and mutton was boiled down to make candles and soap, with chandleries on every corner of the city. As the light source for every night, candles were everywhere and readily available but they were still too expensive for the very poor, who had to resort to more ingenious methods to light the night.

Rushlights

In rural Ireland from the eighteenth to the early twentieth century, shop-bought tallow and wax candles might only have been purchased for special occasions such as wakes, a Station Mass or for Christmas. The cheapest, simplest, yet highly efficient candle used for every day was an unassuming homemade entity: the rushlight.

The common rush is found in wet marshy land and along the banks of rivers and small streams, where it grows in distinctive clumps or tufts. These were once an integral part of Irish rural life; rushes were commonly strewn on the wet mud floors to provide a protective soft layer underfoot, and they were used to provide the natural wick material for the simple candles. The rushes were best cut when they were green and ripe, in late summer and early autumn before the winter frosts turned them brown and useless.

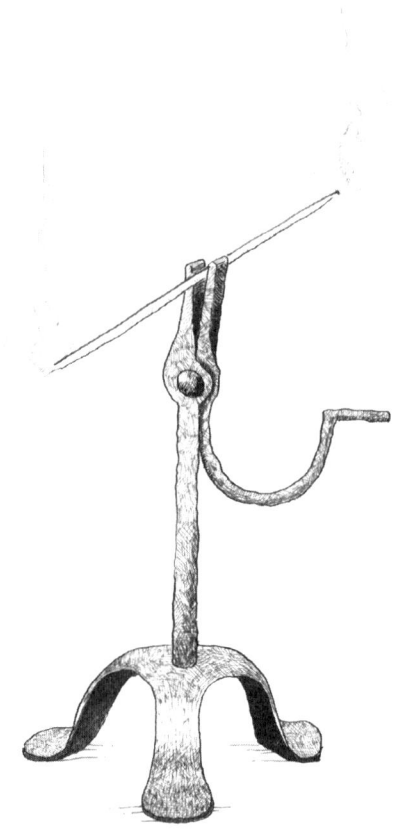

When they'd been cut, the rushes were kept in a bucket of water to stop them from drying out, ready for the slow and deliberate process of peeling off the hard green outside layer to expose the soft pith. Such finicky tedious work, picking off strips of hard shell, as it was termed, was the habitual activity of the weather-worn blind beggars, Martin and Mary Doul, in J. M. Synge's play *The Well of the Saints*. The trick was to peel off most of the rind but to leave a long narrow strip of green skin running down the length of the rush that gave it stability and strength – but it was a task that was easier said than done. The peeled rushes were between one or two feet long and tended to curl as they dried, so tying them loosely to a length of stick kept them straight. They were left for a few days and nights to ripen, absorbing the dew of the morning while bleaching in the sun by day, resulting in a clean, white, dry wick. The peeled rushes were then left in an open airy spot close by the fire to dry out completely.

The dry rushes were ready to be loaded with grease and some of the big farms would have used the fat of home-slaughtered animals or fowl. The suet fat surrounding the kidneys and loins was considered best and it was regularly the humble sheep or goat that became the source of fat for the candle. Pig lard spluttered, smoked and smelled, and it was often easier to buy a dipped tallow 'penny candle' to melt down, which provided enough grease to make anything up to thirty rushlights.

The soft dry sponge of the exposed rush pith soaked up the melted fat instantly. In turn, the fat-laden rushes were laid on a piece of timber or bark to dry and, in some parts of the country, a piece of badger skin, hanging in the rafters, was considered the best for curing and storage. It was important to keep the tallow rushlights out of reach of the cat or indeed, mice and rats, who looked on these lengths of fat as irresistible snacks!

When employed to provide light, the rush tapers were fixed in a special rushlight holder, made by the local blacksmith. These holders took the form of two pieces of iron riveted together to form a set of nips or pincers that stood upright in a solid block of wood. The rushlight was set at an angle of forty-five degrees and needed to be adjusted occasionally through the claws as it burned down. The flame provided a surprisingly effective light and one rushlight could provide enough light for almost an hour. When the rushlight was almost spent, it was necessary to light another from the flame and the chant 'help the candle' drew attention to lighting a new one off the old. If more light was needed it was possible to set a rushlight horizontally – this is the only candle that can do this – and you can, as the proverb tells us, 'burn the candle at both ends'.

Well-to-do farmers could afford to kill an old cow at Christmas and render the tallow in the metal, boat-shaped *grisset* to make a larger candle. They would string a wick through a special metal mould, blocking off one end by sticking it into a large potato. The large quantity of rendered tallow was poured in and left to set. Slightly heating the metal mould enabled the thick candle to slide out, and a quantity of homemade candles could be made in this fashion. Their light was dull, never overly bright, but such candles provided uninterrupted light at night-time across the dark winter months.

There was a season for candles. St Brigid's Day marked the turning point for candle use and the increase in the natural light meant less reliance on artificial light. On 2 February, the feast of Candlemas, people would bring candles to the church to have them blessed. It was a mark in time, as the old saying went, 'on Candlemas day throw the candle and candlestick away', or at least 'half the candle away'. It was a short few weeks to St Patrick's Day and the equinox and the natural light lengthened the evenings.

I have made a number of rushlights to show my students the nature of these simple and ancient candles. Each time I light one, I feel I am re-enacting one of the most seminal moments in human evolution. Even in front of my students in a modern lecture theatre, I have moved out of the everyday and I am no longer in linear everyday time. Neither do I feel like myself, but I take on the role of magician. I am in the role of the druid or priest, and I have ritually returned to cyclical time in reperforming one of the great achievements of humankind's technical achievements.

The Christmas Candle

It was at the winter solstice and Christmastime that the candle was most celebrated. Here, at the darkest point in the year, the candle played centre-stage. In rural Ireland, a special candle for Christmas was rarely bought but formed a core part of what was known as the 'Christmas box' given by the local shopkeeper.

The traditional day when the country came to town was 8 December. This was the day of the live market and the country people who had reared their flocks of turkeys and geese would come to town and sell them. With this hard-earned money, they would settle their account in the local grocer's shop and, in turn, buy small luxuries for Christmas. The grocer would 'draw the line' in the shop account book and when everything was settled, he would give his best customers their Christmas box of a bottle of port wine or whiskey, a half-pound of tea, a slab of currant cake and the all-important Christmas candle. This long candle was as thick as the handle of a pike and some six pounds in weight. They came in different colours in various parts of the country with Limerick and Clare favouring white and the midlands, pink. In Dublin, only blue candles were taken, with Cork and elsewhere content with either red or green.

When it had been brought home, the large candle was set in an improvised sconce, in the form of a hollowed-out turnip and decorated with fancy paper and a sprig of holly. It was lit at six o'clock on Christmas Eve, and this was always done by the youngest in the house. I remember so well as the youngest, being hoisted up by my father and his gentle hand guiding the flame of the match in my small hand to light the candle.

This marked the beginning of the twelve days of Christmas and the lighted candle would stand sentinel for the full festive period until Little Christmas on 6 January. The twelve days of Christmas corresponded to the twelve months of the year and if the candle blew out on a particular day, it was looked on as an omen of some bad luck or a death during that month in the year ahead. If a moth was seen flying around the candle, it meant that there would be news from someone overseas.

In addition to the large candle that remained in the centre of the kitchen table, smaller candles were placed in the windows and their purpose was to guide Joseph, Mary and their donkey on their way to Bethlehem. They were a source of great wonder and excitement when the family would head to town for midnight Mass and the whole countryside was aglow with little lights in every house, twinkling from afar.

Following the Christmas period, the butt of the Christmas candle was carefully kept, as it was thought to be a protection against sickness for the rest of the year and the tallow could be used for curing earaches and rheumatic pains. It was also considered by some to have such efficacy that it could even be used to divine gold. There is an account in the folklore record of a woman who lived near Ballyvourney in County Cork who kept the butts of the Christmas candles for over five years because, with them, she believed that she would be able to find gold. She took two lighted candles in her hands and started walking through the fields; whenever they would go out she was sure there would be gold hidden. The candles kept going out and she thought the farm was full of gold but, after a week or so, digging up half the farm and finding nothing, she gave up on the belief.

Whatever about the ability to find gold, there is still a certain magic about the candle at Christmas and its perpetual presence in the depths of darkness counters our fears and maintains our spirits.

Paraffin Oil and Tilley Lamps

Over the latter half of the nineteenth century, the candle gave way to the paraffin oil lamp with its woven cotton wick and its glass globe. Each evening when lighting the wick, the traditional grace for light was said: 'The light of heaven to our souls.' Some lamps were fixed to the walls with the lid of a tin of paint or a small circular mirror behind it to reflect the light. The tilley lamp with its delicate mantle that glowed white hot provided even brighter light. The tilleys had a large domed brass base into which the paraffin was poured and a small hand pump on the side pressurised the fuel. The tilley lamps hissed loudly and gave off not only a great light, but the overpowering smell of burning paraffin and a considerable amount of heat. When a central bright light was needed, they were ideal for card games, reading a book or doing schoolwork, while the small wax candle in the handheld sconce was still the light that was taken to bed.

In urban centres, gas light pervaded for a time before the ubiquitous electric light bulb, dangling from the middle of the ceiling in each room, became standard. The long, unbroken era of the candle was over, though it might make an appearance at a romantic dinner setting.

I spend a great deal of time and money lighting church candles as a way of remembering those I love who are no longer here. Candles continue to be central in the realm of the sacred and meditative. Without the light of day, the night brings natural darkness in which we are lost, disorientated and vulnerable.

The artificial light radiating from a small candle is a feat of extraordinary magnitude that has kickstarted the technological relationship we have with the planet on which we live. It is the beacon of our aspirations, our primal identifier as humans managing our existence in the natural world. It is no wonder that the candle is at the core of our most sacred rituals and intimate gatherings. I came across a lovely nugget of wisdom in my father's papers that captures the very essence of this achievement. He wrote: 'There isn't enough darkness in the whole wide world that can quench the light of one small candle.'

Pole Men and Sacred Heart Lamps

In the 1950s, my father's sister, my auntie Mary, married John Leary from Portmagee in County Kerry and moved there from Cork City. Life was very different for her in the countryside, not least as she had no running water and had to walk to the well each day to fill the buckets and canisters. More than that, however, she always remarked that at night she used to put her hand on the wall to switch on the light, only to find there was nothing there – electricity had not yet made its way to Portmagee.

My aunt had stepped back into an older Ireland, a world where both farm and household work were confined to the daylight hours and where, in the absence of refrigeration, any perishable food was stored outside in the open air, cooled by the wind but protected in the 'safe', a square framed cupboard with panels of fine wire mesh. To keep it cool and fresh, milk had to be left standing in a bucket of cold water. Her cooking and baking were confined to the black Stanley range that she had to feed continually with turf cut from the bogland behind the house. All the hot water necessary for the daily chores of washing children and clothes had to be drawn from the rain butt and boiled on top of the turf range. When electricity did come to Portmagee, it was truly transformative and liberating, and my aunt moved from a time of continuous toil and hard labour into a new way of living.

~ THE COMING OF THE ELECTRIC ~

In the nineteenth century, Ireland had played its own significant part in the widespread development of electrical power as Nicholas Callan, Professor of Mathematics and Natural Philosophy at Maynooth University, is credited with developing the dynamo, the electric motor and the induction coil in his pioneering work in the late 1830s. In turn, Charles Parsons from Birr Castle, County Offaly, invented the steam turbine in 1884, which would lead to the widespread generation of electricity.

The phenomenon of electricity and its application to everything from lighting the dark streets in towns and cities to powering the public transport trams that replaced those drawn by horses, utterly transformed urban Ireland by the turn of the twentieth century. Bealick Mill on the banks of the River Laney provided public lighting for Macroom in 1899 and, by 1925, there were some 161 different providers of electricity that supplied the main towns in Ireland with direct electrical current. However, the supply of this revolutionising phenomenon was haphazard and piecemeal, and a national strategy was soon called for.

What was to become a seminal achievement of the newly founded Free State was the brainchild of a young Irish engineer, Thomas McLaughlin. In 1922, he had been working with German engineers Siemens-Schuchert, and his plan to build a major electricity-generating station on the Shannon between Killaloe and Limerick was boldly approved by the government, despite vociferous objections because others wanted the scheme to be on the Liffey to better serve Dublin. This was an audacious and extraordinary civil-engineering challenge, employing

over 5,000 Irish workers who were guided by a small cohort of German engineers. It was completed in 1929 and brought Ireland into a new era.

The Shannon Scheme was envisaged as a nation-building exercise and initial objections from a Dublin-centred opposition were quelled when the capital and other urban centres were made a priority. Soon, the large cities and big towns were well served with the new and versatile source of power, though the vast majority of those living in rural Ireland were still left in the dark. In 1945, two out of every three homes were without electricity, and it fell to William Francis Roe, Director of the Rural Electrification Office, to oversee an ambitious scheme that would bring electricity to every home in the country and become a part of everyone's life by the early 1970s.

The acquisition of an epic quantity of wooden poles to carry the electricity wires was the first concern. Given the extensive denuding of Ireland's woodlands over the centuries, our native supply of trees was totally inadequate and with prices high in Norway and Sweden, Finland was to prove the best source. In August 1946, Neil O'Donoghue, the Rural Electrification Scheme's accountant, travelled to Helsinki to negotiate a price for the immense order – this was a huge financial transaction and the price per pole was paramount. In the frequent negotiations, each offer of price was sent by telegraph from the Finnish office back to Dublin. The Finns thought they had an advantage, having full access to the Irish telegrams, but because these were all written in Irish, they found the Irish replies puzzlingly unintelligible. In this manner, O'Donoghue succeeded in reducing an original asking price of £4 per pole to a rock-bottom and very economical £2 for each straight length of the best Finnish pine.

Whatever the price, all the poles needed to be of top quality and on-site inspection was necessary. This task fell to a Dundalk forester, Dermot Mangan, a somewhat naive but wily and spirited man who used his callipers and tape to measure and assess the trees and poles. He travelled to the far reaches to northern Finland and chose the best of trees that were packed in their tens of thousands on to specially commissioned large barges and ships that were dispatched from the Scandinavian ports before the winter seas froze over. The poles were landed in Dublin, Cork, Limerick and Donegal where they were debarked and lathered in creosote to preserve them. It is a testimony to Mangan that some seventy-five years later, many of those original poles are still standing today.

The huge poles were transported by lorry to their various locations, and it fell to teams of pole men to set them in place. This was referred to as 'pegging' and 'pegging someone's field' or land was not without its disputes and stand-offs. Frequently, in addition to local feuds and arguments over someone's right of way, progress was held up because a pole was to be placed in a fairy fort or in the middle of a fairy path, and alternative routes had to be accommodated. In the remote and rocky terrain of the west, the pole men used gelignite to blast their way spectacularly through obstinate terrain while, in the soft midlands, deep holes had to be dug. A pole team consisted of six men with a ganger (the foreman of a gang of labourers) calling the shots. In the span of one day, with their picks and shovels, they were required to dig a hole six-and-a-half-feet deep and a second, half hole, four-feet deep.

The real physical effort came in standing the poles. Horses were often used, but it still fell to the sheer brute strength and brawn of the pole men, along with their guile and determination, to successfully heft and heave the pole into its upright position. At the village dances, the novelty and virility of the pole men drew the attention of the women of the parish and there were often jealous scuffles with the local lads.

The provision of electricity in rural Ireland was a conscious undertaking with a dedicated drive to bring Ireland into the modern world. There were many in rural Ireland however, who were set in their ways and had little interest in a new technology that would not only cost money but was also outright dangerous, carrying, they believed, the risk of death. Stories of electricity seeping out of the wall sockets and electrocuting the occupants while they slept in their beds were rife. Later, when people did get electricity in, it was common to fill the holes of the sockets with plugs of old newspaper as a deterrent against seeping electricity. Such fear of electricity was met by an organised educational campaign that regularly involved the local parish priest speaking from the altar or at a community gathering on the advantages of electricity.

The countryside was divided into manageable areas of twenty-five square miles and while most everyone signed up to have electricity installed, when the pole men arrived, some reneged. These so-called 'back-sliders' hampered the economics of the scheme, and this became the cause of angst and rifts between neighbours. The back-slider's home and land were an obstacle en route to the next, and it was often years later before the latter managed to get access to the new power source. In addition to those who objected out of meanness, fear or conservatism, there were many whose homes were in a dreadful state, living in semi-derelict conditions and so were refused the supply. In truth, the scheme exposed the destitute poverty of many and the challenge of meeting the financial burden of a fixed cost was simply impractical for those with large families and low incomes.

~~ Light and Water ~~

For the great majority who embraced the new technology, there was palpable excitement on the days when their hinterland was being connected. The minimal installation was that each house was to be fitted out with one socket and two lights. The outside feed came in at the front door and the meter and fuse box were fitted just inside. The main socket, black in colour with its gaping openings to take the large three round-pinned plugs, was set in the centre of the wall in the kitchen, just above the kitchen table.

It took no time at all for some enterprising young bucks to start the lucrative sideline of calling to houses and installing an electric Sacred Heart light just above this socket. Over time, this small red bulb, sometimes with an illuminated cross within its globe, became a stalwart of Irish life. Whatever the cost, this perpetual light, illuminating the thorn-enrobed, flaming heart of Jesus was a sound investment and a proud display to neighbours at the Station Mass and when the priest called for the dues.

The main electric light came in the form of a large naked bulb, suspended on its woven insulated electric cord that hung from the wooden matchboard ceiling in the centre of the kitchen. Its Bakelite switch was mounted on a small round of wood that was fixed to the wall inside the door and the stark, bright illumination of the kitchen interior brought both wonder and distress when first in use. The vibrancy of a 100-watt electric tungsten filament brought a clarity and dazzling intensity of radiance that no candle or tilley lamp could match. Night was made day, but now the cobwebs and dust and dirt and the discoloured yellowed paintwork from years of turf and pipe smoke and paraffin oil lamps was fully visible. There were many who had the electricity installed but never used it. I heard an account of one lady who was visited by the ESB because she had used very little power and when she was politely asked if she found the electric light useful, she replied, 'Yes, I find it great, I just have to switch it on for a few seconds to help me to find the matches and the candle!'

There was a definite need to promote the new technology. The Irish Countrywomen's Association started their 'Better Living' campaign where they toured the country with a mobile display kitchen equipped with all the modern electrical appliances. The glamorous women who worked as electrical-appliance demonstrators were as exotic as air hostesses, and became the empowered role models of Irish women in a new Ireland. They could drive, and would arrive in a village or call to a farmhouse with a vehicle packed with electric irons, toasters, hair dryers, mixers and the all-important electric oven. Their biggest challenge was to convince the rural housewife that the electric cooker could produce high-quality brown bread. Under the watchful eye of the doubting housewife, the demonstrators would mix the eggs, buttermilk, salt, wholemeal brown flour and a pinch of bread soda, and place the loaf in the electrical contraption for an hour or so. The resulting steaming crusty loaf was enough to win over both housewife and household, and the electric oven was ordered and fitted beside the range.

The second biggest transformation for the rural household was the radical change in the supply of water. Up to the mid-twentieth century, the water barrel at the corner of the house collected rainwater and this was sufficient for washing and cleaning, but not for drinking or cooking. The constant need for fresh clean water demanded an arduous and time-consuming trek to the nearest well or village water pump with two heavy enamel buckets. This daily task might demand a journey of a few miles and, sometimes, had to be performed several times a day, often in terrible weather.

Most small villages and hamlets relied on one of the thousands of large cast-iron water pumps that had been set up by the local county councils. These pumps, brightly painted in a rich green, with their spiked caps and long cow-tail handles and the little notch on the spout to hold the bucket as it filled, were the favourite meeting places for women. Some might even wash clothes in the small stone trough beneath the spout and the pump was where all the local news and scandal was gathered and consumed. This was the central location where the needs and concerns of the hinterland were openly aired and discussed and where the phrase 'parish-pump politics' originated. Like the

decline of the forge as a gathering place for men, electricity was to rid women of this favourite daily gathering point.

The electric water pump with pressurised water was now piped directly into the house. It was, as if by miracle, available in endless quantities from the twist of a tap on the wall and such a leap in technology and convenience offered quantum improvements in domestic and farm life. The luxury of water-flushing toilets and septic tanks replaced the outdoor earth closet. On a trip to Inis Meáin a few years back, one of the islanders, reflecting on the use of toilets, remarked to me when he saw a group having a barbeque, *'Fadó, bhíomar ag ithe istigh agus cac amuigh ach anois táimid cac istigh agus ag ithe lasmuigh'* ('Long ago we were eating inside and shitting outside, but now we are shitting inside and eating outside').

The provision of boiling water could now be readily supplied by the most popular of all appliances, the electric kettle. The large tin kettle was always on the range or close to the fire but to get it to a boil, to make a proper pot of tea, took time and it was never quite ready or hot enough when called upon. The electric kettle changed everything. Some of the finest were beautifully crafted from sturdy bright copper and fixed with a black Bakelite handle. Mick Forde from Grenagh told me a great story of a woman who was dubious of the electricity and who, in the time of 'waiting to see', decided to visit a neighbour who had just had it installed. When she came in, she was mesmerised by the electric light and as she sat down, she was offered a cup of tea. The woman of the house filled the electric kettle and plugged it into the socket. The two women sat and chatted and in no time the kettle boiled, and the woman plugged it out and made the tea. When she got home, the woman's husband asked her about the electric and she replied, 'By God, it's marvellous. If you want a cup of tea, all you have to do is to tie the kettle to the wall, and it boils!'

Much of the drudgery of the incessant chores of washing, drying and ironing clothes was greatly alleviated by the ready domestic supply of water and the various electric appliances that were on offer. A number of different makes of washing machines and dryers became available in the 1950s and 1960s and these were eagerly sought after by the many housewives. The ESB developed a mechanism where you could pay on what was called the 'never-never', a hire-purchase system of buying appliances paid through your electricity bill.

One very popular washing machine was the twin-tub, which had one large washing tub on one side that was manually filled and emptied via a system of hoses. When the clothes were washed and rinsed, they were transferred by hand to the revolving wringer on the other side that spun the clothes at a terrific rate that made the whole house shake. I had a granduncle who came home from America and with a generous stroke of bravado, he bought my mother and my aunts a twin-tub each. They were absolutely over the moon with such largesse, but when he returned to America his wife insisted that my mother and my aunts return the money. They did, but the twin-tubs remained and went on the never-never.

The washing of clothes was one thing, but drying the clothes was always a major chore. Given the perpetual inclemency of the Irish weather, there was little more satisfying for an overburdened housewife looking after a big household than the sight of a full clothesline of washing, drying in the wind and sunshine. The challenges were severely increased in the era of cloth nappies that had to be washed and dried on a daily basis. Electric dryers came in the form of what were nicknamed 'sputniks', named after the new Russian satellites of the time, and these small, metal, revolving drums were well named. When at full tilt, they took off dangerously across the kitchen, often shredding and shrinking the woollen clothes within.

The wooden clothes horse in front of the fire was a better bet, but nothing could get past the mounting mountain of ironing. Before electricity, the flat irons, heated on the hotplate of the range, or the box irons with their iron inserts, that were placed in the fire and placed within the wooden handled iron, were notoriously ineffective and finicky to manage. The electric iron with its instant heat was a godsend.

The first electric irons had no thermostat, but the temperature was assessed in a time-honoured way of licking a finger and dabbing the spittle on the hot iron and listening to the sound that it made. It was not always plugged into the wall but was regularly attached to a special small adaptor that was fixed into the overhead light fitting and so the lead conveniently came down from the ceiling. The same overhead power supply was used for similar smaller appliances, such as hairdryers or the radio, and such an overload often caused a fuse to go. Standing on a chair at the meter and fuse box by the front door, playing with trip-switches while screwing in and out old, blown and incorrect ceramic fuses was a whole other occasion of danger, a type of electrical Russian roulette.

The availability of running water brought huge changes in domestic plumbing, and the modern Irish home was epitomised by dedicated bathrooms decked out with the triad of sink, toilet and bathtub. The psychedelic colours of the 1960s produced the immortalised avocado, orange and duck-egg-blue suites.

The installation of the large copper cylinder and its hot press was step one in the provision of a large supply of hot water and the electric immersion heater entered into the Irish psyche. There is perhaps nothing more resonant and immediately perturbing to Irish people who grew up at this time than the mention of the phrase, 'Did you turn off the immersion?' The immersion with its chunky white 'on and off' and 'sink or bath' switches, would, whatever the setting, eat electricity and caused endless anguish in the household. There is the story of my sister's neighbours, who when they flew off on one of the first sun holidays to Spain couldn't rest for the two weeks, fretting the whole time that they had left the immersion on.

Electric heating was also a worry and, as people curled around the ubiquitous small bar heater with the coils of red glowing electric heat, they would switch from one bar to two bars and back to one bar to conserve the cost. In suburbia, large, heavy, brick-laden storage heaters running off more economical night meters were popular, but totally inefficient.

The great conveniences of electricity – to provide light, heat, hot and cold water, radio and television, and to make cooking and baking, washing, drying and ironing clothes so much easier – came at a cost, and managing the ESB bill became a new concern. In addition to paying for the ever-increasing electrical appliances on the never-never, each purchase meant more and more power was consumed. The electrical revolution created a new demand for must-have items in the form of electric toasters, hoovers, fridges, curling tongs, record players, food mixers, carving knives, bedside lamps, and so on. The incitement to the new world of electrical appliances was amplified by the Green Shield Stamps of the 1960s and 1970s. This marketing scheme offered one stamp for every six old pence (half a shilling) spent on groceries and petrol in certain shops. As children, we had the job of licking the backs of the stamps and sticking them into a book that never seemed to fill. Each book needed an exorbitant 1,280 stamps and the most sought-after objects, such as cameras and record-players, demanded an almost unachievable fifty or sixty full books. It never stopped us dreaming of a future technological idyll as we looked through the Aladdin's cave of utopian modernity presented in the well-thumbed, full-colour catalogue.

Many families had special coin meters installed in their hallways that enabled the household to pay for their electricity as they used it. There was a mechanism with a small slot into which a ten-pence coin was placed and when the handle was turned, it would drop down into a secure box. Every now and again, the house would be thrown into darkness when the electricity went and I remember as a child standing on a chair in the hall, reaching up to put the coin in the meter. With inflation in the 1970s, the meter needed a deposit of the distinctive snipe-decorated seven-sided fifty-pence coin and my father always kept a small stash in his jacket pocket, lest his television watching be disturbed.

Electricity brought changes to the outside world of cities and towns with streetlights, traffic lights, neon advertising signs and shop windows that had their contents light up and on display at night. Elaborate streams of colourful Christmas lights added a sense of wonder and a warm glow in the heart of the cold winter. Ireland was aglow with the new technology. The combined vision, enterprise and determination of the individuals involved, from foresters to polemen, linemen to engineers, parish priests to demonstrators, all contributed to lighting the dark and changing Ireland forever.

On the Farm

On the farm, the coming of electricity was to catapult Irish agriculture into a whole new era. Simple changes like the provision of the constant warm glow from infrared heating lamps gave the lease of life to the hitherto vulnerable newborn *bainbh* (piglets) and fledgling chickens that might otherwise have perished from the cold. Light was now an amazing facility in the milking stall and the calving shed. In the henhouse, it led to increased egg production as the artificial light fooled the perching hens into thinking that dawn had arrived and, alighting their perches, they started to lay early. With automatic timers not yet invented, the most dedicated poultry mistresses used to drag themselves out of their beds at four o'clock in the morning to switch on the new egg-inducing light.

However, the most significant change in farming came with the provision of electric water pumps. Newly sunk wells were kitted out with the pumps and pressure containers enabled water to be piped not just to sheds but to troughs in fields, doing away with the tedious and inefficient demand of drawing water to animals by hand. Jonathan Bell and Mervyn Watson, the great historians of Irish farming, assert that farmers reported that this one change enabled them to multiply the number of animals they could keep by up to five or six times. Another change came with the electric fence that, in addition to providing effective control over pasture, did much to curtail the habit of cows breaking out and jumping ditches in search of a tasty morsel.

A revolution in milking came with the Gascoigne Milker. This was fondly referred to as the 'bicycle', named for the set of handlebars that guided the small-wheeled contraption into position behind each cow. This portable milking machine relied on a small electric motor that created a vacuum in a glass or stainless five-gallon bucket and the resultant suction was connected by a flexible rubber tube to a cluster of four milking teats. The milking cluster was dipped into a bucket of clean water before being suctioned to the cow's udder where the rhythmic action of the oscillating pump sucked the milk and the bucket filled. Before this revolutionary milker, it could take fifteen minutes or longer to milk a cow by hand, but the small machine brought the time per cow down to no more than five minutes.

Twice the number of animals could be managed in the same amount of time and, very soon, the average number of milch cows kept on farms doubled. The quantity of milk increased and, with an emphasis on quality and freshness, keeping it cool became a priority. In advance of refrigeration, an ingenious system was invented. The electric water pump enabled a steady flow of cold water to be pumped through a long U-shaped pipe that reached deep inside the ten-gallon churns filled with milk. In addition, the same cooling water exited via a series of small holes from the cap of the churn and trickled down its outsides, keeping the new milk extra cool and fresh.

The increase in cattle and sheep demanded supplementary winter fodder in the form of mangolds and turnips mixed with hay to get the animals through the lean months. To that end, most farms were well equipped with one of a variety of robust iron turnip pulpers, mangold cutters and furze choppers that were made by Pierce's in Wexford, among other foundries. The strenuous and tiring chore of endlessly turning the big handle that drove the rotating cutting-blades and teeth of these dangerous machines is well recollected in the memories of recent generations. With electricity, the slow, manual effort of turning the handle was replaced by a flywheel that was rotated by a motor via a drive belt, turning the chopper into an industrial beast and spitting out the feedstuff in effortlessly quick time.

The major advancements brought by electricity in rural Ireland were matched by the major changes brought about by the widespread increase in tractors and their uses from the 1950s. Electricity empowered the farmer in the everyday use of welders, angle grinders, drills and other power tools, whereby ploughs, harrows and the full range of farm machinery could be easily modified and repaired.

It is difficult to perceive how radical a transformation in Irish agriculture was effected by electrification in such a short space of time. From a country that was barley self-sufficient in the post-war years, with a multi-piece patchwork of small family farms, it has now, for its size, become one of the biggest producers of food globally. In 2022, we exported close on €19 billion worth of agriculturally produced food. The advent of electricity in rural Ireland was one of the catalysts and core players that prompted this extraordinary revolution.

FREEDOM

'THE HORSE THAT EATS NO HAY'

When the volcano of Mt Tambora on the island of Sumbawa in Indonesia erupted on Wednesday, 5 April 1815, it inadvertently gave birth to concept of the bicycle. This was the largest volcanic eruption in recorded human history, spewing massive quantities of volcanic dust into the atmosphere and resulting in catastrophic weather conditions throughout the world. The following year, 1816, became known as the 'Year without a Summer', and there were widespread crop failures.

In Baden, Germany, Karl von Drais, a civil servant conscious that the fodder shortage would not support horses, set about creating an alternative means of transport and invented the first prototype of the two-wheeled bicycle in 1817. His wooden construction was not dissimilar to the children's balance bikes of today and did not have any pedals, instead being both propelled and braked by your feet. They were known as swift-walkers and enabled the rider to travel at great speed downhill, averaging eight miles per hour.

Soon, this initially childlike contraption became a very popular fad for the foppish elite in London and Paris where they were known as hobby horses and dandy horses. By 1860, pedals had been added and there were even races of the new velocipedes, as the French called them, on the Champs Élysées.

Nevertheless, the ultimate bicycle design as we know it today had yet to be settled, for it had first to win out against its main design rival, the high penny-farthing.

'The Devil on Wires'

The year 1869 saw the development of the wire-spoked wheel and, very quickly, it was understood that the larger the bicycle's front wheel, the faster you could go. This led to the development of the penny-farthing where the size of the big wheel – the penny – was dependent on the length of your legs. With the rider sitting on the saddle above the pedals, it was as high as a horse and every bit as fast. The small wheel at the back was for balance and was called the farthing.

When these contraptions first appeared in Ireland, people were so astonished to see 'a man riding on a cartwheel' that they thought the world was coming to an end. They would make the sign of the cross, fall to their knees in prayer or even faint when 'the devil on wires' was seen flitting through the countryside. The niece of an army officer in Tralee, speeding along the boreens on a penny-farthing, was known as the 'Flying Girl' and children of the town were convinced that she had to be a fairy and were duly terrified.

As splendid an invention as it was, the penny-farthing led to catastrophic head injuries and fatalities when the riders hit a stone or pothole and were propelled headlong on to the ground at full velocity. From the late 1880s, the safety bicycle with its two wheels of the same diameter, driven by a chain and powered by pedals on a solid metal frame, became the standard.

Ireland played no small part in the popularisation of the bicycle, as all sorts of improvements and innovations were made towards the end of the nineteenth century. In Belfast, the son of veterinarian John Dunlop complained of a sore backside when he was riding his tricycle over the cobbled streets to school. Dunlop was a man of science and, in modifying a rubber garden hose, he is accredited with the invention of a pneumatic tyre that made his son's journey smoother and faster. Up to this point, many bicycles were known as boneshakers because they had solid tyres and no suspension, but Dunlop's inflatable tyres were a gamechanger and became instantly popular, first with racing enthusiasts and then the public at large.

In its new form, as it was first envisaged by Karl von Drais, the bicycle became 'the horse that eats no hay', and many crafts associated with horses became subsumed into the new industry. A notable example is that of the saddler and harness-maker, John Boultbee Brooks from Birmingham in England, who applied his equine leather-working skills to create the now famous Brooks Bicycle Saddle, which he patented in 1882.

In the nineteenth century and the early years of the twentieth century, the mobility offered by the bicycle entered theatres of war, being used by infantry, who were formed into effective cycling battalions.

This application bolstered the production and availability of bicycles. In the heartlands of industrial Britain, bicycle manufacture went into overdrive with Raleigh in Nottingham, Rudge in Coventry and BSA (British Small Arms) in Birmingham amongst the largest producers. In Ireland, Lucania in Dublin and the Pierce Foundry in Wexford made 'Irish' bicycles, and the ownership of an Irish-made bicycle became something of a political statement.

There is still controversy about whether Michael Collins's double cross-barred bike was an English Rudge-Whitworth or an Irish Pierce. Whichever it was, he knew that the bicycle was ideal for discreet reconnaissance and delivering dispatches. It played its part in the 1916 Rising when, for example, Peter Paul Galligan cycled a ninety-mile journey from Dublin to Enniscorthy in eight hours to cut the railway line, preventing the possibility of immediate British reinforcements. In the War of Independence, the bicycle was the means of swift stealthy transport and central to the guerrilla warfare of the flying columns.

The bicycle soon entered every facet of Irish life; the guard and postman began their ongoing relationship with their bicycles and while the car was still only starting to make in-roads, it was now common to see the doctor, the midwife, the parish priest, the curate and the schoolmaster travelling the hinterland on their push bikes.

In the early twentieth century, bicycles were relatively inexpensive, but people were slow to part with their money. One salesman arguing the price of a new bicycle with a farmer who had informed him that ten pounds was the same price he would pay for a cow, remarked 'you'd look very silly riding on top of a cow', to which the farmer sharply retorted, 'I'd look even sillier trying to milk a bicycle.' Regardless of price, the attraction and advantage of the bicycle was that it greatly widened the world for everyone and this new liberty seemed limitless. A neighbour of mine remembers his grandfather cycling from Matehy to Thurles for a hurling match, a round trip in one day of over 160 miles. When he returned, he cycled off immediately to a dance that night in Rylane, another hour away and, to cap it all, he brought his girlfriend home on the crossbar.

The Freedom Machine

The bicycle played a seminal role in the liberation of women, regardless of their class. Those in Victorian high society were constrained from showing any display of athletic or physical prowess and, in keeping with expectations of being weak and feeble, were confined to the pianoforte and bridge table as appropriate activities for their amusement and exercise. At first the tricycle, safer and more modest than the bicycle, opened the door for women who were confined or restricted not only by social expectations, but also their dress. The bicycle was instrumental in ridding women of their bustles, copious petticoats and long skirts and, in their place, they wore the new practical pedal-pushers, knickerbockers or bloomers. For many, this was a step too far and these pioneering women were castigated for such mannishness.

Nevertheless, the speed and freedom of cycling symbolised the ultimate release from constrained convention and, in no time, they were part of the now popular cycling clubs. A number of these clubs were all-female and, at weekends and in the summer months, the countryside was full of bands of women, attired in their practical cycle wear, some taking photographs with another new technology, the box brownie camera. The bicycle was the ultimate freedom machine.

The bicycle also played its part in the search for love. In rural Ireland in the first half of the twentieth century, its widespread adoption facilitated people from farther afield to come together, radically improving the mix of potential romantic relationships and resultant marital unions. Previously, the pickings in the dancehalls were limited by geographical constraints but the bicycle widened this radius beyond the hinterland to villages and towns within cycling distance. Most young men, fuelled by devilment and 'taspy', thought nothing of cycling fifty or one hundred miles to platform dances, crossroad dances, 'hops', pattern days, fairs and every type of social gathering from wakes to regattas in the hope of meeting an eligible woman. The women were always open to meeting a handsome athletic stranger from outside their usual catchment area, dreaming of romance and the potential for a better life.

When arriving at the dancehalls, the men knew to plank their bikes behind a ditch some distance away, lest it be sabotaged by a local rival who might leave the air out of their tyres or 'borrow' it to go home. The bicycle provided an invitation for courtship and in a demonstration of amorous intent, the shiny bicycle pump in the inside jacket pocket was a clear signal of its presence.

At the end of the dance, there was a noble gesture of walking the girl home and if she did not have her own bicycle, she might consent to taking a spin on the crossbar. The crossbar was an intimate setting and with hands on the handlebars, such a cossetted embrace enabled the rider to place his face near the neck and ear of his passenger, whispering his affections. This was the situation on the flat but, as the journey wore on and a few steep hills presented themselves, the whisperings might become a mixture of gasping, breathless panting as the man quickly ran out of puff and his machismo was severely challenged. His ability to pedal up a steep hill with his new cargo on board was a make-or-break scenario.

Giving a lady a crossbar home late at night demanded a light on the bicycle and before the ever-reliable dynamo or battery, the bicycle light was a carbide lamp. These were ingenious devices made of solid polished chrome, and their light was produced by a small jet of gas that burned behind a circular piece of glass. There was a small spherical reservoir on top into which water was placed and as it dripped down onto a store of calcium-carbide pieces held in a bottom receptacle, the gas was produced. The flame of the burning acetylene gas could be adjusted by regulating the flow of water, but it often happened that the water ran out when there was still a plentiful supply of carbide pebbles. In need of light to continue the journey and with no stream or roadside well close by, the long-established secret fall-back of piddling into the water reservoir was regularly resorted to.

Travelling by bicycle has never been pleasant when it rains and in the absence of the modern waterproof gear, the heavy oilskins that were common were uncomfortable and an unbreathable reservoir of sweat. All cyclists know about the barely perceptible wind at their backs on the outward journey that on their return manifests as a cyclonic headwind that they curse at every strenuous push of the pedal. The freezing cold brings the further unwelcomed challenge of sheets of black ice that result in unexpected and potentially lethal falls from the bike.

The bicycle was and is still not without its dangers and pitfalls, but as an instrument of liberation and opportunity it has few equals.

Messenger Boys and Punctures

From the 1950s and 1960s, car ownership became a signal of wealth and modernity, and the bicycle quickly lost out in terms of status and utility. Yet, even in the face of such technical progress, the bicycle remained more practical for those who needed to make quick journeys.

In towns and cities, flocks of aproned, fast-pedalling messenger boys were a common sight. Their modified bicycles were heavy and robust, with an extra-large metal rectangular frame fixed to the front that accommodated a large basket or the base of a cut-down tea chest. Each butcher, greengrocer and retail merchant had at least one delivery boy who could balance the precious parcels, be they pounds of sausages, sides of bacon, or bags of sugar and tea, neatly wrapped in brown paper and tied with brown twine.

You had to be both clever and tough to be a messenger boy, managing the awkward, heavy bicycle with its extra ballast, powering up steep hills, while also knowing the whereabouts of various vicious dogs and how to access side gates. The advantage of being a messenger boy is that you could take your bike home and you had free use of it in your spare time around town. This was, of course, extra marketing for the shop as the messenger bikes had two crossbars and between them was a tinplate with hand-painted lettering proudly advertising the proprietor's name.

In the 1960s, the delivery van put an end to the era of the messenger boys but, despite the ever-increasing ubiquitous presence of the car, the bicycle has remained. There were accoutrements that marked out an avid cyclist and it was a common sight to see someone with their trousers tucked into their socks to stop the flared leg getting oil from the chain.

The dedicated aficionados wore a pair of metal bicycle clips for the same purpose and they were also the ones who attached a little pouch to the back of the saddle to hold the puncture repair kit. Punctures were the bane of the cyclist's freedom and perhaps the most disconcerting was the slow puncture. This was halfway between everything being fine and everything being a disaster, and such self-denial came because fixing the puncture was a complicated and unrewarding ritual.

Removing the wheel was the first ordeal and involved turning the whole bicycle upside down and balancing it on its handlebars and saddle. There were two wheel-nuts to loosen but nobody ever owned the correct tools and instead of the precision 5/8-inch spanner, an old pliers might be employed and the fused rusty nuts ended up rounded and mangled. When the wheel did come off, the tyre had to be levered off using the round ends of the kitchen cutlery, spoons and forks, that were pushed in to the tyre and then fixed behind the spokes and in the process ended up severely deformed, twisted and mishappen forever more. The tube was pulled out, inflated and placed in a dish of water where the air bubbles indicated where the holes were. The bicycle repair kit had different size patches, rubber solution, chalk and a little piece of sandpaper. The chalk marked the position of the hole, and the sandpaper was used to roughen the tube; the rubber solution had to be applied sparingly and left to go tacky and the patch had to be placed firmly in place, making sure it was well fixed down on all sides. This exacting process was known to everyone who owned a bicycle and the idea of anyone else fixing your puncture or buying a new tube was never considered.

A puncture often put a bicycle out of use for some time, but we thought nothing of taking a spin from a friend. I recall ferrying an old pal and neighbour to school on my crossbar for about six months while he contemplated getting around to fixing his puncture. More often, the bicycle was often used to transport your pals on a short jaunt down to the shop or to the pictures. If not on the crossbar, it was common to give someone a 'backer' or perhaps have them perched on the saddle for a 'hopper' while you stood on the pedals. There were occasions when you could also have someone sitting on the handlebars and such overloading of the poor bicycle, combined with constant pounding from the pot-holed roads, led to the marked buckling of wheels.

In fact, most of the heavy-rimmed bicycle wheels were always buckled, not helped when we toyed with the old tram tracks on our way to secondary school and the wheel got wedged in the tracks, bending the metal. The buckled wheel quickly wore the brake pads down to the metal and braking was now back to the original mechanism of Karl Von Drais, dragging your foot on the ground to slow down. A pair of quarter irons on your heels greatly augmented their effectiveness with sparks flying.

The present-day Bike-to-Work scheme, the development of greenways on the old railway lines and urban cycle tracks, along with an increase in environmental and health concerns, has brought the bicycle back into Irish life with gusto. There are pods of Tour-de-France MAMILs (middle-aged-men-in-Lycra), whizzing their way up the mountains at weekends while bemused children are ferried to school on perilously loaded electric cargo contraptions.

Whatever about the prime utility of the car for the long journey, there is still nothing like the pure joy of cycling out in the open air, with the wind in your hair, free-wheeling high on the saddle of the horse that eats no hay, intimately at one with the world around you.

COMMUNICATION

Drop Me a Line

The habitual process of writing with a pen and paper is a technical skill that is radically changing in the internet age. Even the wizardry of email has been surpassed by texting and voice memos on WhatsApp, so there's no need to know how to type or, with auto-predict, how to spell. Without the benefit of what was once a routine everyday practice, our handwriting has turned into an untidy, unintelligible scribble. The ability to form beautiful legible letters on a page that communicates respect in both its appearance and content is extremely rare. Even the thought of having a dedicated supply of nice pens, writing paper, envelopes and stamps seems somewhat Dickensian. This long-evolved seminal component of our civilised world is evaporating before our very eyes.

Pen

It was during a workshop with the great calligrapher Tim O'Neill that I first fully appreciated the complexity of the primal writing materials used in the early Irish manuscripts. Writing first came to Ireland in the wake of the arrival of early Christianity around the fifth century. There was no paper – the writing material was vellum, made from the skins of young calves that were dehaired and stretched and cut in four to provide a surface to write on. Ink was made from small, round, woody oak galls that develop on oak trees around the larvae of small wasps. The oak galls were crushed added to rainwater, boiled and when combined with some iron rust and a little tree sap, a very usable black ink is produced. The Latin for a feather is *penna*, reminding us that the original pen was, of course, a carefully prepared feather. The hollow round of the feather was cut at an acute angle to create a reservoir to hold the ink and shaped to form a narrow tip. A slit to carry the ink was cut down its centre and its tip was cut flat to form a chisel head. All was in place to enable the wisdom of the ages to be shared in perpetuity.

It was this technological mechanism that was at the root of our extraordinary manuscript tradition, which is celebrated in the illustrated gospel books of Kells and Durrow. However, Ireland's literary heritage is far more encompassing than these well-known examples. Ireland boasts an exceptional corpus of medieval manuscripts, incorporating the oldest vernacular literature in Western Europe. This enormous collection details everything from ancient legal texts, saints' lives, the lore of places, genealogies and annals, in addition to the great sagas of mythology and heroic figures and much more. Each manuscript was laboriously copied and reproduced following the maxim of the time, 'to every cow its calf and to every book its copy', which effectively established copyright. It was this mechanism of ink, pen and vellum – and the resulting libraries of manuscripts – that enabled memory and knowledge to transcend the barriers of time and space. From the early seventh century, following in the tradition of the great Columbanus, other Irish monks and their manuscript tradition spread across Europe, founding influential monasteries where great libraries of wisdom were compiled.

The writing equipment changed very little over the centuries. The earliest example of a pen in Ireland was excavated in Caherconnell stone fort in the Burren, County Clare, and dates to the eleventh century. It is a small length of bird bone, most likely the radius bone of a swan, into which a folded copper alloy nib has been set. The user would have dipped the nib into the ink and this example was most likely used for ruling fine guidelines on the parchment. The practice of dipping one's quill pen into ink was the system of writing that continued throughout the medieval period and up to recent times.

The pen as we know it evolved in 1828 when Josiah Mason of Birmingham patented and began mass producing steel pen nibs that conveniently slipped into a wooden holder. By the end of the nineteenth century, the fountain pen, with its internal chamber of quality ink, had been developed in America by Lewis E. Waterman and George S. Parker, both of whose names are still synonymous with writing materials today. These pens were finicky at the best of times and needed to have their ink reservoirs constantly refilled. This could be a messy process while, in addition, the fountain pen often leaked into a

breast pocket, destroying a good wool suit. When writing, they generally did not supply a constant supply of ink and when shaking them to bring out the ink, an unwelcome blob of ink would splodge onto the page. As fancy as they were, the fountain pens remained under constant refinement to overcome their familiar idiosyncratic failings.

It is only since the 1950s that the modern ballpoint biro has become widely available. This pen was developed by the Hungarian newspaper editor, Lászlo Bíró, who, along with his brother, refined and patented the ballpoint ink pen. However, it was the French entrepreneur, Marcel Bich, who bought their patent and mass-produced the Bic biro, which is now so universally available.

Despite such technical advancement, we learned how to write with the steel nibs that were dipped into ink wells. Our school desks had small white porcelain inkwells set into the wooden desk that was covered over with a sliding brass cover. I remember looking at boys in the class, their lips black having succumbed to the childish temptation of drinking the ink. The metal quill nibs scratched and scraped audibly as we wrote, and, every now and again, we would dry our page with a sheet of blue blotting paper. The delicate downward pressure widened the gap at the top of these nibs and for those from a previous era who were well-practised, these nibs enabled them to produce copperplate autography with swirling cursive flourishes that were things of pure beauty.

The whole process of pen and ink was too messy and complex for our poor teachers and for everyday activity we used our pencil, our *peann luaidhe*, along with a parer and rubber. With our pencils, we learned how to write between the horizontal pink and blue lines of our copybooks.

Paper

Glancing at the old maps of my local area, with its myriad of fast-flowing rivers – the Dripsey, the Shournagh, the Martin and the Blarney – what is fascinating is the extent and number of mill complexes that utilised water as their source of power in the early years of industrialisation. In amongst the corn, gunpowder, woollen, spade and flax mills, it is the number of paper mills that jump out at me as something familiar, yet forgotten.

The raw material for this early form of paper was bits of old discarded linen and cotton rags that were collected in the towns by the rag-and-bone merchants and supplied in great quantities to the mills. The bones were sent elsewhere to be turned into buttons or glue while the rags had to undergo a complex transformation to turn them into sheets of paper. The rags were cut, boiled and bleached, and then set in vats of clean water. The water wheel of the mill powered a rise-and-fall system of wooden hammers set over the vats of rags and the mixture was continuously pounded and pulverised, separating the vegetal fibres and turning them into a thick sludge. This wet cellulous sludge was then carefully extracted, bit by bit, by filtering it on to a rectangular close-knit wire frame and moving it from side to side, leaving the water to drip out. The resultant sheet of paper, now in its fully saturated delicate embryonic state, was dexterously flipped onto a sheet of woollen felt and another sheet of felt was placed on top.

This process continued until the large assembled bales of wet paper and felt were placed in a large press and, when under pressure, the excess water was squeezed out. The wet sheets were taken and dried and, finally, they were rolled to give their surfaces the flat polish necessary to stop the ink bleeding when used for both printing and handwriting.

The thin wire frames that drew out the linen paper pulp had an extra arrangement of thin wire formed in the shape of the manufacturer's name and insignia, which resulted in a characteristic watermark on the paper. Society's elite commissioned their own writing paper with watermarks of family crests and political emblems that were visible when held to the light. The general demand for quality paper was fuelled by an ever-burgeoning printing industry for its books, pamphlets and newspapers.

Post

Personal writing paper was in high demand with the great expansion of the postal service, which had been revolutionised by the introduction of the Penny Black stamp in 1840. This was the very first stamp and reformed a hitherto convoluted and expensive postal system, not least because, previously, you'd had to pay more depending on the mileage taken to deliver the letter. Before the prepaid economical penny stamps, it was the recipient rather than the sender who incurred the expense of postage.

The stamps, or labels as they were called, were sold in sheets of 240; one penny for a label, one shilling for a row of twelve and one pound for a full sheet. They were accompanied by a set of instructions: 'Place the labels above the address and towards the right-hand side of the letter. In wetting the back, be careful not to remove the cement.' When the sheets were first printed, they had to be hand cut with a scissors or knife to separate them. It was a Dublin man, Henry Archer, who solved this annoying problem by inventing a perforating machine that divided the stamps by lines of tiny holes that characterise the comb edges of stamps to this day.

Various Education Acts in the post-famine period increased school attendance and greatly improved literacy. In the 1851 census, it was recorded that close to half the Irish population could neither read nor write but, by 1911, this figure had dropped to as low as 12 per cent. However, the improvements in literacy were not universal and, in addition to reading, not everyone could fashion a letter in the way they wished and it was common to ask those with the skills and equipment – the schoolmaster, shopkeeper or parish priest – to write a letter on your behalf.

This was the time of mass emigration and the letter from America or England, perhaps with the price of a ticket enclosed, was eagerly received and read by such a literate person or by the youngest in the family, who was now at school. There is the story of the man who could not read or write, who asked the local curate to write a letter to his old friend and neighbour who had emigrated to America. As he dictated the letter, the curate became rather contemptuous of the illiterate man as he wrote down what the man thought was the important news of the locality, every titbit from the winner of the bowling score, the state of the mangles and the low price of eggs. When he had finished, the curate asked him if he would like to add anything else? The man, not impressed with the curate's attitude, sarcastically replied, 'No, only tell him to please excuse me for such bad writing!'

The Picture Postcard

The picture postcard was a development that flourished from the first decade of the twentieth century. It was the result of the combination of the technical developments in paper and card, photography, printing and the postal service, along with an increase in tourism.

Initially, you could only write the name and address on the back of the postcard, along with the stamp, and people used to secretly write little messages on the image on the front. In 1902, the Post Office rules were changed and it became the standard that a dividing line on the back separated the address and stamp on the right-hand side from space for a personal message on the left. It is fair to say that the sending of pictorial postcards became a crazed phenomenon worldwide and this is reflected by the fact that the Irish post office handled an estimated 33 million postcards in 1906 alone.

There were a variety of British companies, such as Valentine's and Raphael Tuck & Sons, who produced postcards of Ireland, while Dublin-based producers Lawrence and Eason's, along with Louis Anthony of Killarney, vied for the lucrative trade.

Many of the postcards were printed in Germany and one or two Irish manufacturers, in an attempt to appeal to the home market, boasted that their cards were not only designed and printed in Ireland, but their very paper was made from turf. These rustic postcards, their paper speckled with peat, sent from Ireland meant you were sharing 'a bit of the old sod' with relations and friends around the world.

Perhaps Ireland's best-known photographic collection was that amassed by William Mervyn Lawrence, who started his career as a portrait artist in Dublin's Sackville Street, now O'Connell Street. He lost his right arm in an accident and, while not a photographer himself, he employed Robert French, his chief photographer, and number of others to travel the countryside to capture images of every town and village for the postcard industry. Over twenty years, his enterprise produced an incredible 40,000 glass plates detailing beauty spots, streetscapes, ancient monuments, transport, buildings and untold examples of different facets of Irish life.

In addition to these images, other postcards of this time exploited and promoted particular stereotypical caricatures of the Irish. There are thousands of images of pretty bare-footed coquettishly smiling colleens, carrying a basket of turf or trying to avoid a kiss from an over-eager admirer. Similarly, the Irishman is distinguished by his shillelagh, the *dúidín* in his mouth, his companion the pig, and an overall sense of being unkempt and ignorant.

The widespread popularity of the postcards fed into the pervasive British colonial perspective of the Irish, reinforcing our unrefined peasant attributes and casting us as racially different and inferior. The flirty, red-haired colleen and the dim-witted, indolent Paddy were not unique to their postcard incarnations, but were omnipresent in all manifestations from *Punch* cartoons to the stage Irish of the vaudeville shows. It was the reaction against this ubiquitous portrayal of the Irish on these very popular and widespread postcards that was one of the many incentives that drove Ireland into redefining its national identity. The protests against such degrading and insulting portrayals bolstered the cultural movement that directed Ireland towards a different, de-anglicised view of itself.

The great postcard impresario of more recent times, the colourful John Hinde, succeeded in creating a greatly augmented view of Ireland. Hinde was an English Quaker and was a photographer for the Civil Defence during the Second World War, who came to Ireland with his own circus company in the 1950s. When his circus venture failed, he turned to his photography and made his name by introducing heightened vibrant colour into postcards of the Irish landscape. Hinde was not shy about amplifying the brightness and enhancing the colours of the Irish scenes, often to the point of the surreal. The glistening, azure waters of the Aegean Sea had nothing on Hinde's view of Barleycove beach and bright turquoise cars or purple-pink rhododendrons enlivening every Ektachrome image. His postcards of the three men under the currach on the Aran Islands and the red-haired boy and girl collecting turf with their donkey have achieved iconic status.

The technical requirements for mass communication in the form of quality paper, stamps and a postal system came together and developed from the mid-nineteenth century. Letter writing and sending postcards became an everyday activity and the convenience of 'dropping a line' to someone meant literally writing a note and dropping it into the post box. Postal directories were available for each county, and for the country as a whole, and people could look up the name or business and find the address.

The creation of the worldwide postal system that came into being, with its ability to post anything to anyone, anywhere is truly one of the greatest human achievements of all time. I am always reminded of Tadg Ó Buachalla, the tailor from Garrynapeaka, near Gougane Barra, who in a fit of fun and mischief, put a stamp on his forehead, plonked himself outside his door, waited for the postman and asked him to post him to Cork City.

The tailor might have taken things too far, but the marvel of writing a letter or card and posting it, is now something that is on the edge of an existential crisis. Denmark is the first European country to declare that the postage of letters is now officially obsolete and its postal service PostNord will no longer accept letters from the end of 2025. It is removing its distinctive red post boxes and laying off most of its postal staff. There are now so many alternative means of digital communication technologies, with such immediate conveniences – from texting to social media, email and FaceTime – that there seems no need for physical post along with the hard-won craft and skill of handwriting. Pens, paper, stamps and envelopes that were once everyday essential items of home and office, are becoming rare and unused.

It takes time, patience and learned skill to make legible letters on a page, to transfer the ideas from one's brain to a cypher that others can read and understand. This process is the cardinal kernel of our civilisation, and it is a fundamental skill that we learn at school as soon as we can. There is a sincerity in the stream-of-consciousness that comes with an unedited, direct piece of writing. There is something ethereal and special about the process of gathering your thoughts and committing them to paper. The old maxim rings true: 'Letter-writing combines solitude with good company.' The personality of an individual is enshrined in the scribblings and flourishes of their hand and a letter becomes a physical relic of their very existence. It is the empowered vernacular mechanism by which we can preserve our ideas and inherited wisdom and enable us to transcend time and space.

Regardless of modern technology, to be able to materialise your ideas and thoughts is the most accomplished facility of the ages and we might think long and hard about leaving this evolved system of communication behind.

Black and White and Read All Over

When she was well into her eighties, and despite the great effort it took, my late mother continued to walk each and every morning to the corner shop to buy 'the paper', *The Examiner* (as it was then called). Returning home, the kettle was boiled for a cup of tea and, with glasses perched on her nose and her elbows leaning on the broadsheet spread on the kitchen table, her eyes would move up and down the columns, reading and soaking in the news of the day. This was her conscious method of keeping her mind active and staying engaged with what was happening in the world. The daily newspaper was, up to recently, an indispensable item in every household and dedicated time was afforded to a deep critical scrutiny of its contents.

~ THE FIRST MASS MEDIA ~

The widespread availability of newspapers first came when the linen and cotton rag papers were gradually replaced with the cheaper and easier-to-source wood pulp. This pulp was ideal for creating rolls of what was termed continuous paper, and such rolls, combined with new roller-print technology that could print with fast-drying inks on both sides, paved the way for the modern newspaper. As this first exponent of mass media developed throughout the nineteenth century, it was set to influence and change people's views of themselves and the world.

The oldest Irish newspaper, *The News Letter*, first published in Belfast in 1737, was followed by *The Freeman's Journal* in 1763. The *Limerick Chronicle*, established in 1768, is Ireland's longest-running newspaper as most periodicals of the first half of the nineteenth century did not survive.

The advances in printing technology and distribution networks witnessed newspapers – such as *The Cork Examiner* from 1841, *The Nation* from 1842 and *The Irish Times* from 1859 – establish a significant local and national presence, with many regional papers and periodicals rehashing and reprinting the material from other national and international publications. The rise in the popularity of newspapers was the result of, and partly the catalyst for, the major increase in literacy from the latter half of the nineteenth century. Indiscriminate and instant access to the daily publication of contemporary knowledge and information empowered its readers to feel part of the world around them.

In those years, with so many competing political agendas, newspapers were the social media of their day, flooding cities and towns with different papers that all offered divergent perspectives on every issue. Daniel O'Connell set up 'repeal newspaper reading rooms' and openly advertised in both English and Irish newspapers to further his campaign to repeal the 1801 Act of Union. This ideal was loudly vociferated in the weekly newspaper, *The Nation*, the mouthpiece of the Young Ireland movement that was owned and edited by Charles Gavin Duffy and Thomas Davis. It was one of the first newspapers to include female writers, not least Speranza – the pseudonym of Lady Wilde, the mother of Oscar Wilde – a pioneer of Irish folklore and an ardent nationalist.

There is nothing new in the term 'fake news' and not only has propogandist and biased reporting long existed, but as newsprint did not refuse ink, the newspapers were hijacked for political advantage. There was the infamous case of a set of forged letters created by one Richard Pigott designed to undermine the political stance of Charles Stewart Parnell and firmly associate the leadership of the Land League movement with violence. They were published in *The Irish Times* in 1887 but, following a full official government enquiry, they were proven to be forgeries, and instead of undermining Parnell, they united the cause of Irish nationalism around him.

~ Keeping an Eye on Russia ~

As time went on, the quality and appeal of the newspaper content was bolstered by two major technological innovations: the telegraph and the railway network. The telegraph connected the world, and newspapers could now carry important news stories from around the globe as they happened.

Fred Potter, the editor of one small provincial publication, *The Skibbereen Eagle*, which was founded in 1859, demonstrated this new global perspective when his paper famously published a far-reaching editorial on 5 September 1898. Fred was unconvinced of the anti-war assertions of the Czar Nicholas II, who was calling for peace, having just annexed a strategic ice-free port from China. Sitting in his small cramped office in west Cork, Fred Potter penned a timeless piece: '*The Eagle* will keep its eye on the Emperor of Russia and all such despotic enemies – whether at home or abroad – of human progression and man's natural rights which undoubtedly include a nation's right to self-government.' The audacious stance that *The Skibbereen Eagle* would look after us by 'keeping an eye on Russia' has entered into national folklore and is an empowering maxim for anyone, no matter how small, who stands up and scrutinises the seemingly indomitable oppressive forces around them.

The second technological factor to influence newspapers was Ireland's well-developed trunk-and-branch rail system that, by the 1920s, was capable of connecting practically all parts of the country. There was a record 3,442 miles of railway lines crossing Ireland and, in addition to doing its best to standardise Irish time, the railway enabled the swift distribution of both post and newspapers.

The open distribution network was at full capacity and the country was awash with newsprint. Ireland's national and local newspapers invariably sprung from diverse political, social and cultural origins, each espousing varying opinions and perspectives. Whether dedicated to one masthead or several, 'what it says in the papers' has contributed to Irish people's engaged critical and discerning mindset. The *Irish Independent*, with its roots from pro-Treaty Fianna Gael, had a different take on matters when compared to *The Irish Press* championing the opinions of de Valera's anti-Treaty Fianna Fáil. *The Irish Times*, the official public newspaper of record, offered yet another view, while regional titles like *The Kerryman*, *The Meath Chronicle* and *The Connacht Tribune* catered for the interests of its dedicated readers.

Whether international, national or local, daily newspapers, printed in different, updated editions, along with evening newspapers, weekly newspapers and Sunday newspapers, remained a core communication medium of influence from one end of the twentieth century to the other. It was not at all unusual for a household to buy the morning and the evening paper each day during the week and then, at the weekend, buy three or four Sunday papers. Newspapers were read from cover to cover and provided the necessary information fix for a nation addicted to news and stories that would fuel the conversations and informed discussions that followed.

Instruments of Change

∽ A Way with Words ⌒

It is fair to say that Ireland has produced generations of accomplished editors and journalists, who, through the informed choice of content and the quality of writing, have greatly contributed to shaping and influencing public opinion.

A prime example of such journalistic prowess is the contribution of the sports journalist Con Houlihan, who over a career of sixty years until his death in 2012, endlessly beguiled his many readers with the calibre of his writing. All over the country, people could hardly wait for Monday's *Evening Press* to read the back page with Con's account of the latest sporting occasion, be it GAA, soccer, rugby or horse racing. Con's unique style, turn of phrase and polymathic allusions made his recollections of the sporting event even better than being there yourself.

The appeal of his wry wit and intelligence is exemplified in one of his most-quoted quips – 'a man who will misuse an apostrophe is capable of anything' – and is redolent of another journalistic legend, Myles na gCopaleen. Under this pseudonym, the eccentric Brian O'Nolan wrote his regular column 'Cruiskeen Lawn' in *The Irish Times* from 1940 to 1966. This column was a kaleidoscopic mix of intellectual intrigue, comedy and contemporary satire. It was written in Irish, English and other languages (even at times Latin), often written phonetically and functioned as a sort of cerebral conundrum, being rife with puns, word games and outlandish anecdotes that ended with enticingly ponderous punchlines. One story concerning an incident where a small dog was unceremoniously brushed out of the way while on a hurried potato delivery round, ends with the line, 'Why should I let a Pomme-de-terre me?'

Newspapers provided far more than just news and opinion. In Ireland, death notices were often the very first item consulted upon opening the paper. Equally, it was a significant social statement when the announcement of an engagement, marriage or birth was published in the paper. Photographs of the happy couple in the local, provincial or national papers elevated individuals to celebrity status.

Newspapers were also replete with enticing pictorial advertisements for everything and anything: fashion, cosmetics, medicines, furniture, gripe water for restless children, whale-bone corsets, fox fur coats and grand pianos. Notices for dances, local fairs, cinema listings, bullocks for sale, horoscopes, horse races, planning notices, photographs of debutante balls, cartoons, spot-the-ball, weather forecasts and positions available were published along with the personal ads: 'Lonely farmer 50, 5'4", light-smoker, R.C., new bungalow, likes dancing, coursing and home baking, would like to meet sincere girls aged 30 to 40 who are attractive with their own farm. Photo with first letter please, will be returned.'

For many, when the news had been read, they found a quiet corner, folded the paper in four, balanced it on their knee and, over lunchtime, went at the crossword with their biro. My brother, Rory, was one of the very few people I knew who was able to get anywhere with the infamous *Irish Times* Crosaire crossword. *Crosaire* is the Irish for crossroads but, it was in itself, a play on the name of its extraordinary creator, John Dereck Crozier.

From 1943, each and every day, six days a week until his death in 2010, Crozier compiled over 14,000 enigmatic crosswords, each with the most unusual cryptic clues that challenged and flummoxed half the country. One of the few clues that I worked out and can remember was: 'Taxi-drivers at the opera' to which the answer is 'carmen'.

Between crosswords, quality journalistic analysis, thought-provoking editorials, small ads, informative features or letters to the editor, the newspaper has been a constant in shaping Irish life. There has been, and will always be, inevitable biases in the different publications, but we have the choice to decide what we read. As we are now in the digital age of mass media, newspaper content is channelled directly into our smartphones. This has presented advantages where hitherto less-widely broadcast views have now found a forum and exposure.

Nevertheless, what we now experience in respect of our worldview is tailored, personalised and governed by a process of self-reinforcement. It is selected, filtered and fed to us individually by the algorithmic information genie, over which we have zero control. The age of the newspaper is waning and, with it, so is some of our ability to make up our own minds, to distinguish, discern and learn from other perspectives.

Lighting the Fire and Killing Flies

Whichever newspaper was read – and regardless of its content – the actual paper of the newspaper was perhaps the most useful and necessary everyday item in an Irish home. Newspapers were never thrown out but stacked in a corner as a resource that was constantly in demand.

Old newspaper was essential for lighting the fire where a few sheets were twisted into tight batons, placed in the grate and covered with *cipíni* (kindling sticks). Before firelighters, the stock of old newspapers and kindling was the way that the fire was lit every day.

If the day was heavy and the chimney was cold, there was a downdraught and it was hard to get a fire going, the whole kitchen would usually fill with smoke. Here, the newspaper was the solution and holding it in two hands, it was placed flat against the fire surround, causing a powerful upward draught at its base that got the fire going like a furnace. Needless to say, this was a regular, pyromaniacal operation that regularly backfired, with the newspaper bursting into flames, a regular occurrence far outside today's health-and-safety regulations.

Newspaper was called into action for all manner of everyday domestic uses. People used it to line drawers, shelves and the insides of wardrobes. The underlay for lino in the kitchen or new carpets in the bedroom came in the form of neatly laid editions of the *Evening Echo* or *The Clare Champion* or some such local paper – years later, when they were being pulled up, half the day was taken up reading the old headlines. It was usual to paste a few pages of any used newspaper such as the *Longford Leader* or the *Munster Express* to the uneven, matchboard bedroom partitions, as a foundation layer, before pasting on the new floral wallpaper. Excessive over-papering caused the wallpaper to blister and detach, so every now and again it had to be pulled off, which sometimes revealed the early foundation newspaper layers, and one was confronted with an historic headline or the face of Zsa Zsa Gabor staring back at you.

In the 1950s and 1960s, keeping multicoloured budgies, canaries and even parrots became very popular. These were often left fly around the house, content to sit on granda's head, with many escaping through the open window never to be seen again. It was usual to place a rectangle of sandpaper at the base of the cage but for those who did not have the wherewithal, the newspaper served the purpose. The paper was folded exactly to fit into the base, and this was the perfect mechanism to rid the cage of the build-up of scattered waste seed and bird droppings.

The newspaper was also used to toilet train a new puppy, spreading the absorbent sheets all over the kitchen and as the puppy piddled on the paper, each night fewer sheets were left until only a few remained at the back door. Finally, the puppy would equate his needs by going to the back door and he was left out to do his business. Newspaper featured largely in the toilet concerns of not just puppies, but people too. Old newspapers were cut into squares and hung on a six-inch nail in outhouses and used as toilet paper for many years. Before plumbed, flush toilets, the everyday convenience was the earth closet. People sat on a wooden bench with a hole in it, perched over a bucket that was filled with earth. Having cleaned themselves with the newspaper, each user would cover over their deposit with a scoop of earth and when the bucket was near full, it was emptied and the whole mixture composted in a cesspit. To curtail their overuse, such earth closets in public houses were kept under lock and key. On request the publican would present those in need with a large key for the outhouse and a page from the newspaper, the latter serving the double purpose of also providing some reading material.

Spontaneous and unsolicited diverse reading material was also provided when newspaper was used in the local chipper to wrap Friday's fish and chips or the chicken supper on Saturday night. You could ask for your chips to be double wrapped to keep them warm for the walk home and when you opened them, not only did the waft of steaming salt and vinegar assault your senses, but the chance content of newspaper wrapping provided extra distraction and entertainment.

Just the other day, it was warm and sunny, and I was sitting at the kitchen table, the back door and windows open and a fly started buzzing annoyingly around my ear. It drew out a memory from the corner of my mind, of my father in the summer months in the middle of the kitchen, with a rolled-up copy of the *Evening Echo*, standing in a frozen Inspector Clouseau-like stance, listening for the fly, his eyes following the sound before going berserk, bashing and clattering after the offending insect. I had the fly firmly in my sights and I looked around for a newspaper to undertake the same action, but there was none at hand.

I searched the house high and low, but nothing, and I quickly realised that the newspaper, once the most utilitarian and widespread of materials, has unknowingly and silently all but disappeared from our lives.

NEW AGE OF ENTERTAINMENT

The Wireless

When I was a teenager, in the 1970s, we inherited an old Pye radio, a 1950s model that had been presented to my grand uncle Paddy Ryan following a lifetime of working in Cannock's Department Store in Limerick. We had it in our bedroom, connected to an aerial made from a length of wire attached to a metal coat hanger that was affixed to the top of the wardrobe. The radio's wooden casing, with four Bakelite knobs, was emblazoned with a golden metal grill that covered the speaker, while underneath was a long rectangular pane of glass on which was painted the exotic radio locations from all around the world. We would twiddle the tuning knob and skip from Monte Carlo to Luxembourg on to Gothenburg, Rome and Lisbon before switching to Ankara, Minsk and Budapest. With the help of the fine-tuning knob and the little green light, the swishing and swirling of the radio waves would momentarily clarify into an exotic voice or an obscure piece of music and we were transfixed by the wonder of the sounds from the distant world beyond. Lahti in Finland and Hilversum in Holland were outside our geographical ambit, but we took pride that amongst the exotic world capitals of Brussels, Paris and Vienna, our own Cork, Dublin and Athlone stood proud.

2RN: IRELAND CALLING

The technology of radio is barely a century old. Ireland had no small part to play in its development, with Guglielmo Marconi using stations in Wexford and Galway to make the first wireless transatlantic transmission in 1901. Over the next decade or so, numerous radio transmission stations were set up along the west coast in Donegal, Galway and Kerry. The first successful east–west wireless telephony signal from Ballybunion to Louisberg, Nova Scotia, took place in March 1919 and the collective notion of radio was truly born with the establishment of the British Broadcasting Corporation (BBC) in November 1922.

The newly independent fledgling Irish state did not want to be left behind, so, despite misgivings and confusions about the new phenomenon and the extraordinary social changes it would embrace, the Irish station 2RN – a wordplay on Éireann – was established and went on air in November 1925.

It might be argued that radio was to become the first real unifier of Ireland as a nation. Up to this point, widespread communication of local issues was confined to newspapers and with the limitations of travel, most would never have heard the idioms and accents of Donegal, Waterford, Monaghan or Cork. Radio was to prove the mechanism that opened up and brought together the distant varied nuances and traits of the country.

The earliest and cheapest radios were the 'Cat's Whisker' sets, named for the small thin wire suspended over crystals that somehow picked up the radio signals and made them audible in the accompanying headset. As ingenious as these devices were, they were notoriously fickle, with little or no control over what you could listen to or how long an audible signal might last. Nevertheless, they opened up Ireland to itself and to the world with most people hearing the languages of the world for the first time.

Such an extraordinary new medium of open communication and influence was to prove a huge challenge for the newly independent Ireland emerging from years of British rule, coupled with the still very volatile open wounds of the Civil War. Resisting the interests of private providers, Ireland's radio service fell under the care of the Department of Posts and Telegraphs whose location in the GPO on the site of the 1916 Rising, if somewhat impractical, was a powerful symbol.

The Department of Posts and Telegraphs, a legacy from the Marconi radio transmissions, meant that the collection of licences rather than the programme content took priority. The very early content was a conflation of notions of national heritage, with the army band and musicians on violins and piano performing both classical pieces and Irish airs. Tenors and baritones sang Irish songs in both English and Irish and these, coupled with performances on both the uilleann pipes and the harp, were set alongside choirs singing religious hymns.

There were numerous plays in the Irish language, poetry readings and gardening advice, but there was no news, no weather forecast and no discussion of contemporary events. The programming and content were repetitive and uninteresting and, in any case, despite the opening up of a second studio and transmitter in Cork (6CK), the majority of the rest of the country was unable to receive any content. It was the decision to broadcast the Eucharistic Congress in 1932 that led to the setting up of the central high-powered transmitter in Athlone that established radio as something more than a novelty, and it soon became a central part of Irish life. In 1936, following a competition where the public voted by letter, the enchanting tones of 'O'Donnell Abú' became the identifying tune for Irish radio and many an early morning since has been greeted with that sweet melody.

A variety of wireless radio receivers became available for sale and soon there were streams of enterprising salesmen travelling the countryside selling wireless sets to those who aspired to the new world of national and international communication. Shopkeepers, publicans and enterprising households had elaborate aerials attached to their chimneys, and groups would gather to listen in wonder to the transmissions.

With rural electrification some way in the future, the wireless sets were powered by large wet-and-dry batteries. These cumbersome batteries were a health-and-safety nightmare. Firstly, they consisted of a rectangular block of thick glass within which were arranged panels of heavy lead. If that was not dangerous enough, they were then filled with sulphuric acid. The batteries lasted about a week before they would have to be brought to the local shop or creamery where there was electricity and where they could be recharged. Some households had two batteries and would swap one over each week. It regularly fell to one of the children to collect the battery by bicycle as it would have been too heavy to carry. The spectacle of the line of glass batteries, linked up in series as they recharged, causing the acid inside literally to boil, was the epitome of danger itself. Though, this was nothing compared to the perfect storm of danger in the challenge of a teenager carrying the lethal combination of glass, lead and acid precariously attached to a rickety bicycle back home.

The newly charged battery was all important at weekends, especially as this was when neighbours would gather to listen eagerly to the commentary on the hurling and football matches. Many such gatherings were remembered not for the match, but for the emotional trauma experienced when the battery gave up the ghost and died in the vital seconds of a closely fought hurling final.

Sport and Talk

Radio's weekend popularity was directly related to the insatiable appetite for all things sport, and in hurling, football and horse racing, the pioneering and ever-present commentator for over six decades from 1938 to 1985, was Michael O'Hehir, the voice of Irish sport. His commentary was electric, ebbing and flowing with the excitement of an attack or a goal or a well-taken point. In the 1940s and 1950s, on all-Ireland final days or for the Aintree Grand National, large groups would cluster to listen to the spectacle. If the crowd was too big and the kitchen too small, the radio was perched on the windowsill and it was surrounded by the throng, the elders on chairs and the *garsúns* on the ground at their feet. A friend told me that his father used to drag out the large tin bath and put the radio inside, so the reverberating sound would act as an amplifier for all to hear. O'Hehir's signature opening salutation, *'Bail o Dhia oraibh go leir, a chairde Ghaeil'* ('God bless you all, my Irish friends') would announce the programme and, within minutes, the audience was transfixed, hanging on to every detail of the word pictures O'Hehir painted so vividly.

In truth, the commentary was often more entertaining that the match itself and, in later years, when the matches were televised, most preferred to listen on the radio than to watch the television. Sometimes, a frenzied attack at goal would be countered with some foul play and the resultant fracas was a cherished part of the game. O'Hehir described the confusion of such events by coining the phrase 'there is a *shemozzle* in the parallelogram' – 'shemozzle' was a Yiddish word O'Hehir had picked up on one of his many trips to New York – and it has remained a constant both on the pitch and in commentary.

O'Hehir's legacy as a national treasure and as a master of radio commentary was matched, if not surpassed, by his successor Mícheál Ó Muircearthaigh, who continued to broadcast on radio from 1980 to 2010. His off-the-cuff quips and witty colloquial observations during matches have become the stuff of national heritage. 'Anthony Lynch, the Cork corner-back, will be the last person to let you down – his people are undertakers!' or 'Seán Óg Ó hAilpín: his father's from Fermanagh, his mother's from Fiji, neither a hurling stronghold.'

Everything changed for radio with the invention and development of the transistor in the 1950s. The large power-hungry old valve sets were replaced by the new, smaller, more efficient transistor radios, reliant only on a small electrical charge and, in the 1960s, the disposable alkaline batteries made the portable transistor radio an every-day, every-household, every-person commodity. There were radios in cars complementing the Sunday spin to the seaside or scenic spot, with the flask of tea and ham sandwiches and Michael O'Hehir commentating on the match.

From the early years, it was usual that some programmes were sponsored by Sweet Afton Cigarettes, Walton's Music Shop, the Blackrock Hosiery Company or the Irish Hospitals Sweepstakes and these quickly became household names. One of the most influential radio programmes, sponsored by Jacob's biscuits, was *Dear Frankie*, broadcast daily at lunchtime, where Frankie Byrne established herself as Ireland's first agony aunt, introducing each programme with the byline: 'The problems we are discussing today may not be yours, but they may be some day.' From its first broadcast in 1963, the daily *Woman's Page* programme ran for over twenty-two years and its content drawn from the listeners' letters went from conservative general domestic matters in the early days to the first open discussions about the issues of extramarital sex, failed relationships and methods of contraception.

The *Gay Byrne Hour*, which first broadcast in 1973, was even more influential in educating the ultra-conservative, Church-ridden Ireland to the realities and injustices of its unspoken darker side. Radio was especially instrumental in empowering women. Housewives all over the country would take time out with the ritual of boiling the kettle, making a cup of tea and sitting down to listen to Gay read out letters that revealed details of many hitherto hidden aspects of Irish life, including issues concerning alcoholism, domestic violence, incest, child abuse and homosexuality. Throughout the 1980s, Marian Finucane's radio programmes, *Women Today*, *Women's Programme* and, later, *Liveline* fully developed such open discussion and were hugely influential with their finger directly on the pounding pulse of the nation.

These radio broadcasts provided a cathartic platform for disenchanted individuals and a place of persuasive open debate on the major social changes that were to catapult Ireland into the modern world.

Jazz and the Pirates

The power of radio to effect major cultural change was not through talk alone, but also, and perhaps more pervasively, through music. In the early days of 2RN, or Radio Athlone as it was known, the emphasis was on promoting de-anglicised Irish culture and traditional music with slides, jigs, reels and slow airs becoming central to its early broadcasts. This insular, focused medium of radio was designed to celebrate very conservative, folk-centric, non-cosmopolitan, pure Irish culture, but turned out to be the core conduit that would open up the country to the music and complexities of the outside world.

It was during Prohibition in 1920s America that jazz music took off in the underground nightclub culture of the speakeasies, where jazz musicians played free-spirited, uninhibited, wild and exciting dance music – the tango, the rumba, the black bottom and the Charleston. It was enthusiastically embraced by all, and characterised the flappers, the liberated women who sported knee-length skirts and bobbed hair and who danced with arms and legs flying in all directions, embodying the devil-may-care era. In the 1930s, the energetic jazz dance music was popular the world over, though, in Ireland, it was seen by the Church and state to be a major threat to both Irish morals and the sense of Irish nationalism.

The fledgling Irish radio, in need of finance, had sponsored radio programmes and given that these were produced outside Ireland they, of course, included jazz. Those who were vehemently against jazz music and dance were at a loss to explain exactly what it was – one Dáil member when asked to clarify what he understood by the term declared: 'It seems to me to be a cross between a waltz and all-in wrestling.'

'Jazz' became the generic term for any music that was not Irish and was seen as a distilled conflation of the evil mores of decadence from England and America. The chairman of the Gaelic League referred to it as, 'Something that is borrowed from the language of the savages of Africa and its object is to destroy virtue in the human soul.' In 1932, Seán MacEntee, the Minister for Finance, was accused of 'selling the musical soul of the nation for the dividends of sponsored jazz programmes' and, under such pressure, all jazz and crooning were banned on Irish radio.

Such censoring policies could never have hoped to stem the continuing flood of musical influences and dynamism that were to filter into Ireland in the post-war years. Music, through the medium of radio and records, was the catalyst that helped explode the pent-up energies of a repressed nation. My mother used to recount how my father spontaneously let himself go, jumping up on his seat and dancing with abandon to 'Rock around the Clock' at a Bill Haley and the Comets concert in the Savoy in Cork in the 1950s.

The fanatical popularity of the Irish showband scene in the 1960s and beyond was evidence of a newly invigorated generation expressing itself through music and dance. In the 1970s, the youth of Ireland had their transistors tuned to MW 208, Radio Luxembourg, the prime source of new musical influences including rock and roll, soul and Motown. We would sleep with the small transistor under our pillows beguiled by the beats and lyrics of The Beatles, the Bee Gees, The Rolling Stones, Crosby, Stills, Nash and Young, Neil Diamond, The Stylistics, The Carpenters, Rod Stewart, The Who, and Van Morrison. Luxembourg was a commercial station and, given it had the most powerful radio transmitter in the world, its signals were easily picked up in Ireland. Its laid-back presentation of non-stop popular music with celebrity disc jockeys prompted the emergence of the first major pirate radio station, Radio Caroline. The first pirates played music that was outside the control of the big record manufacturers and responded to the tastes of their audiences rather than dictating what that audience should listen to.

Radio Caroline was spearheaded by a young Irishman, Ronan O'Reilly, whose family owned the small port of Greenore in Carlingford Lough, County Louth. Here, he refitted an old Scandinavian ferry with a 165-foot mast, sailed it to a spot off the coast of Essex outside official UK waters and began broadcasting in March 1964. A sister broadcasting ship, whose signals reached Ireland with ease, was located off the Isle of Man and would regularly refuel in Dundalk.

Between Luxembourg and Caroline, the new music was the soundtrack to a liberated and diverse new Ireland and, from 1975, Ireland started its own terrestrial pirate stations. Unsophisticated at first, they operated out of attic rooms in rented flats, with their antennae fixed to the roofs. The gardaí would raid and confiscate the transmitter and gear and the amateur station would be off the air. The station might disappear forever or reappear under a new name when a new financier was sorted. Many a broadcast was interrupted by someone bolting into the studio or, as I remember, the DJ being called downstairs by his mother for his tea.

A host of catchy names – such as Capitol, Galaxy, Nova, Sunshine, Kiss and Telstar – promised a sophistication of production but, in the beginning, the service was haphazard. The 1980s saw the Irish pirates become far more professional and they mushroomed all over the country, speaking directly to the needs and interests of their communities. They went from simple AM transmitters operating out of bedrooms, to fully developed FM stations with the most sophisticated of gear. Despite the recession of the 1980s, the big pirate stations became financially successful as commercial interests were quick to see the advantage of marketing and advertising at relatively low cost directly to the local captive audiences. Prompted by the need to control the liberal agendas and allow bigger business tycoons to cash in on their success, the era of the free-for-all pirate stations came to an abrupt end in 1989. A new, restrictive licensing regime was introduced and a golden age of liberal radio ended as broadcasting came back under government control.

Ireland grew up with radio and it is an essential part of our lives. When we wake up, we turn on the radio to hear the news and the weather forecast. It is everywhere: in the bathroom, in the kitchen, in the car, in the shop, in the background at work. It is the soundtrack to Saturday and Sunday mornings while eating toast and reading the paper. There are programmes with chat and current affairs and magazine programmes that entertain, inform and educate. We can switch between stations and presenters with different musical choices that match our moods and tastes.

With radio, we are never alone. It is the intimacy and familiarity of our everyday presenters, either in their chat or musical selections, that resonate with us and feeds our social and emotional needs. Radio is family, deep in our souls as individuals and as a nation.

Going to the Pictures

After a hectic week attempting to control our wild antics as children with threats of the wooden spoon, Saturday could not come quick enough for my mother. Saturday was my mother's day off and she would stay in bed with *Woman's Own* magazine. In the morning, my father drove us into town and, in a master stroke of tact, he simply deposited myself and my two older brothers at the Savoy cinema. My father was a commercial artist and worked for several cinemas, mounting the large cinema posters while skilfully hand-lettering additional display boards that boldly proclaimed the names of the associated film stars. From my earliest years, I was introduced to the wonder of Panavision and Technicolor, and I spent my entire youth wide-eyed and whole-heartedly absorbed in the never-ending thrills and emotions of the big screen.

My mind and imagination were shaped by the excitement and adventures of Ali Baba, Robin Hood, Pinocchio and Long John Silver. As the years went on, it was James Bond, Clint Eastwood, Superman and Racquel Welsh who babysat me on Saturdays, while my father partook of some refreshment with his friends in the Cubiculo Bar on Drawbridge Street. My father knew the head usherette and she made sure we were brought to the toilet at opportune points between the flickering marvel of the ads, the cartoons, the short film and the main feature. As I got older, my brothers went to music or soccer, but I was happy to sit in the cinema all on my own. On a few occasions, my father would forget about me and I ended up watching the same film two or three times. If he was very late, my eyes grew even wider when I soaked in the first half hour of a slightly risqué over-18s film. The constancy of the cinema experience with its mesmerising large screen and all-consuming surround sound had a profound effect on me and many others in my generation, shaping our imaginations. It was the vehicle that brought us to different times and places, introduced us to villains and heroes, and where our moral compasses were constantly tested and directed.

∽ The Flicks ∾

The development of cinema mirrors Ireland's journey to modernity from one end of the twentieth century to the other. Cinema was the wonder of its age and the first screening of the newly invented Lumière brothers Cinématographe camera system marvelled the masses in Daniel Lowrey's Star Theatre of Varieties in Dublin's Temple Bar in October 1896. *The Freeman's Journal* of 5 January 1897 reported: 'the house was crammed to its capacity each night'. The excitement and sense of incredulity at the extraordinary spectacle of the novel technology is clear.

> *The pictures which this wonderful contrivance throws up the screen are marvellous and interesting in the highest degree. The railway train dashing into the station, the cavalry charges, the bathing scenes with divers leaping into the sea from springboards, the scenes of bustle and commotion in some of the great London centres, are all perfect representations of actual life reproduced before the eye of the spectator with absolute realistic effect.*

In 1909, it was none other than James Joyce, who, having secured finance from some associates in Trieste, came back to Dublin and opened the first dedicated picture theatre, The Volta, at 4 Mary Street.

By the 1930s, Ireland was openly embracing cinema, with entrepreneurs in the cities building large opulent auditoriums to cater for and profit from the ever-increasing popularity of films. For example, the incredible 3,000-seater Savoy Cinema in Dublin's O'Connell Street opened in 1929. Its proscenium arch in the form of Venice's Bridge of Sighs and its fire curtain imprinted with the Doge's Palace manifest an interior that was extraordinarily luxurious. The sophistication of such city cinemas, with uniformed ushers and bellboys, cloakrooms, lifts and relaxing restaurants, offered intense moments of elegance and escape, no matter how temporary, and were open to all for a meagre admission charge. Such inviting exoticism was implicit in the chosen flamboyant cinema names, such as The Coliseum, The Palace, The Corinthian, The Ambassador and The Adelphi. The advent of 'talkie' pictures, along with increased

technical progress in projectors and audio amplification, enabled the ultimate sensual synchronisation of sight and sound that transported audiences into different worlds.

Over the years, regardless of the efforts of the Irish Censorship Board, who banned and cut films that did not chime with the perceived notion of Catholic morals and the nationalistic ideals, the world projected on to the large screen opened minds and ultimately reshaped Ireland.

Cinema was at its zenith from the end of the Second World War to the 1960s. Most small towns and villages had a cinema, and those that didn't were catered to by travelling cinemas, operated by the local circus owners, who were idle over the winter months, or by travelling fit-up theatrical companies. They would set up in the small village halls, and a mobile generator powering a projector was fixed outside the window of the hall with the films projected inwards onto a white sheet. The wide-eyed patrons sat on makeshift benches made from planks of wood set atop upturned butter boxes. Films for children were shown in the afternoons, while in the evenings the wider world entered the Irish adult consciousness. The screen sirens Jane Mansfield, Hedy Lamarr or Ingrid Bergman along with heartthrobs like Jimmy Stewart, Cary Grant or Tyrone Power were on full display.

This dangerous and exciting alternative way of living, projected through the lens of the Hollywood studios, displayed startling and flamboyant lifestyles. In the dark of the picture house, the twirling reels of film presented the frightening, yet alluring, world of femmes fatales and manipulative cads. While still the stuff of distant fantasy, it opened up a vibrant vista of life outside of Ireland and would prove the catalyst to emigration for multitudes.

Those who remained at home were reminded to keep on the straight and narrow when they were chastened from the tempting world of cinema every year over the Lenten period. Given the Catholic ethos, all dance halls and picture houses were closed over the forty days of abstinence before Easter. Towards the end of the period, the owners, in an attempt to recoup lost revenue, would screen religious films, such as *The Song of Bernadette* or Cecil B. DeMille's epic *The Ten Commandments*, and this somehow satisfied the establishment and the punters.

The Ten Commandments and devotion to religion were at the heart the one of the very worst tragedies and loss of human life in Ireland back in 1926 in the town of Dromcollogher in County Limerick. A make-shift cinema was surreptitiously assembled in the disused upstairs of an old wooden building in the village. There was a ready audience for a film from a mix of inquisitiveness and devotion and some bootleggers thought they could profit from the opportunity. From the earliest days, there were strict controls over the safety in cinemas because the nitrate film was highly combustible, but, in this case, all safety regulations were ignored. Following evening Mass on Sunday, 5 September 1926, 150 paying patrons filed up a make-shift ladder, some with their prayer books and rosary beads still in their hands, to the rough-and-ready candlelit auditorium. The reels of film were secretly 'borrowed' and transported by bicycle on the four-hour, forty-mile journey from the Coliseum Cinema in Cork. To lighten the load, the heavy protective fireproof metal cases in which the reels were stored were left behind. An external generator powered the borrowed projector and the magic of the cinema was, for a short time, cast on the screen to the delight of the assembly. On the night, it is thought that a stray candle started a small fire, but this quickly spread and ignited the highly flammable nitrate film – the upstairs of the wooden building became an death-trap. Those close to the door escaped down the ladder but, in all, forty-eight people died in this horrific tragedy. Following the fire, cinema health and safety regulations became strictly enforced and special fireproof projection boxes and well-indicated fire exits became paramount.

In the 1950s, there were some standout made-in-Ireland films that particularly resonated with Irish cinemagoers. One favourite director was John Ford, whose father had emigrated from Spiddal in County Galway to America, and who was the master of westerns, including S*he Wore a Yellow Ribbon* and *Stagecoach*.

He came to Cong in County Mayo and ploughed over a million dollars into what was a quasi-western film. He took the great cowboy John Wayne and cast him as the troubled American, former boxer Sean Thornton, who vies for the love of Mary-Kate Danaher, played by Maureen O'Hara. The feisty red-haired colleen played by O'Hara conformed to the Ford's classic, stage-Irish stereotypes, a mechanism that was brought to a whole new level by Barry Fitzgerald who played the matchmaking, sweet-talking jarvey Michaeleen Óg Flynn. Despite its clichéd American perspective, *The Quiet Man* was a huge box-office hit, offering a full Technicolor panorama of a romanticised and imaginary Ireland. Bord Fáilte could not have wished for a better and more appealing marketing tool and the film was instrumental in attracting huge scores of Irish-American tourists to Ireland from the 1950s onwards.

John Huston's re-creation of the great whaling station of Bedford, Massachusetts, in the waterfront of Youghal, County Cork, for the filming of *Moby Dick* was another memorable occasion. In 1954, Gregory Peck played Captain Ahab and Orson Welles the hell-fire preacher Fr Mapple, while Irish audiences were to appreciate the contributions of the homegrown Noel Purcell, Joseph Tomelty and Seamus Kelly. The town was transformed with dummy whales floating in the harbour and a flurry of tall ships moored at its quays – most of the townspeople secured roles as extras or were employed at set building. Each day, there were ten full trains coming from Cork, the carriages packed to the doors, with onlookers seeking to experience the excitement of the process and looking for autographs. The film was released in 1956 and was very well received by Irish audiences, especially in Cork.

Jam Jars and Usherettes

Cinema was at its apex in Ireland's pre-television era of the 1950s, and it became the focus of social life for young and old. Saturday afternoon at the pictures was the ticket of escape and fantasy for the hordes of children and teenagers who walked, cycled or got buses, and formed long queues outside the cinemas of the big towns and cities. In the 1950s, admission for the matinee was four pence but, in many places, you could gain access by bringing along eight small jam jars worth a ha'penny each and these were passed on to the local jam factories. When a popular blockbuster film, such as *The Magnificent Seven* or *Ben Hur*, was shown, the queues would be all the way down the street, and there was no skipping the queue under the watchful eye of the uniformed ushers who marshalled the masses. The biggest disappointment was when you were nearly in and the usher, in his dickie-bow and jacket, would put his hand across the line and announce that the picture was full. The only thing to do was to run, helter-skelter to another cinema to try to get into another film. There was always next week.

Depending on the cinema, there were different prices for different seats. On the ground floor, you had the stalls, with lines of plush, red-velveted, flip-up seats. Some small cinemas arranged a few wooden benches right up front for the children and these were known as the fleapit. These were the worst seats of all as you had to crane your neck to watch the film. When the lights went off and the usher wasn't looking, there would be a mad dash back to any of the proper seats that were unoccupied. Perched atop the upright flip-up seat without pulling it down was the best vantage point for the youngest kids.

Many cinemas had a balcony and its front seats were highly sought-after. They were a place of great mischief, especially when the film was boring and the temptation to throw a few missiles over the top into the stalls below had to be carefully controlled by the roaming flashlight of the usher. If guilty of any such messing or talking in the cinema, the culprit was isolated and humiliated by being spotlighted in the beam of the usher's torch. In the large city cinemas, balconies were on a huge scale, the Savoy in Cork, for example, was a 2,250-seater cinema and the highest seats had a precipitous climb to the very top, infamously known as 'the hundred steps'.

The cinema was well served by teams of uniformed usherettes with trays, selling cigarettes, chocolate and ice-cream. They balanced their trays of treats with the help of a large strap around their necks and they negotiated their way in the dark with the aid of a torch. There were plenty of intermissions between the short, the cartoon, the newsreel, ads and the main feature, and the usherette's enticing fare was eagerly exchanged for pocket money.

Transactions continued during the film, with patrons beckoning in the dark for a slim bar of Fry's Chocolate or a small bar of chocolate-covered, rose-flavoured Turkish Delight. A small packet of salty, Pete's Peanuts, a packet of Scots Clan Toffees or Iced Caramels, if you had money, were available. Little tubs of ice-cream, vanilla or raspberry ripple, complete with a small wooden spoon were an anticipated treat.

This was also the era where everyone smoked, not only on the big screen, but also in the cinema, and the usherette with her tray was on hand to sell both cigarettes and matches. On the back of each scalloped-shaped cinema seat, was a small brass ashtray for patrons to tap their ash and stub their cigarette butts. When the film was on, the intense beam of projected light was fully visible, filled with a continuous, dense, white clouds of swirling cigarette smoke.

Jumbos, and Cowboys and Indians

The Saturday afternoon matinee began with a short – a brief twenty-minute documentary about some archaeological discovery in Egypt or the building of a dam in Australia that served to quieten and settle the masses of kids. There was also what were termed a follower-upper or cliffhanger serial designed to make sure you came back the next week to see what happened to never-ending woes of Flash Gordon, Batman, The Lone Ranger and many more.

Shorts of Laurel and Hardy were ever popular and, along with a newsreel, adverts for local businesses were looked at in wonder. The most popular adverts, orientated to courting couples, were always by local jewellers' shops encouraging the purchase of iceberg diamond engagement rings and, in turn, the local hotel promoted its facilities for weddings. This made great sense, because, in an Ireland fettered by Catholic guilt and non-public display of affection, the dark private interior of the cinema was an ideal location for courting.

The dark interior of the pictures was the only outlet for casual intimacy for a young couple in love. Those couples desirous of kissing and cuddling had little regard for the picture itself, but would head straight for the seats at the back of the cinema where they were not overlooked. The cinema was cosy, dark and private, and if the film was a scary horror or a mushy romance, it acted as a potent catalyst for fledgling amorous encounters. In the 1970s, several cinemas went a step further and introduced jumbos, a large, double seat that was much frequented for those seeking a comfortable spot for hanky-panky.

The varied range of films shown in Ireland in the pre-television age filled and fuelled the imaginations of a generation. Week after week, the box office presented a fantastical kaleidoscope that encompassed the simplicities and complexities of diverse characters, plots and ethical perspectives. It was the cinema that rewarded, challenged and cultivated our sensibilities. We were in awe of the ways of the Orient and, after watching the exploits of Bruce Lee and Chuck Norris, we would leap down the cinema steps, high kicking and giving each other karate chops all the way home. The following week, it might be the adventures of Sinbad the Sailor or Tarzan and Jane and, as children, we sat on pretend magic carpets or swung out of trees mimicking Johnny Weissmuller's famous cry. Next, we were transfixed in fear following full-length features starring Vincent Price, Christopher Lee and Peter Cushing in some terrifying horror, like *Dracula* or *Frankenstein*. There were the ever-popular re-releases of the 1950s musical classics with Yule Brenner in *The King and I* and Julie Andrews in *The Sound of Music* while, equally, audiences of all ages sang along with *My Fair Lady*, *Hello Dolly* and *Mary Poppins*.

The original hand-drawn Disney cartoons of *Pinocchio*, *Cinderella* and *Snow White* were moments of seminal and lasting enchantment. We laughed our way through the Ealing Studio comedies, the risqué *St. Trinian's*, the double-entendre of the *Carry-Ons* and the hilarious ineptitudes of Inspector Clouseau bringing smiles and levity to our being.

The intrigue of the adventurous and dangerous exotic world of James Bond was complemented by further fantastic journeys to the realms of *Star Trek*, *Superman* and the *Planet of the Apes*.

In equal measure, there were numerous second-rate films that we sat through, but which left a lasting impression. Doug McClure in *The Land that Time Forgot* or James Mason in *Journey to the Center of the Earth* supplied us with new imaginary settings that became the focus of make-believe games.

Perhaps the most resonant genre of film in Ireland right through time has been the western, with stars such as Hop-Along Cassidy, John Wayne, James Stewart, Roy Rogers and Gene Audrey shooting or singing their way into the Irish psyche. The world of the American wild west with its gunslingers, whiskey-drinking, piano-playing saloons, pioneering wagons, a posse setting out on horseback and dusty cowboys rustling cattle was the favourite setting for a host of moralistic, allegorical tales. *High Noon, The Good, The Bad and The Ugly, The Magnificent Seven, True Grit* and so many more filled the picture houses like nothing else. The cowboy and Indian film was ubiquitous in our youth. We understood very little about the plight of Native Americans and the manner in which they were portrayed on the screen, and, in our innocence, they became mere characters in our play.

Such was the popularity of the cowboy film that, at Christmas, we would ask for a cowboy suit and hat along with a cap gun and a holster. I remember in the summer months when I was ten years of age, getting out of bed in the mornings, putting on my buckskin cowboy suit with its frills, slinging my gun and holster and heading out to meet my pals for a game of cowboys and Indians. Those without the cowboy attire and appendages were happy to be Indians, making bows and arrows out of string and bits of bendy hedging and sticking a crow's feather in their hair.

They had the benefit of making the 'wow-wow-wow' sound of the Indians we saw on film while the cowboys, hiding behind garden walls, would shoot them by mimicking the sharp sounds of bullet noises that we heard in the pictures.

The following week, our trip to the cinema had transformed us into the Second World War veterans from *The Guns of Navarone* and our hurleys were reimagined into machine guns as we scattered bullets everywhere by voicing an endless loud cacophony of 'ha-ha-ha-ha-ha'.

When television arrived into Irish life in the 1960s, it robbed the cinema of its novelty. The cinema experience co-existed with television right through the 1970s and remained hugely popular as a recreational experience. However, in the same way that theatre suffered because of cinema, cinema suffered because of television.

In response to the waning numbers, large cinemas divided their auditoriums into multiplexes, but the industry was in decline. By the 1980s, with more sophisticated television programming and increased channels and the increased popularity of video recorders, the world of film moved from the public auditorium to the video shop and the domestic sofa. The large palatial cinemas of the cities and those of the smaller towns and villages that communally fed the imaginations of generations, closed their doors and many were demolished.

Turning on the Telly

My aunt and uncle ran a small grocer shop between Caherciveen and Portmagee that met the needs of the scattered households within that hinterland. It was a focal point in the rural community and, as such, they were the first in the locality to get a television in the mid-1960s. The television was the pure wonder of its day with crowds congregating to marvel at the moving images and especially to watch the televised football matches featuring the rampant Kerry teams of the 1960s and early 1970s.

At that time, many bachelors living on their own would shyly make their way to the shop once a week to pick up the 'messages'. Preferring to keep themselves to themselves, their regular visit, usually outside normal hours, was to replenish their stocks of tea, sugar, biscuits and cigarettes. In the small shop at the back of the house, my sympathetic aunt would fill a cardboard box of everything they might need while they put their head around the door of the living room to say a few words to my uncle. When the television first appeared, they were in total awe of, and genuinely confused by, the spectacle of the talking heads in the box. The television announcer of the day was the glamorous and beautiful Thelma Mansfield, and the first time one of the bachelor visitors saw her looking directly at him from the screen, he was instantaneously transfixed and entirely dumbstruck. My uncle witnessing the poor man's immediate infatuation, mischievously doubled on his awkwardness by remarking to him, 'She's looking at you!' The following week when the man came to call, he was all dressed up, shoes polished, hair combed and wearing his Sunday suit, as if he were on the date with the woman of his dreams. He sat down and waited for Thelma to appear and announce that *Amuigh Faoin Spéir* or *An Nuacht* was about to come on. He would stare at her flowing blonde locks and big eyes, and, with my uncle's continuous litany of, 'she's looking at you', the poor man, thinking that he could be seen, would blush and bow his head in unbearable shyness.

~ TELEFÍS ÉIREANN ~

Television first came to Ireland in the 1950s, long before the first transmission of *Telefís Éireann* on the last day of the year in 1961. Transmitters from the west coast of the UK and in Ulster enabled those on the border and the east coast, specifically Dublin, to access what was termed fall-out signals from BCC and ITV broadcasts. In the mid-1950s, a weekly schedule of *BBC Television Highlights*, catering for Irish audiences, was printed in the *Irish Independent*. By 1958, there were an estimated 20,000 television sets in Ireland and the progress could be seen as aerials were set up on chimneys, even in remote rural areas.

The conundrum now was that Irish people were experiencing the world through a British lens and were being exposed to a more liberal and open-minded content. One overwrought parishioner, worried about the lack of faith on the British television, exclaimed in a letter to the cardinal, that 'a good programme is likely to be followed by the contortions of some dancer, and never will all the arts of Satan be so articulately expressed'. Moreover, several television programmes about Ireland were made by the BBC. For example, a programme entitled *Buried Treasure* celebrating the archaeological site of Lough Gur in County Limerick, was broadcast in September 1954. This state of affairs could not continue. It was clear that there was a need for an Irish television station controlling and broadcasting its own content.

The issue was an ideological one, differing somewhat from the dilemma that the choice and content of films at the cinema had presented. With television, Ireland would have to broadcast its own content and, in doing so, would have to choose who it was and how it wanted to progress. Moreover, how such an entity might come into being and who would hold sway over its identity and worldview was a real issue. There were many who wanted their say: the Irish language revivalists, the Church, politicians, academics, the GAA, journalists, writers and actors, musicians, overseas television experts, and the many commercial interests. The early years of the station were dogged by continuous criticism and interference from the different interest groups vying for control and power.

While the first broadcast of *Telefís Éireann* on New Year's Eve 1961 was officially the beginning of the television age, it was the visit of John F. Kennedy in June 1963 that was something of a catalyst for the major increase in television popularity. His visit was a blockbuster television event and, being followed by his assassination a short five months later, meant that many Irish people accessed a television set to watch the aftermath and the funeral. By 1964, it is estimated that nearly a quarter of million households in Ireland had a television. This figure was to increase as the years wore on but, given the expense of purchasing a new set, it was cheaper to rent the television and a whole industry of television rental began to emerge.

The early sets made by Pye or Bush could be rented for an initial weekly sum of ten shillings and, after six months of regular payment, the sum was reduced. The large glass screen was the slightly domed flat end of a large glass tube that was so big it projected out the back of the rectangular wooden box in which it was set. Peering in the back you could see rows of glowing glass valves and puzzling tangles of multicoloured wires. There was a speaker at the front while there were knobs to turn and circular dials with numbers and fine tuning that were fiddled with endlessly to manifest a picture.

When the television was switched on, it took some time for the tube to heat up and the picture emerged from a grey haze. When it was turned off, the picture collapsed inwards and sank dramatically into a vanished bright dot in the centre of the screen. As children, the screen was a plaything of static electricity and our mothers would warn us to stay well back from it, lest we were irradiated or went blind.

The television sets were notoriously fickle and did not always behave. Before the installation of the large aerials fixed to the chimneys, many relied on the infamous rabbit's ears whose bi-pronged antennae were continually adjusted in pursuit of a clean, clear and constant picture. The picture always had flecks of dusty interference that were called snow and, every now and again, the frame of the picture would start flicking crazily up and down the screen and we battled to adjust that with the vertical hold knob at the back.

'What's on the Box?'

As a child of the early television age of the 1970s, I used to run home from school and turn on the telly straightaway but, despite such fanatical enthusiasm, programmes did not start until 5.30pm. Nevertheless, we were still content to stare at the test card for hours on end. When not transmitting programmes, the television companies broadcast a static image of a card made up of patterned shapes and lines that could be used to adjust the quality of the picture. The early test cards were in

black and white and, one fad at the time was to buy a special sheet of transparent plastic that would magically turn the grey screen into radiant colour. The sheets were taped to the screen, their top blue for the sky, the middle orange for people, while the bottom section was green for grass. This arrangement was less than convincing, but the technical marvel of colour television was introduced in the first half of the decade and, as time went on, colour sets became the norm.

By the mid-1970s, television was omnipresent and we feasted on a curious mix of programmes. There was not enough home-produced content to fill the broadcast schedule, so our television viewing was amply supplemented by cheap American and British films and series. The large Hollywood movie studios who faced a huge decline, given the ever-increasing popularity of television, turned to their back catalogues of old movies as a source of much-needed revenue. Older films, for which they had full ownership and which were long outside any contractual obligations, were sold off in swathes to the television companies. *Raidió Telefís Éireann* was delighted to avail of this resource, as they were cheap when bought in bulk and because they were old, they did not fall foul of the Church-dominated censorship board. Our film digest was markedly anachronistic and consisted of the musicals of Fred Astaire and Ginger Rogers, Alfred Hitchcock's tales of suspense, Shirley Temple, Laurel and Hardy, and the Marx Brothers.

American comedy came in the form of a long series of *I Love Lucy*, with Lucille Ball and the likes of bumbling Maxwell Smart talking into his shoe in the spy comedy *Get Smart*. Science fiction and space travel with Captain Kirk and the crew of the *Enterprise* in *Star Trek*, boldly going where nobody had gone before, had us glued to the screens each week. The adventures of *The Six Million Dollar Man*, *The Invisible Man* and *The Incredible Hulk* heightened our suspension of disbelief, while the sense of the possible was revealed in exciting weekly episodes of *Mission Impossible*.

There were endless detective series that were the entertainment manna of their day. We jumped between Ironside in his wheelchair, Mannix with his sidekick secretary, Peggy, Barnaby Jones and his glass of milk and Columbo and his raincoat. At the end of each episode of *Hawaii Five-O*, the refrain, 'book 'em, Danno' became a schoolyard catchphrase. Telly Savalas, with his distinctive bald head, played the role of the lollipop-sucking tough detective Kojak, which followed the farm report on *Mart and Market*, where the whole country listened with a puzzled interest to long monotonous reports on the trade in different marts, noting whether trade was up or down and the price of hoggets and in-calf heifers. Every now and again, there was footage of men in white coats parading cattle around the ring, but mainly it was the presenter Michael Dillon who carried the show. He also had a bald head and, as he was on before Kojak, he became affectionately known as 'Cow-jak'.

Despite the apparent surfeit of extraneous outside television content, it was the homegrown programmes that left a lasting impression on audiences. Politics and current affairs were openly eviscerated on *7 Days* while deep political satire was provided each Friday night on *Hall's Pictorial Weekly*.

Beside the magnificent lampooning of Irish politicians with the councillors of Ballymagash, the Minister for Hardship and the Cork Mothers of Seven, each programme started with a montage of local footage of a different small provincial town. Shots of everyday life, with close ups of smiling faces, people driving tractors or standing outside the local shop, became a cherished moment of television celebrity for rural communities.

Rural Ireland was the setting for highly influential soap opera *The Riordans* that ran every Sunday night from 1965 to 1979, with over 300 episodes. It was written and produced by Wesley Burrowes and its cast, with characters like Benjy, Biddy, Eamon Maher and Minnie Brennan, became household names, though its impact was far from benign. Its talented cast of actors played out the scenarios marked by the eternal divisions in the rapidly changing Irish society. Its represented and voiced conservative and liberal viewpoints of age and youth, of tradition and change and audiences could relate directly to the dogmas, dilemmas and life choices that had to be made. It succeeded in drawing public attention to the dilemmas faced by women on Irish farms and their plight if their husbands died. It coincided with the enactment of the Succession Act of 1965 that guaranteed women their automatic inheritance and also forced banks to allow women, without permission from their husbands, to open their own bank accounts.

THE LATE LATE SHOW AND BEYOND

The singular most influential television programme that channelled and influenced the highly conservative Irish state in its radical metamorphosis to an open and more liberal society was *The Late Late Show*. Compulsory primetime Saturday-night

– later moved to Friday-night – viewing, its success was down to the genius of its presenter and producer Gay Byrne, who hosted the show from 1962 until 1999. Over the years, *The Late Late Show* slowly and methodically succeeded in breaking the taboos and glass ceilings of Ireland's Church-shackled society. Byrne maintained a benign composure and quasi-central position while teasing out details from well-known celebrities and personalities.

Raconteurs like Peter Ustinov, John B. Keane and Maeve Binchy regaled the country with their anecdotes and observations on life, revealing a spectrum of different philosophies. Comedians from Billy Connolly to Tommy Tiernan and Dermot Morgan pushed the boundaries through irreverence and mocking humour that held a mirror up to our prudishness and duplicity. Byrne also introduced invited unfamiliar guests, who were afforded an open and free forum to tell their own stories. Through a relaxed, probing interview technique, Ireland was exposed to and educated on the concerns and opinions of influential minorities, including punks, rockers, defrocked clergy, environmental activists, naturists, thrill-seekers and atheists.

The content of *The Late Late Show* was never revealed ahead of broadcast and, each week, the show switched from pure light entertainment with music and comedy to serious debates on such previously unmentionable matters of contraception, marital relationships, sex and domestic violence.

An incredibly benign remark by a married couple that has become known as the bishop-and-the-nightie affair caused a countrywide furore in the 1966. In a segment of light entertainment, different married couples were asked how well they knew each other. A question asked to one man was what colour his wife's honeymoon nightdress was. The husband replied that he remembered it as see-through while his wife recalled that she did not wear one at all. This prompted the Bishop of Clonfert to send a telegram to Gay Byrne stating that he was disgusted by the disgraceful performance and, as the days went on, he promoted a virulent campaign against Gay Byrne and the television station.

The bishop led the attack, saying: 'I am asking people to register their protest verbally, by letter and by phone – even by cancelling their subscriptions to Irish television … we as good Catholic citizens do not stand for this kind of programme.'

This controversy and the many other supposedly 'amoral' items that followed, such as appearances by lesbian nuns, playboy bunny girls, and the showing of sex aids and condoms, simply served to make the programme compulsory viewing. Gay Byrne's catchphrase, 'remember it started on *The Late Late Show*', was a maxim not just confined to the new musical bands or authors or actors who started their careers on the show, but to the debates on real-life personal and social issues. There were many who reviled Gay Byrne and refused to watch the programme but who invariably heard about its controversial content from the pulpit or from the gossip-mongers the following Sunday morning.

Seasonal events covered on television were catalysts that charged Irish youth with purpose and focus. Not only did we kick the soccer ball around the back garden or out on the road and simultaneously mimic the exaggerated television commentary in an English accent when we scored a goal inspired by *Match of the Day*. When Wimbledon came on, the football was temporarily put away and the tennis rackets were brought out. We learned the umpire's calls of out, thirty-love, deuce and match point, while some took up the roles of dedicated ball boys, kneeling at the edge of our make-do nets. We pleaded with our mothers to buy us Robinson's Barley Water for those tennis days and never at any other time in the year.

Then, it was the turn of the Aga Khan, televised from the RDS in Dublin and, although we did not have any horses, we made make-shift fences and set about trying to get a clear round. We would tap our backsides, the way we saw the riders hurrying the horse with a short whip and very often, for no reason whatsoever, other than we saw it on the telly, we, as both horse and rider, would do a refusal and get two faults. Every four years, we had the Olympics and on each summer Olympian evening, there were hordes of children running and sprinting, passing batons, doing the high jump and long jump and only wishing they could find a pole long enough to try the pole vault.

While *The Late Late Toy Show* is now the great modern family event, the halcyon night of childhood television in the 1970s was the night of the *Eurovision Song Contest*. This was a major television event with family and friends and scores of children gathered for a Eurovision party, all sitting around the television. We would pick a country out of a hat and as each act came on there would be much cheering and jeering while the assembly ate biscuits and drank tea in good company.

The inclusion of Ireland as an equal player in a competition amongst the towering countries of Europe – France, West Germany, United Kingdom, Sweden and so on – made us so proud of our small nation. We were in shock when Dana, a smiling innocent colleen from Derry, won it in 1970 with 'All Kinds of Everything'. Dana and the Eurovision represented a moment when Ireland began to widen its sense of self. We were coming of age, standing on our own feet and not entirely suffocated by our colonial past.

It chimed with the referendum of May 1972 when Ireland voted overwhelmingly to join the European Economic Community. As a must-see television event, the Eurovision continued to captivate the nation with its variety of music, the startling outfits and the often-outlandish performances. Abba erupted into our lives in 1974, singing 'Waterloo' while, in 1980, Johnny Logan endorsed Ireland's Eurovision pedigree with 'What's Another Year?' He won again in 1987 and then wrote the winning song 'Why Me?' performed by Linda Martin in 1992, bringing the television spectacular back to the small rural Cork town of Millstreet in 1993.

A win that year by Niamh Kavanagh saw RTÉ move to The Point in Dublin in 1994 where Ireland won again with 'Rock 'n' Roll Kids'. As incredible as this was, that year was remembered for the seven-minute spectacular interval act, *Riverdance*. This was a seminal moment in Irish life with the whole television-watching country experiencing an enchanting modern evocation and reimagining of our national identity. It was a unique and captivating new mix of spirited music played on traditional instruments augmented by drumming and choral singing, that conjured up a tangible sense of ancient and mystical Ireland. This music was coupled with a ground-breaking reinterpretation of Irish dance along with eye-catching costumes, freedom of expression and a finale made-up of an imposing chorus line of spectacular dancing. Riverdance, at Eurovision in The Point, epitomised how Ireland now saw itself. Its expression through the international medium of television was a principal moment in our ever-developing story.

EPILOGUE

In the teaching of archaeology, there is a traditional method of dividing prehistoric time by referencing the technologies of the past. Ireland has its .Palaeolithic, Mesolithic and Neolithic periods of the Stone Age, that give way to the Bronze Age and on to the Iron Age, and so on. I was contemplating this methodology of combining technology and time and began to ponder what my era and that of my ancestors has been.

My grandparents, born in the nineteenth century, would have hailed from the time of horse transport, bicycles and the influence of the newspaper. The world of my parents, born in the 1920s, was characterised by the age of the car, cinema and radio. Born in the 1960s, I am the product of the television and video age, along with the first computers and supermarkets. In my lifetime, many previously unheard-of phenomena such as budget air travel, dishwashers and garden centres have emerged. We are presently in the throes of the generation born into the age of the internet, the mobile phone, wi-fi and social media. Next on the horizon is the dawn of artificial intelligence.

Each and every generation welcomes and bemoans the changes that time brings. We are at once delighted and relieved by the ease on life's burdens that each new technology facilitates. We are equally saddened by the dilution of the familiar subtleties of living and culture that are eroded and rendered obsolete by such progression. We know from our collective life experiences that nothing ever stays the same. In every adjustment of life, nothing is gained without something being lost. Change is unstoppable, but there are times when we can be in control of what we adopt and what we let go.

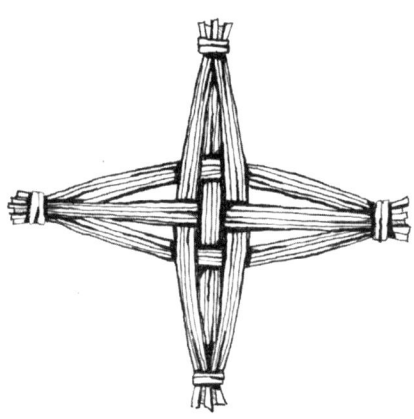

Glossary of Irish Words and Phrases

Ag cur foirc agus scaena	'It's raining forks and knives', the Irish version of raining cats and dogs
An bhfuil cead agam dul go dtí an leithreas?	'May I go to the toilet?', one of the earliest Irish expressions learnt in primary school
An Cailín Ciúin	*The Quiet Girl*, Colm Baireád's 2022 Irish-language film adapted from Claire Keegan's short story 'Foster'
'An Chúalainn'	'The Coolin', traditional slow-air, considered to be one of the most significant in Irish traditional music
An Claidheamh Soluis	'The Sword of Light', an influential, early twentieth-century publication championing Irish culture and language
An Pota Phadraig	(St Patrick's Pot) whiskey drunk on St Patrick's Day into which a person had dipped the shamrock being worn for the saint's day
An Tostal	countrywide celebration of Irish life in the 1950s
An tSean-Bó Riabhach	'The Old Brindled Cow'
Atal	stillness, calmness after a storm, cessation from rain; cheerfulness, pleasantry
Bachachdaig	bandy-legged
Báinín	(1) white, homespun, woollen, cloth
	(2) jacket made from the same material
Banbh	piglet
Banshee	English for *bean sidh* (literally 'fairy woman'), the Irish death messenger
Bárín breac	speckled cake (barm brack)
Bata scóir	tally stick
Bealtaine	May 1st, the beginning of summer
Bean an tí	woman of the house; wife

Bean bhán	corpse washer
Bean chaointe	keening woman
Bean feasa	wise woman
Bean ghluine	kneeling woman (midwife)
Bean leighis	herbalist
Bearradh caorach	fleecy clouds, portending rain
Booleys	summer mountain pastures
Bórachán	a bow-legged person; the joker in a deck of playing cards
Borekeen	name that derives from *bórachán*; organises games at wakes
Brádarnach	slight fall of rain or snow, hazy weather
Braoille fearthana	heavy shower of rain
Braon báistighe	little shower of rain
Brat Bríde	Brigid's cloak, an unwashed piece of cloth hung up on Brigid's Eve
Brideóg	small, straw doll, 'Little Brigid'
Brideóg	the Biddy Boys
Buachaillí bréige	ban-beggars
Buarach	a spancel, length of rope for restraining an animal, usually a cow during milking
Buaradach bháis	spancel of death
Buntús Cainte	A book series written by Tomás Ó Domhnalláin in the mid-1960s and illustrated by William Bolger, used to teach Irish in schools
Cabán	tent that surrounded the corpse at the wake made of the white wake sheets
Cabúis; cabúisíní	small cubby-holes on either side of the hearth
Cailleach	(1) a hag: used for the last sheaf of the harvest
	(2) a hag: an old woman who uses magical charms
Cailín	colleen; a girl

Glossary of Irish Words and Phrases

Cam reilig	'the crookedness of the graveyard': lameness said to come to a child if their mother enters a graveyard while pregnant
Caoráns	small nuggets of best of the hard turf
Céilí	dance, social gathering
Ceobhrán	heavy dew or a drizzling rain
Chomh lom le gé bhearrtha	'as naked as a plucked goose'
Cillíns	unofficial burial grounds
Cipíní	kindling; dry sticks collected to light the fire
Cleamairí	Strawboys
Cliamhain isteach	negative term for someone who marries into property and money, specifically a man marrying a woman with her own fortune
Conradh na Gaeilge	The Gaelic League
Corrchogailt	embers that burn bright blue and green
Couvade	man helping woman give birth/treating the husband of a woman giving birth as if he were bearing the child
Crosaire	(1) name of *Irish Times* cryptic crossword writer
	(2) crossroads
Croisín na leanbh	'the crossroads of the children', areas of 'no-man's land' between townlands that functioned as cillíns
Crubeen	pigs' trotters
Cúilteach	back of the house, small bed outshot found in the northwest of Ireland eventually changed to *cailleach* (the old woman's bed)
Cuinneog	butter churn
Cuiniu	Old Irish linguistic term for a woman
Cúlóg	pillion
Díleannta	deluge-like
Draghnánach	drizzling of rain
Dúidín	a chalk/clay-pipe, often acquired at wakes

Féinín	selfie taken on a phone
Flaithiúil; flaithiúilach	lavishly generous
Fomhar na nGéan	Harvest of the Geese (Michaelmas 29 September)
Gaeilgeoir na seachtaine	Irish speaker of the week (In *Gaelscoileanna*)
Gaelscoileanna	schools that teach through Irish
Garsún	boy
Giolc	tweet (on social media)
Gríosach	ashes of the fire containing small hot embers
Grisset	metal, boat-shaped vessel used to melt tallow
Halloween guisers	groups in disguise who went from house to house on the night of 31 October
Is liom-sa leath do choda-sa	'half of your portion is mine', a *piseog* for stealing butter
Keeler	a wide, shallow wooden vessel used to let the milk and cream separate
Leaba Bríd	Brigid's bed; a collection of rushes or straw brought into the house on Brigid's Eve
Leaba chabh	bedding made from a sack of chaff
Leaba cocháin	bedding made from a sack of newly thrashed straw
Loganimneacha	placenames of Ireland
Lugnasadh	1 August, ancient quarter day that marks the start of harvest
Magairlín Meidhreach	purple orchid, tormented root
Malartán	fairy changeling
Mar dhea	'as if it were so'
Marbh le tae agus marbh gan é	'We're dead from tea but we'd be dead without it'
Meitheal	a group of workers who come together to help each other at harvest time or cutting turf
Mná Caointe	keening women
Mocky-ah	(adj.) something that is pretend or false

Mummers	Groups who, over the Christmas period, dressed as different characters and performed vernacular drama that centred on regeneration
Mún an tsean duine	piss of the old people
Oíche na Gaoithe Móire	The Night of the Big Wind
Olagóning; olagón	loud, verbal, lamenting, keening
Ón oíche a tháinig mé ar an tsop	'since the night I landed on the straw', 'from the day I was born'.
Pattern Day	'*Lá an Patrún*', 'The day of the Patron Saint'; a religious festival of prayers and festivity held on the feast day of a patron saint, most often centred at a holy well
Peg	throw
Peist	worm; monster in early medieval literature
Peann luaidhe	pencil
Pisheog; piseóg(a)	superstitions but, more specifically, items used for magical effect, often negative, e.g. eggs hidden on someone's land
Poitín	poteen, illegal whiskey
Pooka	*púca*, shape-shifting otherworld figure of terror, most often in the form of a wild black horse
Ribín Bríd	Brigid's ribbon
Scairbhín na gCuach garbh í agus fuar	The scaraveen of the Cuckoo, rough and cold – scaraveen is an anglicisation of the Irish, *garbhsíon* (rough weather)
Seanfhocal	proverb, saying
Seoithín-seo	part of an Irish lullaby and used to indicate bed
Séibín	small wooden mug used as a quart measure for ale and grain, from which we get 'shebeen'
Sheebeen	an illegal pub
Sheela-na-gig	medieval carvings of older women in birthing postures

Síbín	bad or stale ale
Sí gaoithe	fairy wind
Síofradh	fairy changeling
Sleán (slane)	special spade used for digging turf
Slua sidh	fairy host
Snas	shine
Sopiní	tall, conical straw hats/masks
Spéachán	spit or kick of rain
Sráideóg	(1) a bundle of straw
	(2) a tradition of multiple people sleeping on straw 'sleeping in stradogue'
Station Mass	a Mass said in a person's home
Tá eitleán sa spéir	'there is a plane in the sky'
Tá sé ag caitheamh sceana gréasaí	'it's throwing down shoemaker's knives'
Tá se ag clagarnaigh báirlighe	it is pattering down rain
Taspy	high spirits, ardour
Tuit	tweet (on social media)
Wren boys	Groups dressed in straw costume who went from house to house with a wren on St Stephen's Day, 26 December

Acknowledgements

I want to wholeheartedly acknowledge and thank all who have encouraged and helped me to bring this book to fruition. My wonderful family and many close friends and work colleagues have been a constant source of inspiration and energy as I laboured through the writing process.

I am similarly indebted to a whole generation of my family, old friends and characters who have all now sadly passed away. When writing this book, recounting many of their stories and anecdotes, I think of their smiling faces, egging me on, their sense of fun and wonder at the world, emboldening me to tell their stories.

I owe much to my innumerable students, both young and mature, whose learned probing questions, learned insights and clever witticisms have bolstered my own learning and enquiries and shaped many chapters of this book.

I wish to acknowledge everyone involved with *The Today Show* in RTÉ Cork over the last number of years, including the presenters and all the many crew behind the cameras who have been nothing but positive in celebrating Irish folklore and social history.

I am most grateful to Ciara Considine and all of her team at Hachette Ireland for their tireless patience, constant positivism and careful attention in reconfiguring my sometimes-disjointed ramblings into a coherent and meaningful text. I am delighted with Sara Baker for producing beautifully crafted line drawings that capture the spirit of the book and embody my family's tradition of conveying things both 'wise and otherwise'.

Finally, my most profound thanks and gratitude go to my long-suffering partner Máire for her reassuring fortitude and constant support not only in listening to my incessant prattle, but also by offering stimulating suggestions and proof-reading the various initial drafts.